China Red Star Design Award Yearbook

中国创新设计红星奖年鉴

中国创新设计红星奖委员会 主编
China Red Star Design Award Committee Edit

中国书店
Cathay Bookshop

图书在版编目（CIP）数据

2012中国创新设计红星奖年鉴 / 中国创新设计红星奖委员会主编. -- 北京 : 中国书店, 2012.10

ISBN 978-7-5149-0583-0

Ⅰ. ①2… Ⅱ. ①中… Ⅲ. ①工业产品－造型设计－中国－2012－年鉴 Ⅳ. ①TB472-54

中国版本图书馆CIP数据核字(2012)第239592号

2012中国创新设计红星奖年鉴

中国创新设计红星奖委员会　主编

责任编辑：刘 深

出　版：中国书店

社　址：北京市西城区琉璃厂东街115号

邮　编：100050

经　销：全国新华书店

印　刷：北京朗翔印刷有限公司

开　本：850×1168　1/12

版　次：2012年10月第1版　2012年10月第1次印刷

印　张：18

书　号：ISBN 978-7-5149-0583-0

定　价：118.00元

目 录

004 评审现场
006 中国创新设计红星奖至尊金奖
010 中国创新设计红星奖金奖
028 中国创新设计红星奖银奖
042 最佳团队奖
044 最佳新人奖
046 红星奖
168 中国创新设计红星原创奖银奖
174 优秀设计师奖
176 未来之星奖
180 红星原创奖
188 2012中国创新设计红星奖获奖名单
202 2012中国创新设计红星原创奖获奖名单
204 主办及专家委员会
212 中国创新设计红星奖组织机构
214 中国创新设计红星奖委员会
216 创新设计服务创新型国家
218 中国设计 国际标准

Content

004 Jury
006 Best of The Gold Prize of China Red Star Design Award
010 Gold Prize of China Red Star Design Award
028 Silver Prizo of China Red Star Design Award
042 Best Team Prize
044 Best New Designer Prize
046 Excellcnt Prize
168 Silver Award of China Red Star Original Design Award
174 Best Designer Award
176 Future Star Award
180 Excellent Award
188 Winner List of 2012 China Red Star Design Award
202 Winner List of 2012 China Red Star Original Design Award
204 Organizer & Jury Committee
212 Institute of China Red Star Design Award
214 China Red Star Design Award Committee
216 Innovation design serving innovative country
218 Chinese Design, International Standard

红星奖
Red Star Design Award
2012中国创新设计红星奖
CHINA RED STAR DESIGN AWARD 2012
红 星 照 耀 中 国

CHINA
RED
STAR

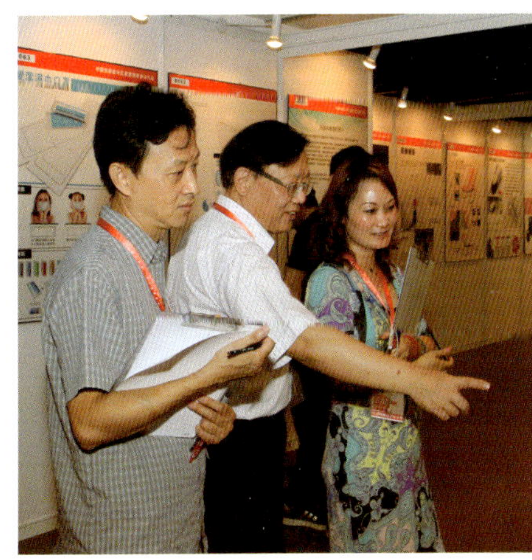

中国创新设计红星奖至尊金奖

Best of the Gold Prize of China Red Star Design Award

消防机器人
Fire-fighting Robot

生产 / 苏州海伦哲专用车辆有限公司
设计 / 上海轱辘轩工业设计有限公司

Manufacture / Suzhou Handler Special Vehicle Co.Ltd
Design / Shanghai Guluxuan Industrial Design Co.Ltd

消防机器人以一种独特的功能造型语言，生动地体现了消防车强健、有力、无畏的特色，在全面实现各种喷洒、排烟、灭火等功能的同时，塑造了崭新的消防机器人形象，是形式追求功能设计理念的最佳表现。该产品是一种用于消防作战的车辆，可以经遥控进入消防员无法靠近的危险场所中进行消防作业，有效保护消防员的人身安全，提高了消防作战效率，其消防功能主要有：在远距离遥控模式下进入火灾现场向火场喷洒水雾、排除烟尘、喷射水柱或泡沫灭火等。

The Fire-fighting Robot uses one special functional modeling language to show the characteristics of the fire truck: strong, powerful and fearless. It fulfills the function of spraying, ejecting smoke and putting out fire. At the same time, it constructs a completely new image of the fire fighting robot which showing the best result of displaying functional design concept. This vehicle is used for fire fighting, can be remote controlled to reach the dangerous places that firefighters cannot reach. It can protect the firefighters, also improve efficiency. When using long-distance remote control, enter into the fire fighting place, the vehicle can spray water mist, remove smoke dust, spray water or foam.

JP18
举高喷射消防车
消防
海伦哲
HANDLER

中国创新设计红星奖金奖

Gold Prize of China Red Star Design Award

LG6210E液压挖掘机
LG6210E Hydraulic Excavator

生产 / SDLG (山东临工工程机械有限公司)
设计 / 沃尔沃集团上海设计中心

Manufacture / Shandong Lingong Construction Machinery Co., Ltd.
Design / Volvo Group Design Center – Shanghai

LG6210E液压挖掘机以它近乎艺术品的气质，给坚硬、冰冷的工程机械业抹上亮丽的一笔。其尊重人、尊重环境与自然以及对科技的热烈拥抱，让它革命性地改变了使用者与机械的交互方式；充满现代气息、外观自信但不夸张、低能耗但不简陋的系统结构设计与材料应用。它不仅仅是机器，更是满怀信心的现代中国品牌。
这是第一台在中国市场应用产品设计特征专为工程机械行业设计的液压挖掘机，新的发动机、液压系统结构，使其成为高效的工程产品，高精度的电源管理系统使其具有前所未有的燃油效率。新的零件设计降低了产品能耗总量。

LG6210E Hydraulic Excavator, with its nearly perfect artistic temperament, brings vigor to the hard and cold engineering machines. Showing respect for people, environment, nature and embracing the technology, it revolutionizes the way people interact with machines. It is full of modern character, with its confidence but not exaggerated appearance, low power consumption but not rough systematic structure and application of materials. All the above brings people the visual and physiological evaluation: it is not only a machine, it is a Chinese modern brand full of confidence.
The LG6210E is the first hydraulic excavator in the Chinese market to unveil a product design character specifically designed for the construction machinery industry. In that context, it revolutionizes the way customers engage with this type of equipment. The new engine, hydraulic systems and structure make it to be an efficient engineering product, high precision power management system providing unprecedented fuel efficiency for its segment. Its new parts are designed in such a manner reduce the total energy consumption.

SDLG

KTM KOMUTER
KTM

马来西亚城际动车组
Malaysia SCS EMU

生产 / 南车株洲电力机车有限公司
设计 / 南车株洲电力机车有限公司&TRICON Design AG

Manufacture / CSR Zhuzhou Electric Locomotive Co.,Ltd
Design / CSR Zhuzhou Electric Locomotive Co.,Ltd&TRICON Design AG

马来西亚米轨线路、马来虎、马来西亚的南亚伊斯兰文化独特风情，都要求一款与之匹配的“马来化”城际动车组，该车辆设计结合马来西亚地域元素进行创新性设计，外型美观，以“马来虎”为创意灵感，各个细节都体现了马来西亚的本土文化与人情风俗。采用自主设计的ZUA120型转向架，创新地将盘式制动方式应用到米轨转向架上，填补了120km/h速度级轮盘制动米轨转向架的空白。而此动车组的AAR头设计既适应马来西亚米轨线路，又与其现有车辆连接；车身的马来虎雄风与车内人性化的柔性设计恰到好处地尊重了地域文化、宗教习俗，更将现代材料科技、电子技术等给人类带来的方便与快感发挥到极致。

The Malaysian meter gauge line, Panthera tigris jacksoni and the unique style of the Malaysian South-Asian Islamic culture all require a SCS EMU which can be symbol of the "Malay". The Vehicle combines the Malaysian culture elements to innovate, it is inspired by the Panthera tigris jacksoni, all the details show the Malaysian local culture and customs. It adopts the ZUA120 frame which is self designed, innovatively applies the disc braking system for the meter-gage railway which fills up the blank of 120km/h wheel disc bogie frame. The design of the EMU's AAR head both adapts to the Malaysian lines and can be connected to the existing trains. The awe-inspiring train body is like the Panthera tigris jacksoni and the humane and flexible interior design perfectly respects the regional culture and religious practices. What's more, it utilizes the modern material and electrical and other technologies.

茧–天津万通生态城新新家园零能耗会所
Cocoon–Zero–energy Sale Center of Tianjin Vone Shangbei Legacy Homes

生产 / 天津生态城万拓置业有限公司
设计 / 北京墨臣建筑设计事务所

Manufacture / Tianjin Eco–City Wantuo Properties Limited
Design / Mochen Architects & Engineers

该会所很好地体现了建筑和设计之间的跨学科交融，建筑产业离智能化和生态化的目标还很远，这样的智能化思考对建筑行业本身等级的提升有非常重要的意义。此外，该产品体现了可持续发展的理念，对于解决生活需求和生态环境的相互关系方面很有帮助，同时，采用大量先进的绿色节能技术，大大降低了建筑能耗，采用了"零成本"的风能、太阳能作为能源。空间划分较为合理，结构布局和环境系统结合较好。该会所以"树状"支撑结构替代多根柱子，节省空间，形成了大厅独特的视觉效果。

The design of this product is the only one that is related with the architecture in 2012 China Red Star Design Award, excellently reflecting the interdisciplinary blending between architecture and design. Since the architecture industry is far from intelligent and ecological, hence this kind of intelligent thinking plays an important role in improving the architecture industry. Moreover, this product reflects the concept of sustainable development and helps a lot in the interrelation between the solution to the needs of daily life and ecological environment. Meanwhile, it is combined with the technology of solar energy and rational special partition. It also well integrates the structural layout and environmental system. Adopting "tree–style" structure replaces many pillars, saving space and forming a special visual effect.

G型透视手术系统
G-type Perspective Surgery System

生产 / 北京东方惠尔图像技术有限公司
设计 / 北京智加问道科技有限公司

Manufacture / Beijing Oriental Whale Image Technology Co., Ltd.
Design / ZCO Design CO., Ltd

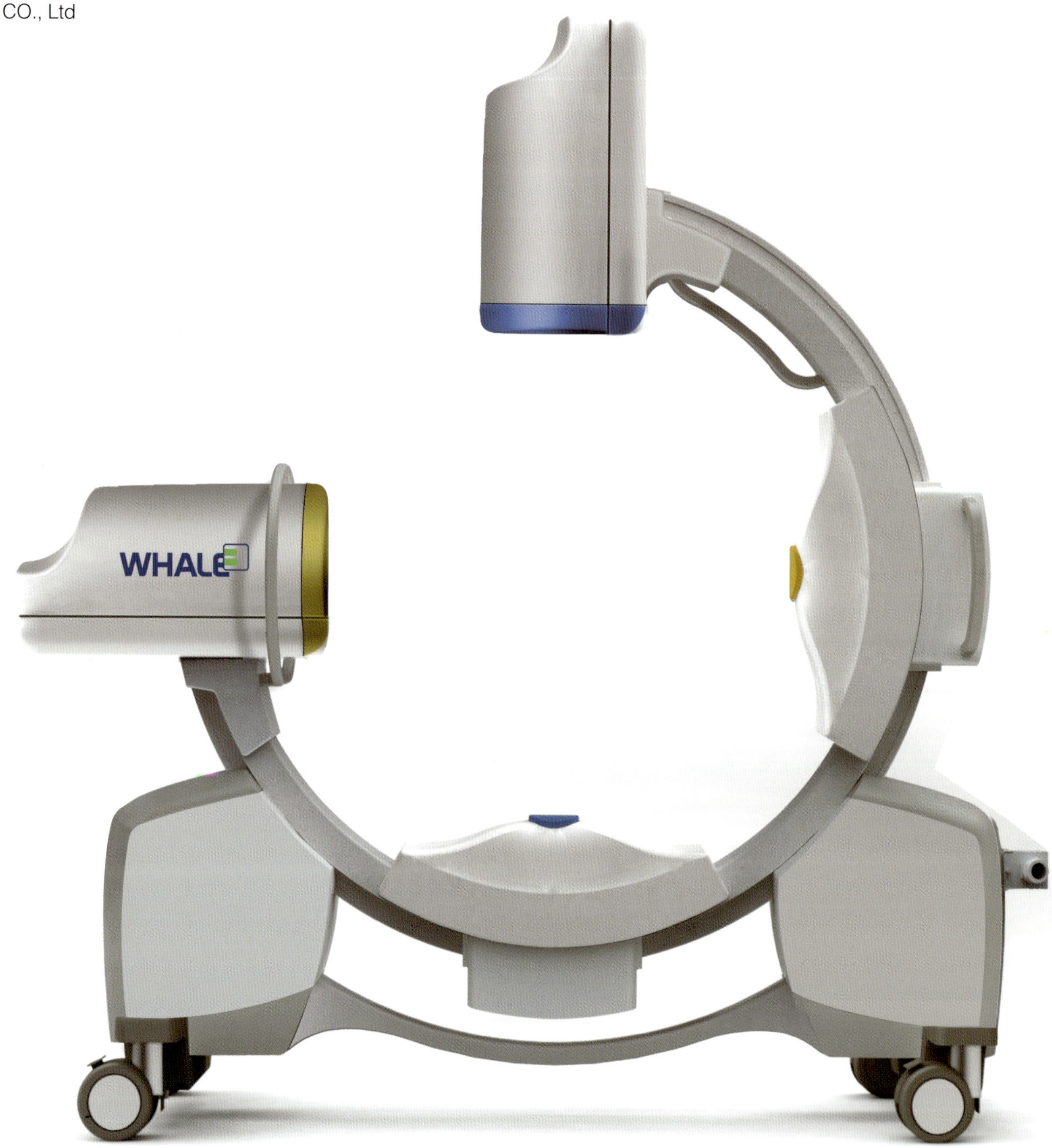

突破单一产品的模式，把组合的手术系统概念引入设计中，通过对医护人员在手术过程中的操作，记录使用轨迹，符合最佳人机使用方式。采用多维G型臂X线发射及接收技术用于骨科手术在线观察、定位医疗过程，在系统结构设计方面具有新颖性和创新性，综合技术方面将影像成像技术和手术系统有机结合，使医疗过程记录得更加准确、详细。设备外观设计美观实用，圆润的造型更适合于手术过程的细节，产品表面使用可降解塑料，采用无伤害的表面喷油技术，人性化设计贯穿于每一个细节。产品创新性明显，为未来骨科手术提供很好的产品。

The G-type perspective surgery system can be used at Orthopedics Department operation room and introduces the combined operation system to the design. By operating during surgery, it records the track of the usage, in line with best of man-machine use pattern. The product adopts multi-dimensional G-arm X-ray emission and receiving technology for the medical processes of orthopedic surgery online observation and positioning. It is creative and novel in systematic structural design. In comprehensive technical aspects, it organically combines the video imaging technology with the surgical system, making the surgical process records more concise and detailed. The appearance design is practical and pleasing to the eye. The rounded shape is more suitable for the details of the surgical procedure. The surface adopts the degradable plastics and the unharmful oil injection on the surface, which shows the hommization in details. The product is creative, and it will be a very good orthopedic surgical equipment in the future.

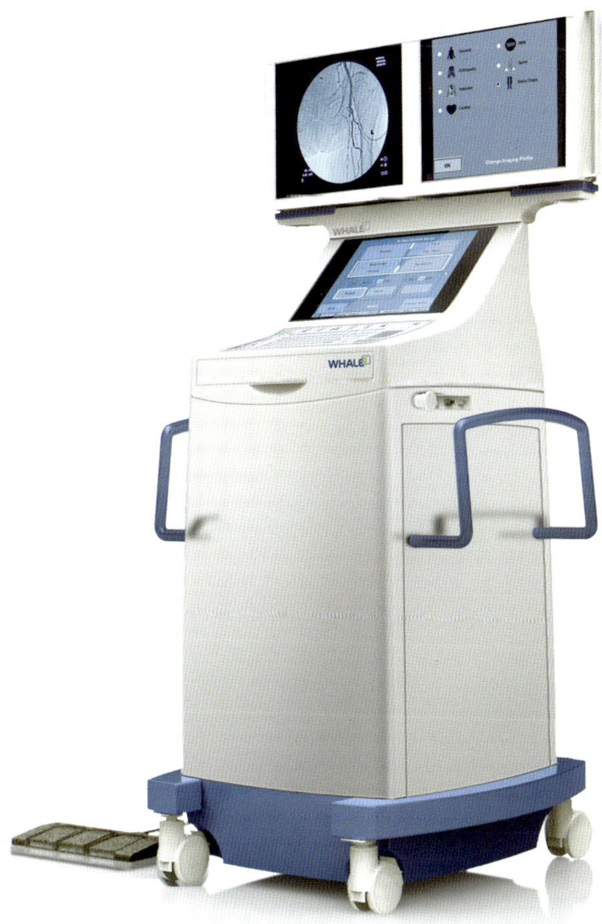

低频磁旋治疗系统
Low-Frequency Rotating Magnetic Therapy System

生产 / 山东超瑞施医疗科技有限公司
设计 / 深圳市无限空间工业设计有限公司

Manufacture / Shandong CRS Medical technology Co., Ltd.
Design / Shenzhen ND Industrial Design Co,. Ltd.

磁旋治疗作为一种新型的治疗方案，具有无痛无创伤的特点，主要通过改变人体磁场来激发人体自身的修复能力达到治疗疾病的目的。该产品采用磁旋治疗方法，设计了一套造型独特、外观新颖的医疗设备，其结构形式采用多维悬臂床方式，方便患者上下，制造工艺方面采用了双面精细磨具负压成型，提高了生产效率和产品精度，该工艺一般用在帆船与游艇领域。流线型造型将机床和控制系统融为一体，材料采用可降解环保合成树脂，美观、大方，在设计上具有创新性，同时具有很好的市场前景。

As novel treatment regimens, the magnetic rotation of the Multi-dimensional cantilever bed system has the characteristics of painless and woundless. Through changing the magnetic field of the human body the product is to stimulate the renovation of oneself. This product adopts gyromagnetic treatment method, designing a set of medical equipment of unique shape and novel appearance. The structure of multi-dimensional cantilever bed facilitates the patients´ up and down the bed. It adopts the manufacturing process uses a double-sided fine abrasive negative pressure molding which is generally used in the field of producing sailing boat and yacht. Streamlined shape integrates the machine bed with the control system. Made with biodegradable environmentally friendly synthetic resin, it is beautiful and natural. The design is creative. This product has good market prospects.

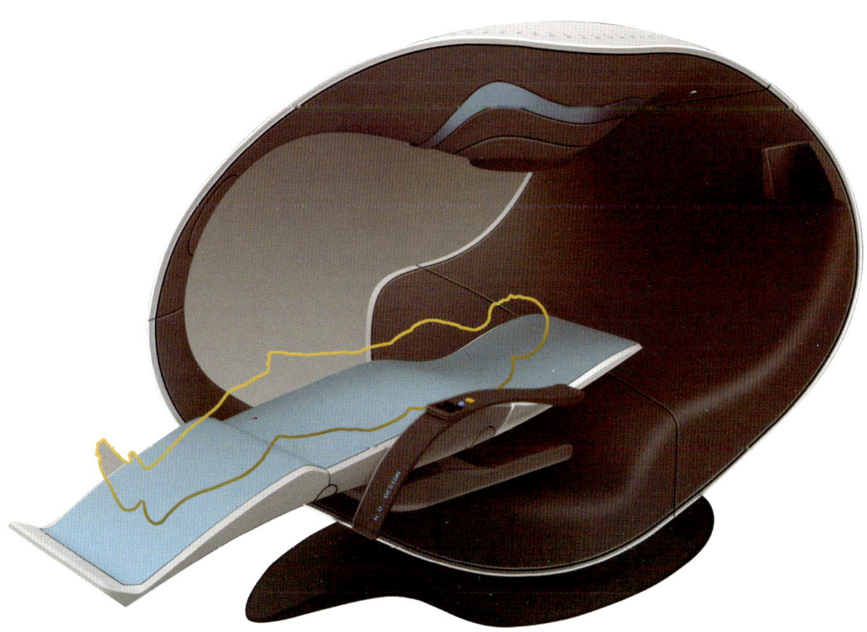

小天鹅比佛利滚筒洗衣机（06外观）
Little Swan Beverly Front-loading Washing Machine

生产 / 无锡小天鹅股份有限公司
设计 / 小天鹅工业设计团队

Manufacture / Wuxi Little Swan Company Limited
Design / Little Swan ID team

该产品设计较智能化，外观和使用系统的结合较合理。自动控制系统方便用户使用，产品造型完整，突出智能化操控系统，非常简单、直观。产品具有首创的自动添加洗涤剂技术，根据衣物量的多少,自动感知洗涤剂的添加量,进行自动添加；人性化设计，让用户随时保留所喜爱的洗衣程序；创新的触摸彩屏技术，不仅使界面更加清晰、生动，而且使枯燥的洗衣操作充满乐趣；能耗低，节能节水。

The design of this product is intelligent. Its appearance and usage system is rationally combined. The automatic control system is relatively convenient for the users. The integrated shape stresses the intelligent control system, easy and intuitive. The device of creative automatic detergent dosing technology can automatically sense and dose the right amount of detergent according to wash load to free people from chores of washing clothes. The customized design can save the personal favourite washing procedure of the user; the creative touch color screen makes the interface more clear and lively and full of fun. It has a low energy consumption, save energy and water.

LittleSwan
BEVERLY

IdeaCentre A720

生产 / 联想（北京）有限公司
设计 / 联想创新设计中心

Manufacture / Lenovo
Design / Lenovo Innovation Design Centre

这是一款较为出众的一体机，创造性地解决了用户和机器之间的交互性，可最大程度地进行变化，机身和基座的相关附属设施有很好的结合，可以降低干扰。该产品是业内唯一实现-5°至90°最大屏幕调节角度的一体台式机，可使屏幕以水平-5°的角度拉近，并以90°以上的角度折叠。正常垂直角度可以作为PC或电视机显示器，倾斜角度支持轻松的触碰使用，完全水平角度可实现多人互动游戏。

This product is an excellent integrated computer. It creatively solutes interactivity between the user and the machine and can be modified to the largest extent. It well combines with ancillary facilities of the machine´s body and base, reducing interference. Its smartly designed display mount can be adjusted across a huge range – from –5 degrees to 90 degrees. Users can watch it in a vertical position like a PC or television, slope it gently for relaxed touch screen use, or slide it into a fully horizontal position to play multi–person touch games.

金奖 Gold Prize

3D显示器
DM92 Series LED Premium 3D TV monitor

生产 / LG电子
设计 / LG电子中国设计中心

Manufacture / LG Electronics
Design / LG Electronics Design China

该产品是一款具有3D功能的电视显示器，产品设计精良，将传统材料和现代科技相结合，其外形设计并不趋同，具有很强的市场竞争力，底座设计灵活，用户可以根据需求进行改变，实用性非常强。在外观上突出超薄和无边框的设计，同时机身厚度也达到了1毫米的同类产品之最。这款产品将3D电视功能集成在显示器中，让用户可以在使用电脑之余体验高画质的TV节目。真正达到了游戏影音视频的全3D化。

This 3D TV monitor is well-designed, combining traditional materials and modern technology. Its exterior design has its own features, with strong market competitiveness. Its base is flexibly designed and can be modified according to the users´ demand, highly practical. The product uses the Ultra-thin and no border style for exterior design. This TV monitor is 1mm thick, it makes it the thinnest one of the similar products. It integrates the TV function into a monitor, makes it possible for the users to enjoy high quality of the TV show. The products achieves the real 3D in the integration of games, video and TV.

真三维道路智能设计系统
Real 3D Intelligent Road Design System

生产 / 设计 / 中交宇科（北京）空间信息技术有限公司

Manufacture / Design / China Trans Geomatics Co.,Ltd.

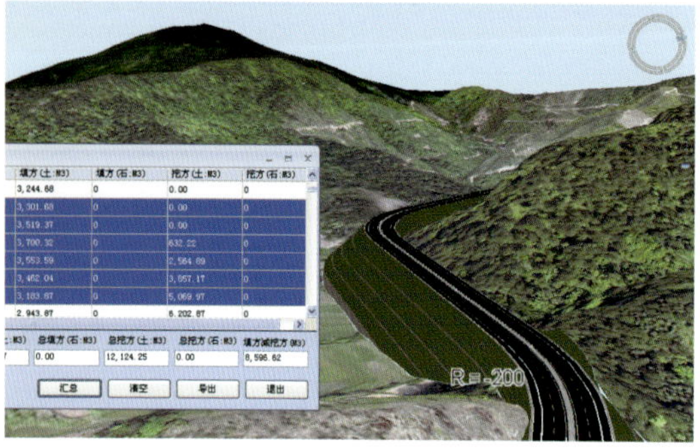

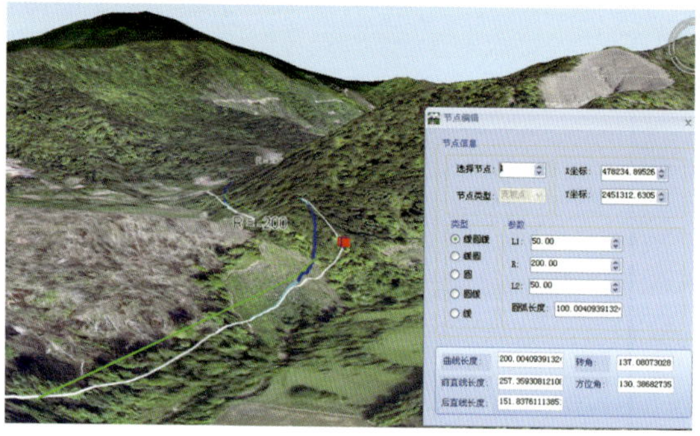

真三维道路智能设计系统采用多种高新科技，构建高精度真三维环境，提供新型道路设计环境；最大程度地优化设计方案，以提高设计效率和质量，节省工程造价；本系统根据需求制定，有效地填补空白。可使道路设计变得更简单、精确、有效率；与现有道路设计软件的数据接口相比不仅为设计提供了方便，更为建设后道路系统化管理提供了可能；利用高精度三维仿真技术，为合理保护环境和节约建设成本提供了更直观和科学的依据。

The system uses a variety of high-tech to build true high-precision three-dimensional environment and provide new road design environment to achieve the maximum degree of optimization of the design program, improve design efficiency and quality, save project cost. This system is formulated based on this demand and effectively fills the blank. The product makes the road design more simple, concise and efficient. Its data interface with the existing road design software not only makes it easier to design but also makes it possible for systematical management after the construction of the road; in using high-precision three-dimensional simulation technology, it also provides more intuitive and scientific basis to rationally protect the environment and save the construction cost.

行程
由起点向终点行驶
由终点向起点行驶
起点->终点、终点->起点循环行驶
初始速度
120
km/h
行驶车道
1
车道
视线高度
2
m
开始行驶位置
0
m
确定
退出
R = -800

内后山隧道

中国创新设计红星奖银奖

Silver Prize of China Red Star Design Award

木质拼装榫卯车
Wood Assembly Tenon Car

生产 / 北京中奥之光科技发展有限公司
设计 / 高天宇

Manufacture / Beijing China-Olympics light Technology co.,ltd
Design / Gao Tianyu

这是优秀设计的最典型代表。此种设计寓教于乐，让孩子在游戏的同时，还能够了解中国古代设计。该产品符合所有的评审标准。安全、简单，使用环保材料，拥有所有优秀产品的属性。该产品运用榫卯特殊结构与鲁班锁的形式，创新出新的玩具；不但有利于开发大脑、灵活手指，而且老少皆宜，从中了解到中国古代建筑的精髓。是一种很好的科教益智玩具，是木质榫卯玩具的一个新秀。采用榉木制作，环保安全，加工简单，采用切割加工。

This is a great example of good design. The design encourages children to play and learn about ancient Chinese architecture at the same time. It meets all the judging criteria, it is safe, simple and made from environmental friendly material – all the attributes of a successful product. The product applies for special structure of the tenon joint, combined with Luban lock form and creates new tenon toys. It is not only conductive to the development of the brain, nimble fingers, and all ages, but can be very good for young people to learn about the essence of ancient Chinese architecture and thus hand down which can be an upcoming star of the tenon toy.

QCAR
QCAR

Kolumb
KEEP DISCOVERING
35L

Airflow空气背包背负系统
Airflow Inflatable Outdoor Backpack System

生产 / 设计 / 福建哥仑步户外用品有限公司

Manufacture / Design / Fujian Kolumb Outdoor Equipment Co., Ltd

Airflow空气背包背负系统采用空气作为主要的缓震填充材料加入分级支撑的概念，引进了一种可充气的缓震方式，在负重时可同时兼顾缓震和支撑的功能，从而提升使用者的旅途舒适度。根据背包类型分全背负式和半背负式，由于使用空气取代传统的填充材料，产品整体重量降低；高密封性能的气嘴设计，可根据使用环境及使用者身体特性调整背负。

Using air as the primary cushioning filler material and using the concept of hierarchical support which can do cushioning and support in weight-bearing function, it introduces the inflatable way of cushioning and adopts the concept of grading support, realizing the function of cushioning and support at the same time, thus improving the travelers´ comfort level. Full-size and half size backpack carrying system. Traditional EVA and sponge material was replaced by air. Backpack weight was reduced, high sealing performance of the air valve design based on the use of the environment and the user physical characteristics of the rapid adjustment to bear.

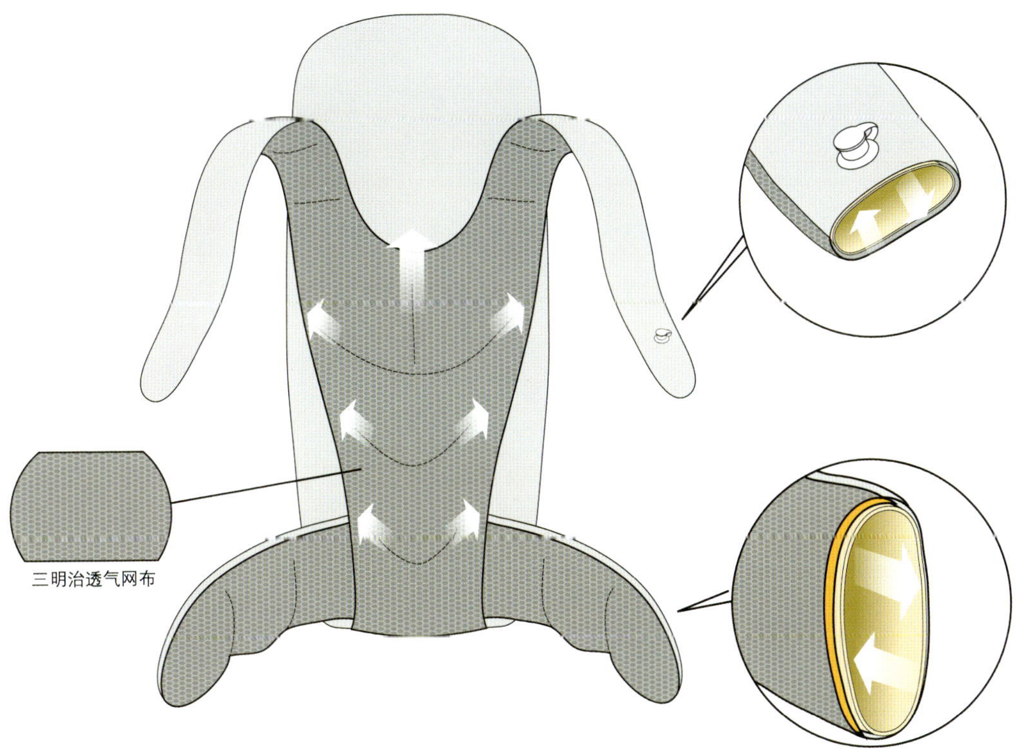

雅生布鲁克面盆及龙头
Axor Bouroullec Basin and Mixer

生产 / 汉斯格雅欧洲股份有限公司
设计 / 罗南和埃尔文•布鲁克兄弟

Manufacture / Hansgrohe SE
Design / Ronan and Erwan Bouroullec

该产品的设计创造了一种全新的浴室景观，台盆的设计以立体的岛状造型分割使用空间，在方便使用的同时，也为用户的个性化龙头布局提供了可能性。 该产品采用EcoSmart智能节水技术，流量始终保持保持5升/分钟，与不含该技术的龙头相比节水达60%，矿物铸造材质的面盆，聚酯凝胶表面，可在面盆上随意开孔安装龙头。

This design creates a brand new bathroom landscape. The basin uses the three-dimensional island shape to divide the spaces. While easy to use, it is possible for the users to personalize the way to position the faucets. The product adopts the EcoSmart smart water-saving technologies, traffic is always 5 liter / min. Compared with faucet without this technology, it saves 60% of the water. The basin uses mineral casting material and the surface is polyester gel. You can make openings anywhere on the basin to install the faucet.

银奖 Silver Prize

油烟机CXW–200–F16
RANGE HOOD CXW–200–F16

生产 / 设计 / 宁波欧琳厨具有限公司

Manufacture / Design / Ningbo Oulin Kitchen Utensils Co., Ltd

该油烟机的设计非常简约，产品将中国特色和西方的简约设计理念进行了完美的结合，在细节方面处理合理。功能体现丰富、健全，且使用方便，品质很高，外观设计简约大方。该产品采用四位瞬吸技术，彻底分离油烟。配有节能1W低功率、高亮度的冷光灯照，吸力大，噪音小，能耗低。45度黄金斜角敞开设计，不碰头。外型时尚新颖，采用钢化黑玻璃与白色航空铝材相结合，给厨房带来更多的艺术气息。

The design takes the principle of simplicity. It thoroughly combines the eastern characteristics and the western sketchy design philosophy. It treats very well in the details and rich and sound in functionality. It is easy to use and has high quality. The design of the appearance is simple and generous. This product uses four–instantaneous–absorption technology making the complete separation of soot. Equipped with energy–saving of 1W low power, high brightness of luminescence, high suction, low noise. It adopts gold bevel of 45 degrees open design protecting the head. The innovative, stylish appearance adopts tempered black glass and white aviation aluminum combined to bring more art sense to the kitchen.

垂直对流散热LED路灯
Vertical Convection LED Street Light

生产 / 勤上光电股份有限公司
设计 / 清华大学美术学院设计战略与原型创新研究所

Manufacture / Kingsun Optoelectronic Co.,Ltd
Design / Institute of Design Strategy and Prototype Innovation, Tsinghua University

利用蜂窝煤的空气对流原理设计出的新型散热结构，打破传统LED散热结构，让散热片之间存在缝隙并形成自然对流，提升了灯具的热交换率和散热效果，延长了灯具的工作寿命，并形成了独特的造型效果。灯具结构实现了照明和驱动的双重模块化，在灯具的设计和生产上更具灵活性，并降低了成本。

Unlike most traditional LED street lights, the design adopted this air convection principle from honeycomb briquette, which makes air go through the gap between each modular and takes away heat on fins. This vastly optimizes heat dissipation effect and improves the working efficiency and prolongs the life of each LED, also in a special shape. The structue realizes the dual modulars of illumination and drive, more flexible in lighting design and production, reduces the cost.

银奖　Silver Prize

模块化办公及展览展示系统
Modular Office and Exhibition System

生产 / 宁波布特坦姆文化传播有限公司
设计 / 宁波柯怡工业设计有限公司

Manufacture / Ningbo Beilun Dongren Industrial & Trading Co.,Ltd.
Design / Co-Yes Industrial Design Co.,Ltd.

模块化办公系统设计，是可以将室内空间进行模块化分割的策略，同时提供了更多的使用可能性，更好地和空间设施进行结合，可以在建筑和产品之间找到一种中间点，可以丰富在生活和办公之间的想象力。该产品设计安装方便，零部件减少到极致，简洁、美观、时尚，安装快捷，容易拆除，高效环保，可重复利用。该系统从一定程度上打破了传统的环境空间装修方式，成功地应用于展览展示、办公空间、博物馆、展示厅、商店和户外场所，具有一定的趋势引领性。

The product uses modularized product design which is a strategy that can partition the space into different modulars and at the same time provides more ways of usage, better combining with space facilities. This strategy can construct a middle point between the architecture and the product and enrich the imagination between life and office space. Modular office and exhibition display system is safe and convenient for installation; also this system is simple, beautiful and modern. It saves more energy and can be recycled. To a certain level, it is a breakthrough of the traditional construction way, widely used in exhibition, office, museum, shops and outer space.

康佳9000系列电视
KONKA 9000 Series TV

生产 / 康佳集团股份有限公司
设计 / 康佳9000系列设计团队

Manufacture / KONKA Group Co.,Ltd
Design / KONKA 9000 Series design team

采用的节能3D屏、OPC节能芯与PMS节能系统，大大提高了其产品的节能性能，系统节能可达52%，智能操作Android 4.0系统，支持语音识别、面部识别、手势识别、全网搜索，底部的触摸感应按键增添了整个产品的科技感。整体设计简洁大方，细节设计突出，圆角设计，材质使用合理，支架设计巧妙，产品完成度高，整体感很强，基座处理很出彩。

The product uses energy-saving 3D screen, OPC energy-saving core with PMS energy saving system, which greatly improves the energy performance of the products. The system saves up to 52% of the energy. The smartphone operating Android 4.0 system supports voice recognition, facial recognition, gesture recognition, network search, touch-sensitive buttons at the bottom also adds up to the sense of science and technology. The overall design is simple and generous, a lot of detailed design is prominent. It is good to design the angle rounded, the material application is reasonable and the design of the stand is ingenious. This product has a strong sense of the wholeness and high completeness. The base is done excellently.

银奖 Silver Prize

【有余•祝福中国】渔具设计
YOUYU•Blessings China Fishing rod

生产 / 设计 / 北京光彩无限管理咨询有限公司

Manufacture / Design / Shine Design Consultation Center

本产品竿体采用100%高级碳纤维与特种裁制工艺手工制作而成，轻盈耐用，使用方便，提升了用户的使用体验。本品的包装体现了中国传统的鱼文化，与产品设计相得益彰，采用透明塑料与印刷纸，内包裹印刷纸板，竿体内置于纸板与塑料包装之间。以“鲢鲶游鱼”、“寿之以渔”为主题，配合透明塑料与印刷图案的纸板，整体为现代的传统中国风。

The product uses 100% carbon fiber and special tailoring process craft, it´s light and durable. Packing with transparent plastic, within wrapped in printed cardboard, product is placed in between the cardboard and plastic packing. Products use the Chinese traditional culture " lian nian you yu", which makes a wish of "living a happy and contented life"; and "shou zhi yi yu", which means "live a longlife" as the theme and coordinate the transparent plastic and printed cardboard. The packaging is modern traditional Chinese style.

MI
23:45

小米手机 MiOne
MiOne

生产 / 北京小米科技有限责任公司
设计 / 刘德

Manufacture / Xiaomi Corporation
Design / Liu De

MiOne市场定位清晰，很好地把握了高层次手机发烧友的DIY能力，不仅仅在竞争十分激烈的手机市场上开辟了属于自己的领地，更是因此创造了新型的高端手机用户的定制服务和销售模式。MiOne手机突出了高端用户DIY设计的灵活性和个性化的用户体验，它的生产工艺、包装设计甚至利用社交网络的推广都是值得称赞的。MiOne作为典型的新型IT行业代表，很好地为其他创业者做出了榜样。小米手机发布时为国内首款双核1.5g高性能智能手机。独创无锁双系统分区，采用独特的半反半透防眩光技术和石墨散热技术。1G Ram大内存，Adreno 220图形处理芯片，4寸大屏，800万像素、f/2.4大光圈摄像头，1930mAh大容量手机电池。售价仅为1999元。

MiOne has a very clear market target. It well grasps the DIY capability of the high-level mobile phone enthusiasts, not only opening up new areas of its own in the highly competitive mobile phone market, but also creating new type of customized service and sales model for high-level mobile phone users. MiOne stresses the flexibility of high-level users´ DIY and personalized user experience. Its production crafts, packaging design and marketing through social networking is worth recommending. MiOne, as the typical new type of IT industry representative, sets a good example for other entrepreneurs. It was the very first Chinese mobile which at its launch, supported a 1.5GHz dual-core chip, powered by the dual-partition update system. Semi-transparent reflection film is adopted to ensure a better vision under direct sunlight. Also, graphite film is adopted to improve radiating effect. The phone is a smartphone with 1GB RAM, eight megapixel camera, Adreno 220 processor, 1930mAh-capacity lithium polymer battery. Exclusively distributed through web store; the retail price is 1999 Rmb.

最佳团队奖

Best Team Prize

轱辘轩工业设计团队
2012 Best Team Prize – Guluxuan Design Team

轱辘轩是一个充满活力的年轻工业设计团队，成立于2009年，由5名成员组成，成员平均年龄28岁。团队秉承“术业有专攻”的发展理念，专心致力于大型专用车辆、工程机械、轻载交通车辆以及车辆内外装饰、附件的设计工作，涉及趋向研究、造型创意、结构设计、数模构建、人机应用、色彩标识、2D/3D展示和图纸绘制等多项产品研发流程。

团队近年来承担了海伦哲消防车系列造型设计、宜工CY957装载机整车造型等多个重大项目，并为由中国工程机械工业协会主办的“2011年度首届BICES中国国际工程机械及专用车辆创意设计大赛”提供技术支持工作。

由轱辘轩设计完成的消防机器人荣膺今年中国创新设计红星奖至尊金奖。该消防机器人是一款颠覆传统、具有全新外型的消防机器人，打破了现有同类产品的同质化。团队以“理性重构”为设计理念，大胆应用新材料和新工艺，兼顾外观和功能。通过设计研发，使得消防作战变得更为安全、迅捷和有效，赢得了广大官兵喜爱。

Guluxuan Industrial design team is a young and vigorous team, which was established in 2009, composed with 5 young members and the average age is 28. The design philosophy is to "be specialized in pursuit". They design specifically on special purpose vehicle, engineering machinery and light load vehicle; they also do the accessories and exterior & interior decoration design for the vehicles. The design process concerns trend research, modeling originality, structure design, mathematical modeling, ergonomics, color identification, 2D/3D display and drawing.

The team has undertaken the exterior design for Haizhelun fire truck series, Yigong CY 957 loader carload and other programs. In 2011, the team provided the technological support for 2011 First Beijing International Construction Machinery Exhibition & Seminar (BICES) which was organized by China Construction Machinery Association (CCMA).

The product "Fire-fighting Robot" designed by Guluxuan design team has won the Best of the Gold Prize of 2012 China Red Star Design Award. This product is highlighted with a whole new appearance comparing with the traditional products, which breaks the homogenization of the congeneric products. The team takes the philosophy of "rationality reconstruction", applies new materials and new craft for the appearance and function. Through their design, the product makes the fire fighting safer, quicker and more efficient, and achieves popularity of the fire fighters.

最佳新人奖
Best New Designer Prize

张青
Zhang Qing

『好的设计一定是源于设计师对生活环境的感知与积累。通过设计创作，把脑中的抽象感觉转化为实物传递给产品的使用者，以此满足使用者在精神和物质两个层面的需求。

A good design must originate from the perception and accumulation of the environment. Through design, designers pass the users an object which transferred from the abstract feeling hereby to satisfy the spiritual and material demands.』

1987年生于北京，毕业于天津理工大学。2010年加入北京智加工业设计有限公司，担任设计师。先后为联想集团、南车集团、国家电网、中国科学院、中国运载火箭研究所以及美、韩、日等国企业设计产品，涉及医疗、电子等多项领域。期间多次参与筹划设计创新盛典、国际峰会及世界华人创新设计大赛。

作为2012年中国创新设计红星奖金奖产品——G 型手术透视系统的主要设计师，她以“越近越贴心”为设计理念，跨越技术与美学的界限，从文化、激情和实用性等角度来定义产品，采用仿生的设计手法，运用流畅圆润的线条，使得产品富有亲和力和感染力，表现出“关注生命、关爱健康、心怀梦想”的设计思想。

Zhang Qing was born in Beijing in 1987, graduated from Tianjin University of Technology and joined ZCO Design in 2010. She has designed products for Lenovo, CSR Group, State Grid, CAS, China Carrier Rocket Institution as well as enterprises from USA, Korea and Japan. The products involve various fields, such as health care and electronics.

As the primary designer of "G-type Perspective Surgery System", she believes "the closer the better", stepping over the boundaries of technology and aesthetic, defining the products with culture, passion and function. The products applies for bionics, looks smooth, easy to approach and full of affinity, showing the design philosophy "care about life, concern health, cherish dream".

中国创新设计红星奖

Excellent Prize of China Red Star Design Award

装备制造、工业仪器、医疗器械 048
Equipment & Manufacture, Industrial Instrument, Medical Apparatus

交通工具 064
Transportation

公共设施、建筑装饰 074
Public Facility,Architecture and Architectural Ornament

信息和通信产品 080
IT & Communication

消费类电子和家用电器 096
Consumer Electronics

家具与家居用品、照明器具、服装服饰 132
Furniture and Home Supplies, Luminaire, Fashion & Accessory

工艺美术品、产品包装 160
Arts and Crafts, Packing

电池移动仓
Mobile Storage Battery

生产 / 国家电网
设计 / 杭州汉度工业设计有限公司

Manufacture / State Grid Corporation of China
Design / HUMTA

这是一款国家电网的配套产品，用于电动汽车的电池充电和储存，并可以自由移动。采用全不锈钢板设计，内部采用钢梁结构，电气功能较多、模块化使得更换电池方便快捷，拿取的方式也变得更加，协调，方便管理。

This product is the complementary product of the national grid for charging and storage of electric vehicle battery which can be moved freely. It adopts the design of all stainless steel plate and interal steal beam structure realizing more electrical functions. Modular makes replacement of batteries quick and easy, way to pick up more convenient, coordinate and easy to manage.

SY5250GJB3A/12NR搅拌车
SY5250GJB3A/12NR SANY Concrete Truck Mixer

生产 / 三一重工湖南汽车制造有限责任公司
设计 / 湖南大学设计艺术学院

Manufacture / SANY Group Hunan Automobile Manufacturing Co., Ltd
Design / School of Design Hunan University

这是一款颠覆了传统模式的搅拌车，采用“工程机械轿车化”的设计理念，流线动感，风阻较小；全覆盖式设计保证了整车与地面清洁，有效防止混凝土残渣污染；扶梯和尾翼连贯式设计，让整车浑然一体。采用欧三排放标准发动机，节能环保。易于装配。

This product changes the traditional way of concrete truck mixer. The all overlay design makes the truck very clipper-built and dynamic. The staircase and empennage´s link up and streamline design makes the mixer one integrated mass. And this product is refined and elegant by the fashionable and streamlined exterior.

能量隧道
Energy Tunnel

生产 / 香港宝龙科技有限公司
设计 / 北京智加问道科技有限公司

Manufacture / PORON International Ltd
Design / ZCO Design CO., Ltd

能量隧道可为普通土壤调节微量元素。通过传送带将原料从设备隧道入口送入，设备本身的不同微量元素发射器将元素辐射入原料内，再由传送带从隧道出口送出。椭圆隧道的造型如同太空来物，充满科技神秘色彩，简洁大方的圆弧体现整体顺畅的视觉效果。

The energy tunnel can be used in the eco-agriculture products production workshop. The energy tunnel can regulate the trace elements for the soil, and change it to be the nourishing soil to meet the various needs. And this oval-shaped model with a mysterious feature looks like the alien from the outer space that gives us a fluent impression which embodies a sense of honor and veneration.

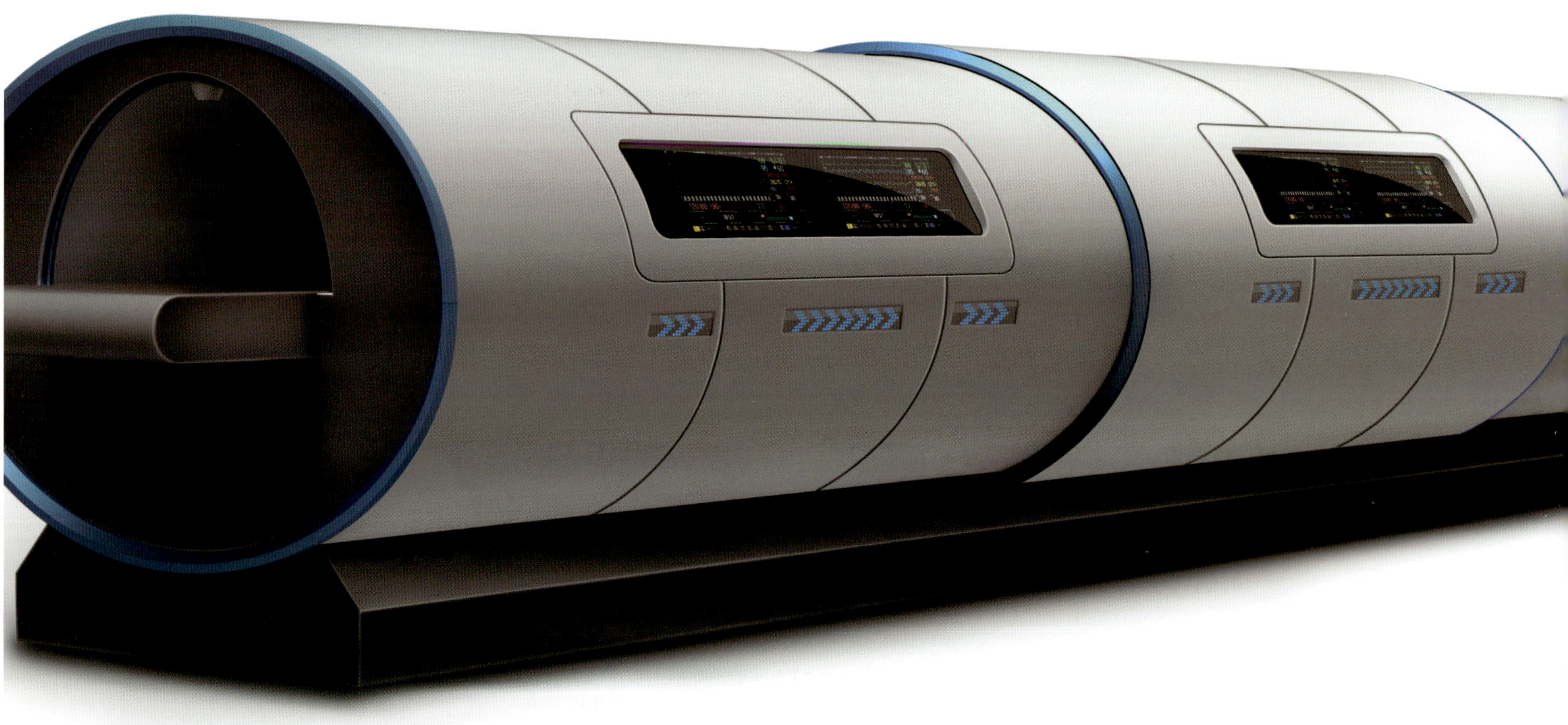

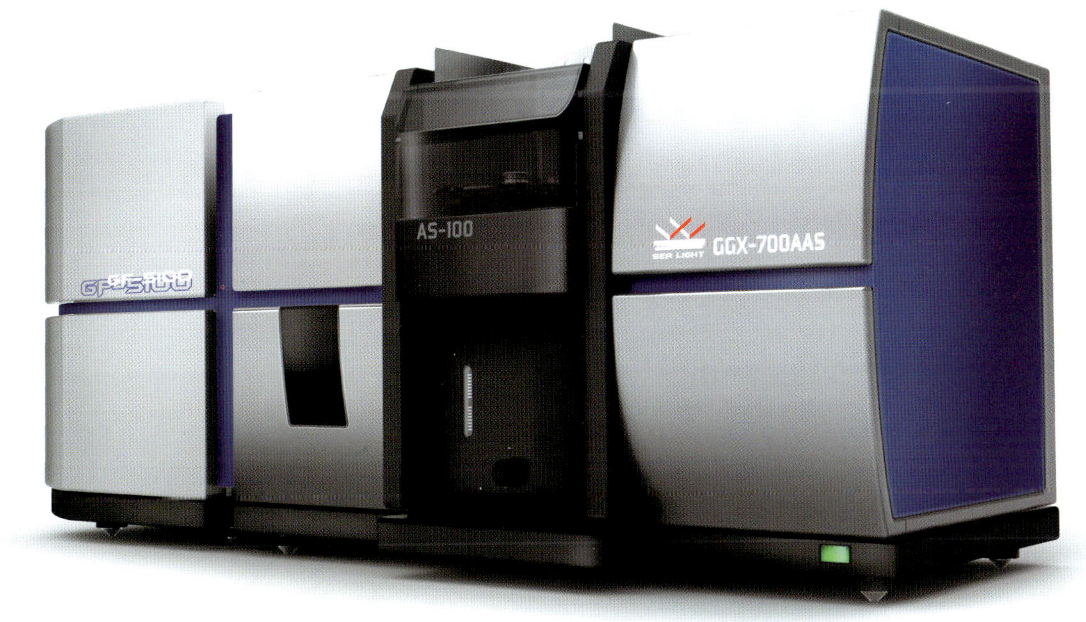

石墨炉原子吸收分光光度计
Graphite Furnace Atomic Absorption Spectrometry Photometer

生产 / 北京海光仪器公司
设计 / 北京智加问道科技有限公司

Manufacture / Beijing Kechuang Haiguang Instrument Co.,Ltd
Design / Zco Design Co., Ltd

该产品主要用于检测样品中的钾、钠、钙、镁等微量元素含量。它有单光束、双光束、双波道、多波道等结构形式，灵敏度高，选择性好。采用整体模块设计，电源部分与整体可以分开使用，也可组合使用。

The product can be used in the lab for R&D institutions. It is mainly used to test the trace elements such as K, Na, Mg, Ag, Cu, Pb, Zn, Mn, Fe, Cr, Ni, Cb in the sample. The device adopts a modularization design with a white and silver appearance.

数控环保锅炉
Numerical Control Eco Boiler

生产 / 河北新华鑫锅炉制造有限公司
设计 / 北京致翔创新

Manufacture / Sunhouse Boiler Manufactory Co.,Ltd
Design / Aestech Design

该数控锅炉打破了常规锅炉的结构设计方式，将反向燃烧原理和多回程烟管绕动技术等以全新的思路融入到燃煤锅炉设计之中，使锅炉的实际运行热效率高达80%以上、彻底改变了传统燃煤锅炉的工作原理。8种专利技术，燃烧更充分，保温效果更好，更省煤。

Numerical control boiler breaks through original engineering design approach. Brand new ideas, such as reverse burning system and flue pipe thermal energy recycle system are applied. Actually, thermal efficiency is higher than 80%. The new NC boiler thoroughly changes the traditional work principle. The boiler has 8 patent technologies. Full fuel utilizing and temperature control system can reduce coal usage when temperature reaches setting.

精密数控电火花成型机 FORM 20
FORM 20 CNC Die Sinking EDM

生产 设计 / 北京阿奇夏米尔工业电子有限公司

Manufacture Design / Beijing Agie Charmilles Industrial Electronics Co., Ltd.

智能控制平台集合多项化的革新，紧凑的外形设计充分地减少占地面积。自动液位液温控制、防夹手设计等，使机床具有更好的安全操作性能。放电加工采用先进的无电阻脉冲电源，降低了加工成本。符合CE标准。采用无电阻电源减少能源消耗。

This product leads intelligent control platform, setting a number of innovations. Its compact design saves space. Automated control of liquid temperature and worktank door automatically lock make the machine tool having a better safe operation performance. The use of advanced non-resistant pulse power greatly reduces processing costs. It is in accord with the CE standard.The adoption of non-resistant power reduces the energy consumption.

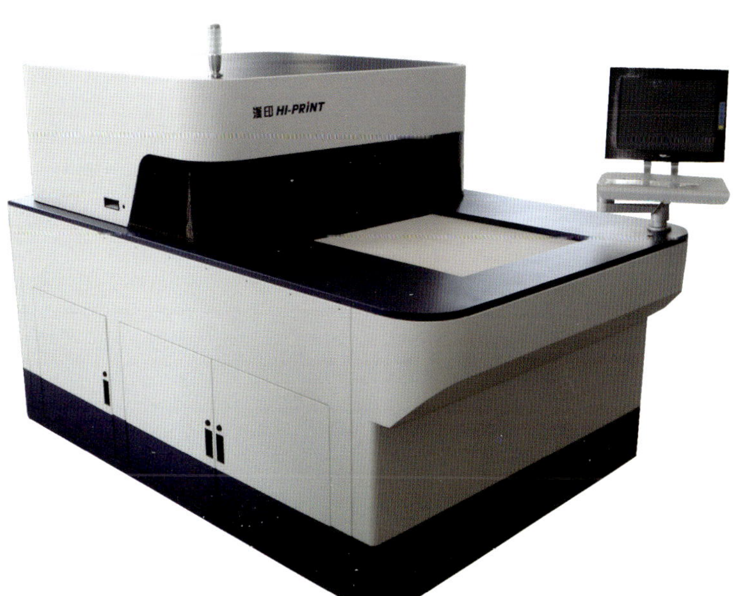

汉印——PCB字符喷印机
Hi-print-PCB Legend Inkjet Printer

生产 / 汉印科技
设计 / 贤信堂设计

Manufacture / Hi-print Technology
Design / Sincere Tone Design

采用加成法数字化高速喷印工艺，制程工序减少，生产周期缩短，有利于降低制造成本，保护环境，是实现PCB绿色制造的有效手段。油墨回收系统降低油墨消耗，简化冗长的文字印刷制程。简洁的外观及配色设计，人性化工序式操作界面，自动定位，即时预览，准确引导作业人员。

It adopted digital high-speed printing technology to reduce production cycle time and is good for reducing the manufacture cost and protecting the environment. Also its interface, automatic positioning and instant preview accurately guide the boot of the operating professionals.

无人侦察机
Unmanned Reconnaissance Aircraft

生产 / 北京观点航空设备公司
设计 / 姜辛

Manufacture / SKYCAM AIR MATERIAL CO.
Design / Jiang Xin

采用仿生学流线型设计，与空气动力学相结合，体现出产品的科技感及价值感。该侦察机可用以帮助警方侦查、缉毒、抢险救援、维护社会治安。

The product adopts bionic streamlined design combined with aerodynamics, reflecting the technological sense and sense of value of the product. Helping the police with investigation, drug enforcement, rescue, and maintain social order.

希盟健康护理监控系统
CIM Health Care Monitoring System

生产 / 希盟（中国）科技有限公司
设计 / 上海木马工业产品设计有限公司

Manufacture / CIM (CHINA) TECHNOLOGY INC.
Design / Shanghai Moma Industrial Product Design Co., Ltd

此系统内储存了50副头戴式健康监测仪，设备强大的运算和处理功能能够同时无线监控50名头戴式健康检测仪使用者的健康数据，并及时对健康数据出现异常的使用者做出警示和诊断。同时，将使用者一段时间来的各种健康参数曲线打印出来供医生参考，智能化程度很高。

This system has stored 50 head set monitoring equipments. Its strong function of operation and processing can monitor 50 users´ healthy data wirelessly. Meanwhile these healthy data can be printed for doctors´ reference; its intelligent degree is much higher than others.

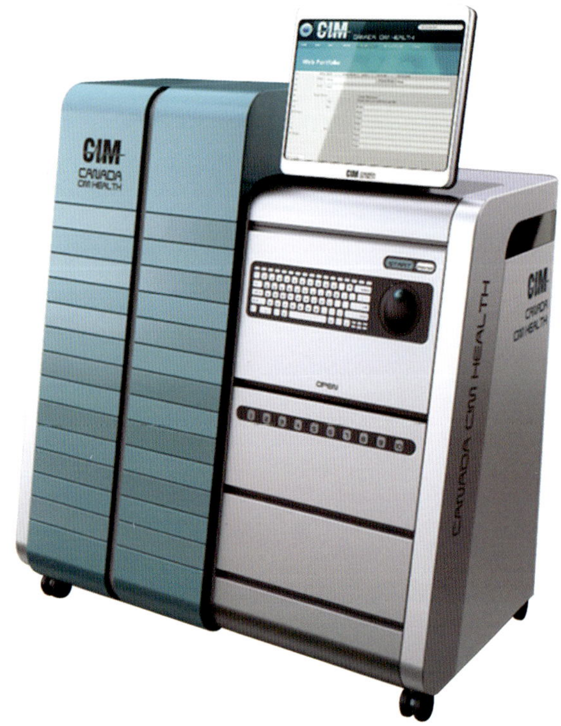

利德曼化学发光分析仪
LEADMAN Chemiluminescence Analyzer

生产 / 北京利德曼生化股份有限公司
设计 / 博砚清艺(北京)工业设计有限公司

Manufacture / Leadman Group Co., Ltd.
Design / Beyondesignlab Industrial Design Company

通过检测患者血清从而对人体进行免疫分析的医学检验仪器。卓越的智能化和自动化设计。优化设计的自动传送机构帮助反应杯进行定向排放。巧妙运用低成本的板金加工工艺，突破了医疗实验室设备冰冷的形象，给用户全新的实用和情感体验。

Through the detection of serum immune, Chemiluminescence analyzer tests human body health condition. Optimized intelligent and automated design of the automatic transfer institutions to help the reaction cup targeted emissions. Ingenious use of low cost sheet metal processing breaks through the rough visual sense of the traditional sheet metal process and gives users a new practical and emotional experience.

KG系列全封闭全自动石油干洗机
KG Series Fully Enclosed Automatic Oil and Dry-cleaning Machines

生产 / 美国百丝特国际集团有限公司
设计 / 北京赛佳图工业设计有限公司

Manufacture / U.S. Best International Group Co., Ltd.
Design / Beyon Design Lab Industrial Design Company

百丝特的干洗设备溶剂回收速度有明显的提高，溶剂损耗率明显降低，符合2010年国家提出的节能减排的发展目标。在电功率不变的情况下，烘干回收性能比普通风道结构的回收率提高了23个百分点，彻底解决了电加热式蒸馏系统回收不彻底的问题。

The recovery rate of the solvent of Best has increased significantly, which makes the solvent loss significantly reduced. So our product meets the 2010 national energy-saving emission reduction goals. In the case of constant electric power, the performance of dry recycling of per product can get 23% recoveries more than others. It completely solves the incomplete recovery of electrically heated distillation system.

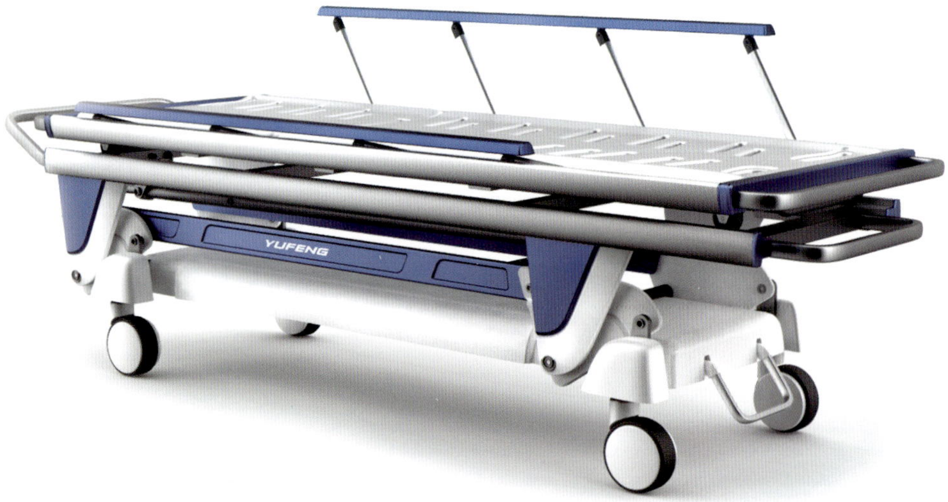

顿力多功能医疗床
Dunli Multifunctional Medical Bed

生产 / 杭州顿力医疗器械有限公司
设计 / 上海木马工业产品设计有限公司

Manufacture / Hangzhou Dunli Medical Instruments Co. Ltd
Design / Shanghai Moma Industrial Product Design Co. Ltd

在该设计中，从患者的生理和心理出发，通过解决需求的方式进行该款产品的设计。采用了仿生学的设计方法，解决了病患心理上的不安全感。包裹式的设计能够满足病患更加安全舒适的心理诉求。

This product design focuses on the patient´s physical and psychological needs. It adopts bionic design ways to solve patients´ insecurity of psychological problems. Also its packing design can make users feel more comfortable.

牙科综合治疗椅
DENTAL UNIT

生产 / 佛山市思福特医疗设备有限公司
设计 / 佛山市尚致设计有限公司

Manufacture / Foshan Safety Medical Equipment Co.,Ltd.
Design / Foshan Bob Design Co.,Ltd

这是一款融合变形金刚和牙科综合治疗仪，营造科技感和未来感，把患者就医时的心理恐惧降到最低。智能化操作、图形化显示减少医生的误操作。管路消毒系统防回吸和智能全自动，把交叉感染风险将为零，满足医学临床对医疗产品的最高要求。产品生产和装配环保低碳。

Crossover design fusion transformers and dental treatment instrument for the integration, create a sense of science and technology and the sense of the future, and reduce the patients´ fear during the treatment. Intelligent operation and graphical display reduce physician misoperation. With pipeline disinfection system and intelligent automatic suck-back preventing cross infection, the risk will be zero, satisfying the clinical medicine for medical products of the highest requirements. Low carbon products manufacturing and assembly process.

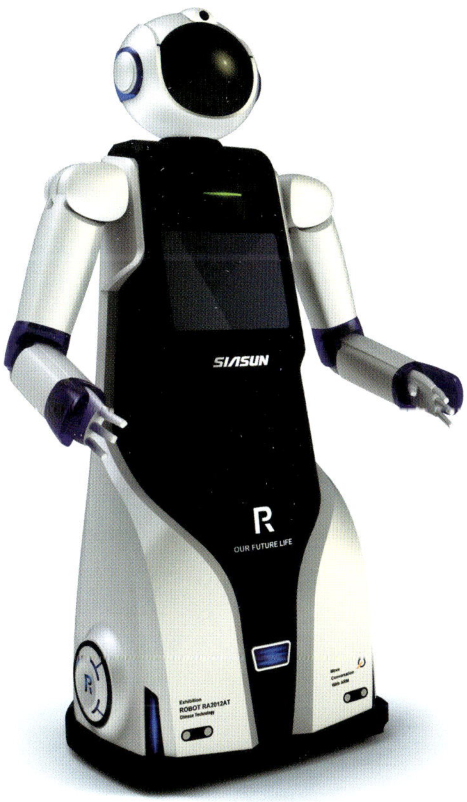

新松智能服务机器人
Siasun Intelligent Service Robot

生产 / 沈阳新松机器人自动化股份有限公司
设计 / 崔亮生

Manufacture / SIASUN Robot & Automation Co.,Ltd
Design / Cui Liangsheng

运用大弧形和切割曲线的造型设计，使产品更加人性化，大尺寸屏幕交互界面带给使用者更好的使用体验；产品外壳为塑料材质，减轻整体重量的同时也具有可回收循环利用的优点，市场性价比高。

Big arcs and cutting design being more humanized, larger interface brings the users a better experience. Plastic is applied for reducing overall weight, which is also a good sample of recycling.

光盘库yeq-001
CD-ROM Library Yeq-001

生产 / 武汉楚活汉工创意科技发展有限公司
设计 / 武汉也琪工业设计有限公司

Manufacture / Wuhan Chu&Han Seiko Creative Technology Development Co.,Ltd
Design / Wuhan YEQ Industrial Design Co,.Ltd

此产品由光盘架、自动换盘机构和驱动器LED灯、接口单元组成；可以多光盘收录，存储和直播重放的理想应用设备，还可以容纳高清录像机；可使用2000张光盘，60太比特，光盘库系统拥有XDCAM，基于文件的操作和元数据功能，具有可靠性高、寿命长、体积小等特点。

This CD library is composed of CD rack, wrapping theplate bodies and driving LED lights and the interface unit. It is the ideal application for multi-disc collection, storage and playout equipment and it can also accommodate high-definition video recorder. It can contain 2000 CDs, 60-terabit, its system having the XDCAM, file-based operation and data capabilities.

数位演讲台
Digital lcctcrn

生产 / 河北海捷现代教学设备有限公司
设计 / 深圳市舵手工业设计有限公司

Manufacture / Hebei Haijie Modern Educational Equipment Co.,Ltd.
Design / Shenzhen Helmsman Industrial Design Co.,Ltd.

融合电脑技术、显示技术、音频技术、触控技术、自动化控制技术等于一体，可同时处理视频、音频、图片、文字等信息并能自动调节高度，满足各种演讲环境需求。自动升降控制机能，可控范围900-1160MM，能充分照顾到使用轮椅的弱势群体以及特别身高的人群。

Digital lectern - It integrates the technology of PC, display, AV, touching, auto control into one. So it is easy to deal with AV files, images, texts etc. It is easy and comfortable to use by adjusting the height at your will. With the ultimate experience of fun and humanity, dignified style is suitable for multiple use environments.

消防式氧气呼吸器
Fire-Type Oxygen Respirator

生产 / 深圳昊泰气体设备科技有限公司
设计 / 深圳市柏斯工业设计有限公司

Manufacture / Jiangsu Oxtek Air Equipment & Technology Co.,Ltd.
Design / Shenzhen Perth Industrial Design Co.,Ltd.

此款呼吸器采用AB壳锁扣设计，佩戴和使用维护时简易方便。以人体呼出的二氧化碳和水蒸气为原料，整个产氧过程无有害气体产生和排放，是一款环保型的单循环呼吸器。

This respirator uses AB shell locking design, simple and easy to wear and maintain. Using the carbon dioxide and water vapor people exhaled as the raw material, the whole oxygen production process produces no harmful gases. It is an environmentally friendly single cycle respirator.

电焊机
Welding machine

生产 / 浙江台州竟添机电有限公司
设计 / 天津市易诺威工业产品策划有限公司

Manufacture / Taizhou Genteck Electric Co., Ltd.
Design / Innova industrial product planning Co., Ltd.

在机电行业中首创使用硅胶标贴，通风孔为防水性设计，广泛地应用于各工业领域。与产品的使用环境相契合，突破了电焊机的一贯造型。

This product first uses silicone stickers in the electromechanical industry and its ventilation holes uses waterproof design. This product has been widely used in various industrial fields fitting with the using environment and breaking the consistent modeling of the welding machine.

煤矿探水雷达
Groundwater Detector System for Coal Mine

生产 / 广西百色美联能源科技有限责任公司
设计 / 洛可可设计集团

Manufacture / Guangxi Baise Myland Technology Co., ltd
Design / LKK Design

设计的形态便于堆叠，管状形态便于搬运，与支架的结合最适合野外地面操作环境，产品的每个细节点均以人为中心；产品可以准确地探测水资源，今后在矿业和水资源探测领域将成为必备产品，耐高温、防撞击材料与完善的结构制作完美结合，防水、防尘、抗撞击。

The product is with combination of impact-resistant materials and the structure of waterproof, dustproof and impact resistant. The shape of cases is designed for easier stacking; the iron tubes are designed for both the workers convenience during transporting and the placements of outdoor environment. This product can accurately detect groundwater sources.

名菱工业缝纫机
MingLing Industrial Sewing Machines

生产 / 名菱工业自动化科技有限公司
设计 / 广东华南工业设计院

Manufacture / MingLing industrial automation technology Co., Ltd.
Design / South China Industrial Design Institute of Guangdong

采用新式缝纫机线架结构，将线架内置于一侧机壳中，简化穿线方式，空间结构更简洁统一；新式打版机造型，增加使用的舒适度，更有利于使用者操作，保护触摸屏在跌落过程中不受冲击而损坏；降低机体组件重量，减少能量消耗，减少零件，降低成本，机械性强。

New sewing machine line frame structure is built into the side of the chassis to simplify threading way. New pattern shape protects the touch screen in the process of falling from impact damage. Reduce the weight of the body components and the reciprocating motion is to save energy.

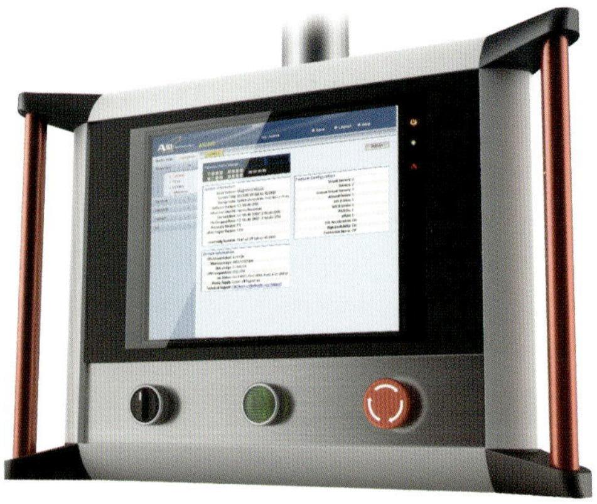

上海珅铼机电操控箱
Shanghai Sunrise Mechanical And Electrical Control Box

生产 / 上海珅铼机电成套设备有限公司
设计 / 上海木马工业产品设计有限公司

Manufacture / Shanghai sunrise complete sets of m&e equipment Co.,Ltd
Design / Shanghai Moma Industrial Product Design Co., Ltd

本产品将重点放在了控制箱的四个角上。用一种横向伸展的造型语言使产品更有气势和力量感，但又显轻盈。把手和箱体也因此有更强的关联性。兼顾了横向与垂直两种使用模式，如此一来通过更换不同角部配件能够方便地适应不同客户的使用要求。

Machine tool control box as an important human-computer interaction modules, its functionality and appearance directly affects the productivity and security operations. The electromechanical design of rhenium subscriber control box, after in-depth study of existing products on the market in lots of features as well as look to find a new balance.

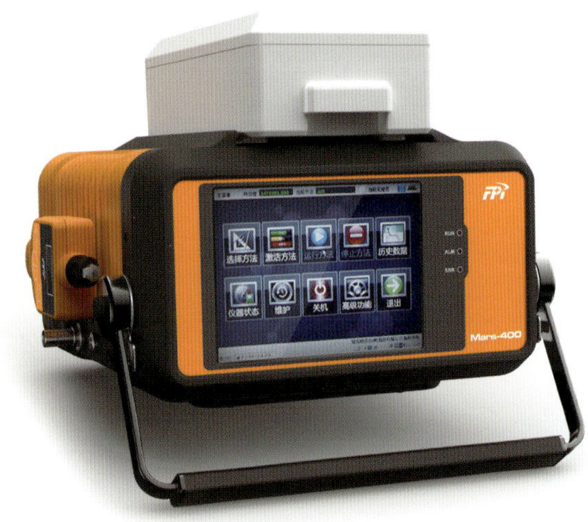

便携式气相色谱——质谱联用分析仪
Portable Gas Chromatography-Mass Spectrometry Analyzer

生产 / 聚光科技（杭州）股份有限公司
设计 / 杭州汉度工业设计有限公司

Manufacture / Focused Photonics(Hangzhou),inc
Design / HUMTA

采用国际最先进的快速气相色谱技术和离子阱质谱分析技术，可广泛应用于突发性事故的现场。外壳材料采用符合UL94和RoHS要求的高强度聚氨酯，符合绿色环保要求，外壳采用低压注塑工艺，强度可靠，工艺精湛。

This product uses the most advanced fast gas chromatography and ion trap mass spectrometry technology, which can be widely used on the site of sudden accident. The shell adopts high-strength polyurethane in accordance with UL94 and RoHS requirements, in line with environmental protection requirements. Its shell adopts low pressure injection molding process with reliable strength and exquisite workmanship.

全智能水表
Radio Frequency Water Meter

生产 / 浙江甬岭供水设备有限公司
设计 / 天津市易诺威工业产品策划有限公司

Manufacture / Zhejiang Younio Water Supply Equipment Co., Ltd
Design / Innova Industrial Product Planning Co., Ltd.

具有智能系统，自动将水表数据上传到管理系统的全智能水表，为厂家争取更多的订单，销量同比去年增加约35%。注塑工艺，适于批量生产，整体时尚的外观领先于市场现有产品，透明材料的搭配使用凸显科技感，翻开式保护盖设计，方便实用。

It has the intelligence system which automatically uploads the meter data to the management system. It wins more orders and sales increase of 35% year on year. Injection molding process is suitable for mass production. The overall stylish appearance is ahead of existing products on the market. The use of transparent materials highlight the sense of science and technology. The protective opening cover design is convenient and practical.

碳清风
Car Air Purifier

生产 / 广州市龙曦生物科技有限公司
设计 / 广州深山产品设计有限公司

Manufacture / Guangzhou Longxi Biota Technology Co., Ltd
Design / Guangzhou Sunine Product Design Co., Ltd

该产品外观采用铸造、冷热处理、喷漆及热压等工艺。能迅速改善汽车内的环境，净化空气，持久留香，价格实惠，使用再生材料，可循环利用。

This product can rapidly improve the air environment inside the car cleaning up the air, lasting fragrant and affordable. It is made with recyclable materials. It is processed with craftsmanship of casting, hot and cold processing, painting and hot pressing. It´s compact and generous.

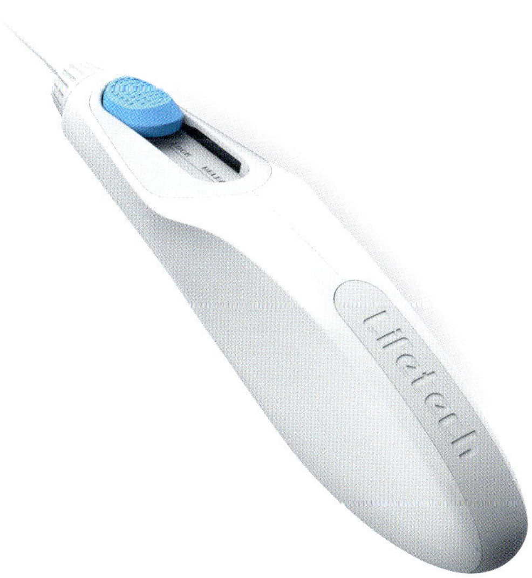

介入医疗器械手柄
Interventional Medical Device Handle

生产 / 先健科技（深圳）有限公司
设计 / 深圳市四六区工业产品策划有限公司

Manufacture / Lifetech Scientific (Shenzhen) Co., Ltd.
Design / Shenzhen April 6th Industrial Products Design Co.,Ltd

创新在于更适合医生快速安全操作的功能设计，手感设计以及美学造型。使用安全锁扣设计，防尘防细菌处理，使得手术过程安全性提高；性价比高，提升医疗品牌形象，环保塑胶注塑成型，工艺简单无其它喷涂处理，废弃之后可以回收。

The innovation point is that the functional design of the quick and safe operation of doctors, handle design and aesthetic shape. The use of safety interlocks, dust-proof anti-bacterial treatment makes surgical procedures improve security. Environmentally friendly plastic injection molding, the process is simple and no other spray processing, which can be recycled.

工业级信号浪涌防护单元
Unit Surge Voltage Protection

生产 / 北京欧地安科技股份有限公司
设计 / 洛可可设计集团

Manufacture / Beijing Allday Science and Technology Co.,Ltd
Design / LKK Design

“X”式的外观造型打破了原有产品规整保守的造型方式，突出高压防护设备产品安全性及高可靠性的产品属性；独特的前端燕尾槽卡接设计，在实现产品单体可自由取放的前提下可保证所有产品整齐有序地固定；同系列两款产品通过共同造型PI的继承，使它们组合在一起。

The "X" style appearance breaks the conservative shape of the original products in order to highlight the security and reliability of the high voltage protection equipment. By the unique front-dovetail card plug design, the product unit is free to install and set in order.

北京地铁昌平线车辆
Metro Cars for Beijing Metro Changping Line

生产 / 设计 / 南车青岛四方机车车辆股份有限公司

Manufacture / Design / CSR QingDao SiFang CO.,LTD.

产品采用国产具有自主知识产权的列车控制网络，轮盘制动，改善车轮工作环境，降低车轮踏面异常磨耗的发生机率，提高车轮使用寿命；实现了ATO自动驾驶；外观设计：线条简洁、明快，上下两条粉色带贯穿全车，具有时代气息。设计理念：人性化、模块化、标准化、通用化、国产化，安全、环保、时尚。

The train control network with our own intellectual property is adopted which is complied with IEC61375 standard. Both the train bus line and vehicle level bus line (MVB) adopt redundant double channel structure. Adoption of disk brake improves the operating conditions.

广州地铁自主知识产权直线电机车辆
LIM Metro Cars With Independent Intellectual Property Right for Guangzhou Metro

生产 设计 / 南车青岛四方机车车辆股份有限公司

Manufacture Design / CSR QingDao SiFang Co.,Ltd

这是国内自主研发的首列轻量化、低能耗直线电机车辆。整车的国产化率达到90%以上，该车辆的成功下线运营标志着我国直线电机车辆整体设计和制造技术达到国际先进水平。与传统地铁列车相比，它有着工程造价低、爬坡性能好、噪音低、曲线通过能力强等诸多技术和性能优势。

The LIM powered metro train applies for numerous technology and performance advantages such as low construction cost, high gradient performance, low noise and excellent curve negotiation ability etc. It is suitable for service in areas with higher gradients, more turns and more complicated geographic structures.

混凝土湿喷机外观及人机优化设计

Concrete Wet Spraying Machine Exterior and Human-computer Optimization Design

生产 / 成都市新筑路桥机械股份有限公司
设计 / 徐伯初、高朋飞

Manufacture / Chengdu Xinzhu Road and Bridge Machinery
Design / Xu Bochu, Gao Pengfei

以包裹的设计形式来保证外部件的整体性。对整车的造型、色彩、材质进行了优化设计，以求达到既安全适用，又美观大方。

The product uses the design of package to ensure external integrity. We optimize the design of the whole shape, color and material of the vehicle in order to achieve safety and beauty of the appearance.

长安重汽M系列新能源重卡
CCAT M Series New Energy Heavy Vehicle

生产 / 太原长安重型汽车有限公司
设计 / 周力辉

Manufacture / Taiyuan Changan Heavy Vehicle Co., Ltd.
Design / Zhou Lihui

长安重汽M系列新能源重卡造型设计具有完全自主知识产权，以煤层气为燃料动力的轻量化新型重车，和燃油车比较其消耗量可节约成本50%。

The new energy heavy truck of Changan Heavy Truck M series possesses complete independent intellectual property rights. It is a new heavy truck that uses coalbed methane as power of fuel. Compared with feul vehicles, it saves up to 50% of energy consumption.

S4200商务艇
S4200 Commercial Vessel

生产 设计 / 太阳鸟游艇股份有限公司

Manufacture Design / Sunbird Yacht Co.,Ltd

S4200采用多混复合材料节能环保双体船艇技术研究成果，属国内首创产品，填补了我国建造大型纤维增强塑料船艇的空白，创国内最大玻璃钢船艇记录。

S4200 is the first of its kind in domestic market. This catamaran boat adopts the research technology of mixed composite, energy saving and environmental protection. It fills the gap of the construction of large fiber reinforced plastic boats. It sets the record of the largest fiberglass boat.

扬帆之星1
YANG FAN ZHI XING 1

什刹海游船
Shichahai Pedalo

生产 / 北京市西城区园林市政管理中心
设计 / 北京博蓝士科技有限公司

Manufacture / Garden Municipal Administration Center of Xicheng District, Beijing
Design / IDC design

一改传统脚踏船的造型，注入了游艇的设计理念，船体内饰设计更加舒适，增加了休闲桌、专用杯架、挂钩、废物收纳架等人性化设计。船体和遮阳顶采用流线型设计，既符合什刹海的人文特征又符合空气动力学，减小风阻，提高了船的安全性，曲面流畅且富有动感。

To improve the kind of board installed solar panels, through the actual operation, its power is fully able to meet the needs of lighting at night; structural design in the foot while rotating impeller water supply of Riga, oxygen, allowing visitors to play while involuntarily waters surrounding environment.

传祺suv GS5
TRUMPCHI SUV GS5

生产 / 广汽乘用车公司
设计 / 广汽集团汽车工程研究院

Manufacture / GAC Motor
Design / GAC Engineering

传祺GS5拥有2.71米的大轴距，内部空间宽大舒适，优异的操控性与安全性，契合目前SUV消费城市化的主流趋势。通过细节设计和间隙面差控制，使内外造型的实车装配品质达到一流水平。融汇经典坚毅与现代光影设计理念，外造型动感美观，线条流畅修长，整体造型充满了时尚与现代感。

Trump chi GS5 continues to follow all the good features of GAC family, and takes SUV´s toughness and contemporary automotive design principles into account in the meantime. With dynamic form and graceful yet powerful feature lines, the overall styling delivers a sense of fashion and modern.

Z-one

生产 / 重庆宗申机车工业制造有限公司
设计 / 重庆蓝海时代产品设计有限公司

Manufacture / Chongqing Zongshen Automobile Industry Manufacturing Co., Ltd
Design / Chongqing Ocean Time Industrial Design Co.,Ltd

将Gp赛车的运动造型元素运用于150cc排量中，创造出适合中国国情风格的街跑车。匹配新型节能发动机，将经济油耗降至1.9L/100km。

The product applies the sports style of Gp racing into 150cc to create a street sports car style suitable for China. Equipped with the new energy-saving engine, it lowers the fuel consumption down to 1.9L/100km.

XMQ6125造型设计
XMQ6125

生产 设计 / 厦门金龙联合汽车工业有限公司

Manufacture Design / Xiamen Kinglong United Automative Industry Co., Ltd

采用下沉司机区域，做到乘客区域面积最大化，最大地体现商用车的价值，同时造型大胆突破传统的处理方式。公司新采用的智驱节油系统，可以比传统的客车节油10%左右，作到真正的经济环保。整车线条和细节设计上运用了美学和数学CAE进行优化。

Sink type driver area maximizes the passenger area and embodies the value of commercial vehicles to the utmost. The bold shapes that break through the traditional approach create a more personalized appearance. The new intelligent oil saving system uses 10% fewer oil than traditional buses and has fewer carbon emissions. In the vehicle lines and detail design, it makes use of aesthetics and mathematics CAE optimization.

生态迷你树屋
Eco-Mini Treehouse

生产 / 合肥德佳节能科技有限公司
设计 / 程曦

Manufacture / Hefei Deka Energy-saving Technology Co.,LTD
Design / Cheng Xi

颠覆传统路由器外观设计仪器设备类造型思路，赋予产品以纸飞机的灵动温情主题造型风格。产品性能强大，信号穿透力强，体积尺寸设计小巧，天线可收纳折叠，预留有线用户插口；产品信号抗干扰性能强，该产品造型以纸飞机为设计主题，上部的装饰件模拟纸飞机的形态。

This ecological mini tree house is the innovative prefabricated mini construction made with natural environmentally friendly materials; recycling of rainwater for plant irrigation; the use of solar, wind and other renewable energy sources; factory precast production greatly reduces material waste; the facade mainly made of green plants, blending with the natural environment.

鸣趣
Street lamp–pigeon

生产 / 四川华体灯业有限公司
设计 / 董石羽、王超

Manufacture / Sichuan Huati Lighting Industry Co.,Ltd
Design / Dong Shiyu, Wang Chao

该产品灵感来自于电线杆上的鸽子，在大都市再现仿自然界生态情景的景观性灯具。组合式多灯头的运用，有效的解决光的单一性，多层次、多角度对路面及周围景观进行照明渲染。也可融入红外线感应功能，做到间隔式感应照明。LED光源节能、环保、耐用，强弱可控。

Inspiration from the poles of pigeons, it is designed for the metropolitan reproduction imitation common natural ecological scenarios landscape lighting. Combined lamp use, it can effectively solve the problem of unicity of light, multi–level and perspectives illumination rendering the road and the surrounding landscape. It can also be integrated into the infrared induction function and do interval type induction lighting. The use of LED light source realizes energy saving, environmental protection, durable, strong and weak controllability.

高速公路绿色通道车辆检查系统
Freeway Green Corridor Vehicle Inspection System

生产 / 北京华立兴科技有限公司
设计 / 曲建全

Manufacture / Beijing Huali Xing Technology Co., Ltd.
Design / Jianquan Qu

该系统检查速度快、全自动运行、全天候工作、安全可靠，并实现了对鲜活农产品运输车辆的快速检查；系统模块化结构设计，占地面积小；可添加违规车辆信息到黑名单数据库中，自动报警；根据客户需求和情况，定制解决方案，提供数据接口，可集成到客户现有业务管理系统中。

The system implements a quick check of the fresh agricultural products vehicles, designed as modula structure. Information of the illegal vehicles can be added to the blacklist database, alarming automatically It provides customized services according to custome demand and on-site solutions.

Modular Traffic Light System

生产 / Modular Traffic Light System
设计 / Barry Geer

Manufacture / Modular Traffic Light System
Design / Barry Geer

通过其模块化功能和设计减少遭遇交通事故时的坍塌以及对交通工具的冲撞和损伤，对人行道和交通工具的伤害降到最低。在事故之后能够较快、较容易且低消耗地进行搭建和替换。较之现用系统安装费用将节省大约30%。较之现用系统维修费用和事故后的替换费用将节约大概80%。

It is designed to collapse on impact with a motor vehicle thereby preventing injuries to passengers. It is also designed to break away from the road surface thereby eliminating damage to the road surface. The system can then be quickly rebuilt by a small work crew. It is on average 30% cheaper and requires no maintenance.

电动巴士电池快换设备
Quick Change Battery Device

生产 / 电动巴士科技有限公司
设计 / 北京智加问道科技有限公司

Manufacture / Shanghai Dianba New Energy Technology Co., Ltd.
Design / ZCO Design CO., Ltd

此款产品最大的创新点在于代替现有的能源（石油）以电为动力，缓解用电高峰期电压不稳所造成的断电情况。在巴士和电池架之间更换充完电和待充电的电池，快速换电，电池体积大，能在较短的时间内为巴士换电，大大提高了工作效率。数字化操控，大部分过程无需人力。

The quick change battery device can be used at bus station and other public territory, located between the bus and battery cupboard and displaced vertically and rotationally. Meanwhile, the device displaces charged and uncharged battery between the bus and battery cupboard.

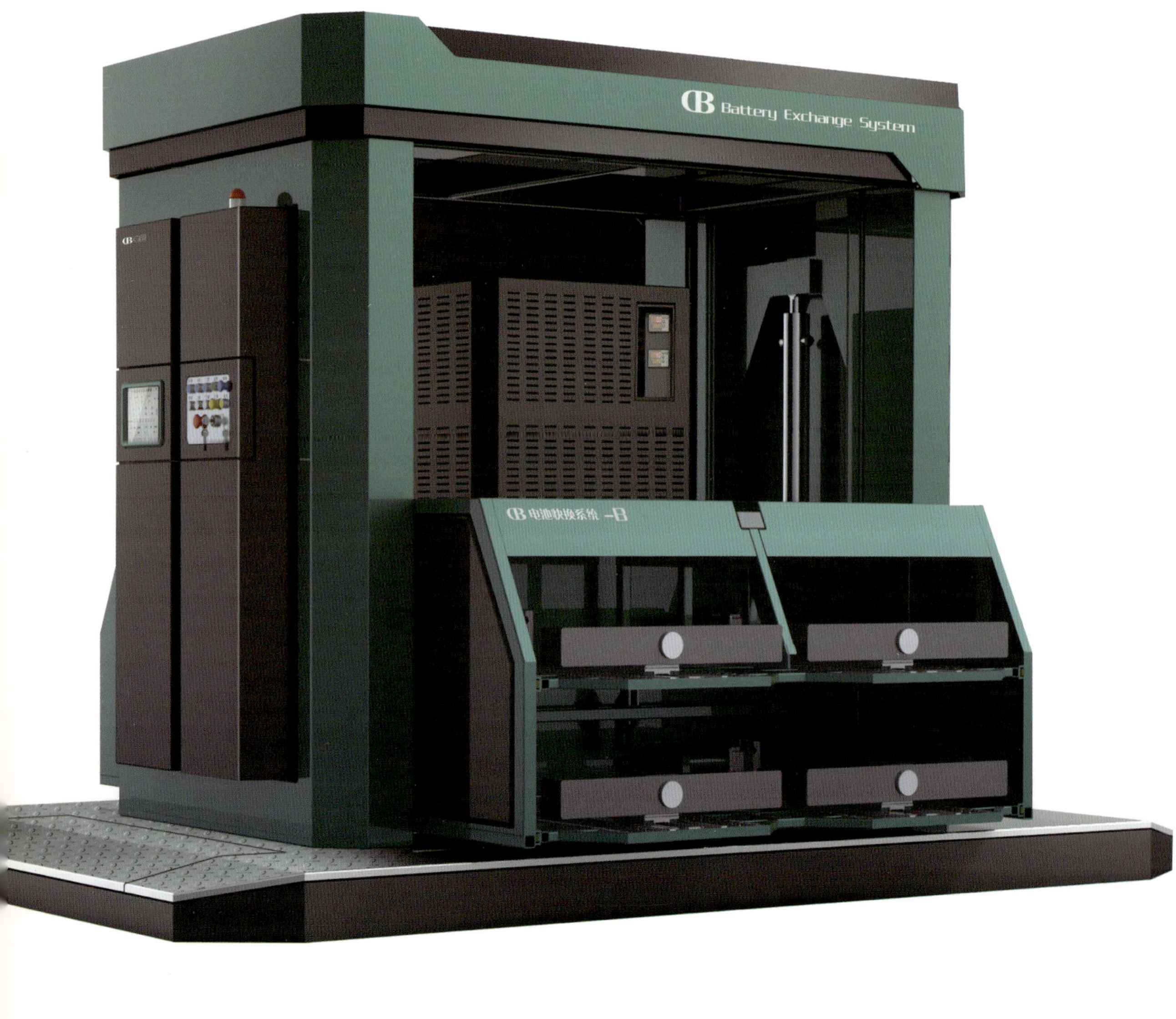

ATS自助办税服务终端
Automated Taxation Service Machine

生产 / 广东金赋信息科技有限公司
设计 / 佛山市顺德区潜龙工业设计有限公司

Manufacture / Guangdong Kamfu Information & Technology Co.,Ltd.
Design / Chinno Industrial Design Co.,Ltd

将办税系统与服务终端结合,实现24小时自助税务办理。功能模块化，标准化设计，实现以极少的投入对功能进行定制式增加裁剪，可在不整体换机的情况下，对各功能部件进行更换和升级；LED屏功能显示屏可折叠，降低运输成本。

Combining the Tax System and the service terminal it is to achieve 24-hours self-help tax issue. It realizes the functional modular, standardized design: customized to increase cutting with minimal input function to meet the local tax geographical differences and the diversity of needs: tailor-made for the local tax services.

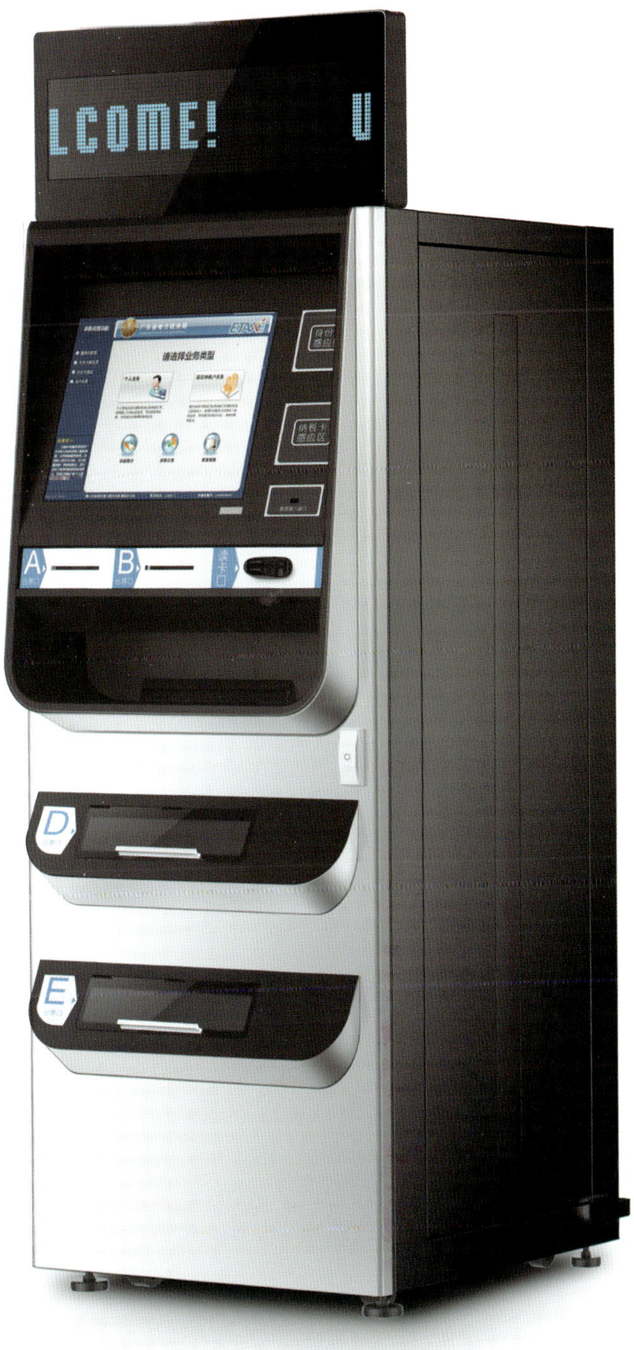

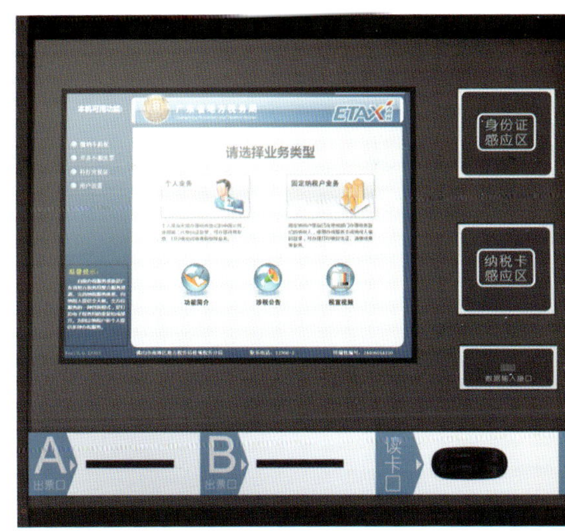

CP16老人手机
CP16 Eldly Phone

生产 设计 / 成都嘉兰图设计有限公司

Manufacture Design / ChengDu Newplan Design Co.,Ltd

这款老人手机的彩色屏幕对比度极高，采用专用光谱显示，长时间查看不会眼花、疲劳；LED灯即使在关机状态也能随时开启，SOS键能在紧急情况下提供求救功能；SAR辐射值只有0.6w/kg；手机外壳融入了IML工艺；通过调研定义出合理的字体大小。

This old mobile phone has a color screen with a high contrast, which uses special spectrum display, so long time not to view with vertigo, fatigue and other issues. The LED lamp, even in critical condition, can always open. The SOS key can not only serve for the elderly in emergency situations to provide rescue function, but also support the health detection equipment to expand the function of the mobile phone. Its SAR emission values only 0.6w/kg. This mobile phone on the screen casing design, integrated into the IML process. It is through practical investigation, virtual reality and other means, in a limited area, defining reasonable font size.

摩托罗拉锋芒 V (MT887 / XT885)
Motorola RAZR V MT887 / XT885

生产 / 摩托罗拉（北京）移动技术有限公司
设计 / 徐国伦

Manufacture / Motorola Mobility
Design / Vincent Shyu

结合工程上的设计创新及复合材料的运用，实现了紧凑尺寸及高强度机身的完美结合；第一款内置安卓ICS 4.0的中国移动TD中端智能手机；背面采用立体复合材料凯夫拉纤维，其更薄更强韧的材料特性使该产品兼具科技感与质感同时提供极佳的手感。

The product uses innovative composites and high performance materials engineered & designed to deliver minimum dimensions with maximum strength. The latest Android ICS UI complemented with unique widgets and smart application shortcuts that keep the users informed. Composite materials (Kevlar) combined with glass, metal and soft touch housings create a sophisticated expression of a modern smart phone.

手机防辐射听筒GR02
Radiation Receiver for Mobile Phone GR02

生产 / 深圳市高迪信科技有限公司
设计 / 想象力产品策划有限公司

Manufacture / Shenzhen Supertempo Technology Co.,Ltd
Design / Imagination Design Co.Ltd

为降低电磁辐射而设计的防辐射手机听筒，运用降噪技术，减少背景噪音，提高听筒的声音质量。使用防辐射听筒能有效减少92%–99%的手机辐射，环保实用。采用低碳、可回收的材质和无毒的颜色处理，丰富了产品的视觉效果，用户感受上更加温和亲切。

In order to reduce the electromagnetic radiation, advocating individuality life and design of radiation mobile phone handset, simulation of the design of household telephone handset modeling.The receiver uses the noise reduction technology which can greatly reduce the background noise, improve the sound quality.The use of radiation receiver can effectively reduce the 92%–99% mobile phone radiation, which is environmental protection and practical. The use of low–carbon, recyclable material and non–toxic color processing enrich the visual effect of the products, users feel more gentle.

康佳T621芒果手机
Konka T621 Mango Moblie Phone

生产 / 康佳集团通信科技有限公司
设计 / 成亦辉

Manufacture / Shenzhen Konka Telecommunications Technology Co.,Ltd
Design / Cindy Cheng

从印度的芒果文化遗产为切入点，背面造型与概念主题相匹配，芒果弧面造型，机壳色彩运用芒果黄，整机造型与概念神形相似；产品能支持多种软件功能，应用动画UI菜单设计，符合内销外销市场年轻，时尚人群定位。

The concept theme of mangoes is from Indian cultural heritage and the back of the modeling match the concept theme, mango arc shape, chassis color uses mango yellow. Product supports a variety of software, and applies for animation UI design to meet the market of young guys.

康佳V95
KONKA V95

生产 / 康佳集团通信科技有限公司
设计 / 周雷

Manufacture / Shenzhen Konka Telecommunications Technology Co.,Ltd
Design / Zhou Lei

正面采用QR二维码识别用户信息；机身造型轻巧，顶部配有挂绳孔，方便用户携带；设计人性化，遇到紧急情况可以一键求助；正面镜片的透明区域可以放置用户的照片和联系信息；带有和手机配套的充电套，充电套采用双色注塑的工艺，增加手机的时尚性。

The QR code is to identify the user´s info; the lanyard hole leads to be portable and user–friendly. The ´one–key´ function is designed for emergency. The transparent area of the front lens can be placed with photos and contact info. Charging sets of two–color injection molding process makes the product more fashionable.

运动三防手表手机
Waterproof sports watch mobile

生产 / 深圳市浪尖设计有限公司
设计 / 张东阳、蔡渊洸

Manufacture / Shenzhen ARTOP Design Co.,Ltd
Design / Toyio Zhang, Cai Yuanguangi

防水等级达到水深1米/时，可以适应各种天气下的各种运动的手表手机；采用可循环材料，较强环保性，采用全钢外壳，拉丝、抛光与喷砂工艺的结合使产品具有极强的品质感和精致感；将天线集成于表带上，避免了钢壳对天线的影响，表带上采用三次注塑的成型工艺。

The waterproof level reaches a depth of 1 meter / 1 hour, and it can adapt to a wide variety of sports in a variety of weather conditions. Using all-steel shell, it features wire drawing process technique, combined with polishing and sand blasting process. To avoid the negative impact of steel antenna, watchband uses the three injection molding process.

家用型信息终端
Household Multimedia Phone

生产 / 惠州纳伟仕智能媒体技术集团
设计 / 深圳市柏斯工业设计有限公司

Manufacture / NIVS IntelliMedia Technology Group, Inc.
Design / Shenzhen Perth Industrial Design Co., Ltd

家用信息终端是新型的多媒体设备，配有强大的娱乐功能和上网功能，材质上采用铝镁合金和ABS环保型塑胶，材料安全、环保、耐用，符合国际环保标准，在使用的过程中不会产生任何有毒、有害物质。

The home information terminal is a new multimedia device with powerful entertainment features and Internet capabilities. It uses safe materials of aluminummagnesium alloy and ABS green plastic. It concerns environmental protection, durability which is compliant with international environmental standards. In the process of use, it will not produce any toxic and hazardous substances.

方位D800智能VoIP视频电话
Fanvil D800 Smart VoIP Video Telephone

生产 / 方位实通（深圳）科技有限公司
设计 / 广州极至设计有限公司

Manufacture / Fanvil Technology Co.,Ltd
Design / Guangzhou UTOP Design Co.,Ltd.

基于Android OS的视频电话，自动化配置，可轻松提供对电信供应商和服务器提供商的定制服务，支持720P视频解码，H.246高清视频标准，G.722高清语音标准，具备4CIF视频通讯品质，采用最新的Broadcom芯片组。产品畅销全球二十多个国家。

Video phone is based on Android OS, automated configuration for different telecommunications service provider. It supports 720P video decoder, H.264 video standard, G.722 HD voice standard, 4CIF video communication quality, newest Broadcom IC chip set. This product sells well all over the world over more than 20 countries.

家联网终端
Home Network Terminal

生产 / 石家庄火木科技有限公司
设计 / 北京智加问道科技有限公司

Manufacture / Shijiazhuang Home Technology Co., Ltd
Design / Zco Design Co., Ltd

这是一款专为老人家庭设计的家用联网终端设备，可以通过室内视频监控，让老人儿女或监护人及时了解老人在家时的生活健康状况；本终端包含Zigbee协调器，Zigbee无线网络所包含的控制节点内容包括烟雾传感节点、煤气泄漏检测节点、红外感应防盗节点、开窗器、心脏监护仪等。

It is a home network terminal, based on the solution for home networking system, work with a Zigbee Network Coordinator, which is responsible for the entire networking timing, and resource allocation. This device is very convenient for the old people.

无线路由器
wireless router

生产 / 成都飞鱼星科技开发有限公司
设计 / 成都浪尖工业设计有限公司

Manufacture / Chengdu flying fish star science and technology development Co., Ltd.
Design / Chengdu ARTOP Industrial Design Co.,Ltd.

颠覆传统路由器的外观设计思路，该产品以纸飞机为设计主题，上部的装饰件模拟纸飞机的形态，赋予产品纸飞机般灵动温情的造型风格；产品性能强大，信号穿透力强，抗干扰性能强，造型设计小巧，天线可收纳折叠，预留有线用户插口。

It subverts the traditional ideas of appearance design of instrument and equipment. The router is with small volume size design, powerful performance and strong signal penetrability. The antenna, which has a cable subscribers´ socket, can be received and folded. The routers have strong ability of signal anti-interference.

物流PDA
Logistics PDA

生产 / 北京维信通科技公司
设计 / 曲建全、易安定

Manufacture / Beijing Vsimtone Technology Company
Design / Qu Jianquan, YI Anding

这款产品大大降低了劳动强度，提高了工作效率、准确性、快递速度；专业的人机工程学设计让手持更加舒适；为了体现对女性快递员的关爱，我们在设计中特别进行了流线型的造型处理，加入了柔软的Softtouch材料。

The product greatly improved work efficiency and accuracy. The professional ergonomic design provides a more comfortable and more suitable experience for longtime holding in hand. The streamlined shape processing, and softtouch materials reflects the care of female couriers who can work with a joyful sense.

3防PDA
3 anti-Personal Digital Assistant

生产 / 北京华夏民生科技有限公司
设计 / 曲建全、赵彻

Manufacture / Beijing China Minsheng Sci & Tech Co., Ltd.
Design / Qu Jianquan, Zhao Che

3防PDA防尘、防水、防摔，工业化外型设计,外壳坚固，防水抗震，适应高低温环境，适于恶劣的作业环境;具有大容量存储，超长使用时间，多种通讯及扩展接口，硬件模块可以根据不同的需要进行配置，软件可以全面定制等特点。

Superior protection structure design, greatly expands the PDA outdoor use. It is dustproof, waterproof, adapting to bad working conditions. It has multiple communications & extension ports, whose hardware module could be configured according to different requests, and software could be customized.

亘业世纪-多功能工业手持机
Hy-Multifunctional Industrial Handheld Computer

生产 / 北京恒业世纪科技股份有限公司
设计 / 品物（北京）科技有限公司

Manufacture / Beijing Heng Ye Technology
Design / PER Design&Consultants

机身与天线部分设计为一个整体结构，天线机身一体化后，减少了磨具数量，大大降低了生产成本，使用寿命长，各部分可分别回收、注塑，结构整合后使产品线条更加流畅。

The product integrates the body and antenna into a overall structure. This integration reduces the number of abrasives greatly reducing the cost of production. It has long duration, the various parts can be recycled seperately for Injection molding. The integration makes the structure more flowing.

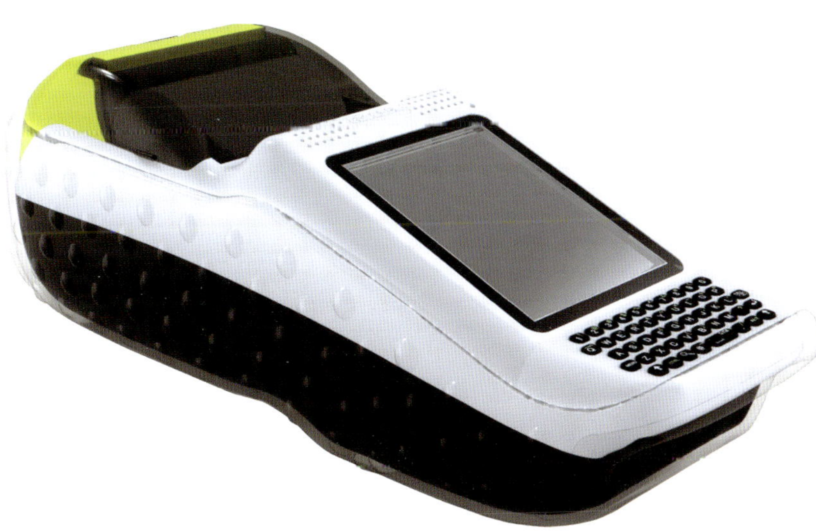

HHT无线POS
HHT

生产 / 深圳市海维海工业设计有限公司
设计 / 印度 Geoamida公司

Manufacture / Shenzhen hvhi Co.,Ltd
Design / Geoamida

该产品可以无线网络打印，实时读取信用卡，可用指纹触摸、手写笔、键盘三种输入；指纹和摄像头识别人脸系统，可以外接USB交换信息；可以用中国移动、中国电信、中国联通3G网络，多语音多国家语言识别；使用环保ABS材料。

The product holds a world's first biometric & smart card enabled, integrated multi-lingual real time and computing & transaction platform. The product is small and runs with high speed, using ABS, streamline design.

FOTA 点钞机
FOTA Money Counter

生产 / 浙江方泰电器有限公司
设计 / 杭州热浪科技有限公司

Manufacture / Zhejiang Fota Electrica Company Limited
Design / Hangzhou Hotid Technology Co.,Ltd

拥有22项国内外专利的点钞机，根据中国人的习惯，设计研发人机交互式屏幕。产品用料环保，零部件可靠性强，大大提升机器使用寿命。

This product has 22 domestic and foreign patents According to the habits of the Chinese people, interactive screen is designed and developed. Products use environmentally friendly materials and, components are reliabe, greatly enhancing the life of the machine.

智能购物车终端
Intelligent Shopping Cart Terminal

生产 / 北京中汉儒臣国际技术有限公司
设计 / 程旭锋

Manufacture / Beijing China Human International Technology Co.,Ltd.
Design / Cheng Xufeng

内置RFID无线功能，可通过无线接收厂商的广告和推荐产品信息，可提供交互操作；内置条码扫描，可在到达结账柜台前预先结算商品。产品安装在超市购物车上，坚固、耐用；性能稳定，耗能低，使用寿命长。L型装饰条使整个造型生动、流畅。

With the wireless function RFID, it can receive advertising and information of products recommended by the manufacturers via the wireless internet. People will use it easily with the benefit of interaction system. The product is fixed on the shopping cart, sturdy and durable L-shaped trim makes the whole modeling vivid and smoothly.

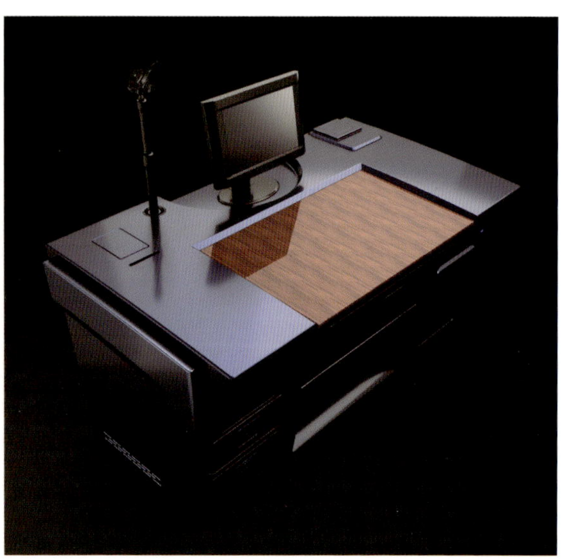

警用一体化信息采集工作台
Police Integration Information Collection Workbench

生产 / 北京东方金指科技有限公司
设计 / 北京东西创新工业设计有限公司

Manufacture / Easten Golden Finger System
Design / East&West Industrial Design Co.,Ltd

突破性地将警务工作所需信息采集集中于一个工作台上，功能多样又条理分明，大大提高了警务人员工作效率，降低其工作强度。经过深入的人机工程研究，采用一体化的紧凑设计，整合各设备位置，小到按键与指示灯的位置都高矮适中，便于操作与查看。

It is a breakthrough that collects the police work information on a table, functionally diverse and clear, greatly improving the police officers´ work efficiency and reducing its intensity. The integration of compact design sets the various equipment position. The height of the product and the position of the light are suitable, easy to operate and check.

WIA工业无线仪表
WIA industrial wireless instrument

生产 / 中国科学院沈阳自动化研究所
设计 / 洛可可设计集团

Manufacture / Shenyang Institute Of Automation Chinese Academy Of Sciences
Design / LKK Design

WIA工业无线仪表的成功推出具有重要意义，使我国在工业无线技术领域占据了至高点，彻底摆脱了对国外核心技术的依赖。产品更换电池周期为10年，周期较长达到环保目的。非对称设计形成产品大特征，造型锋利的天线意味着仪表的精准性。

The WIA–PA specification has been published as a national standard and the IEC standard is already into the CDV stage. China has relied on the international industrial automation for a long time. The cycle of battery achieves to 10 years. The design of non–symmetrical is the main feature of the product; the sharp antenna represents the accuracy.

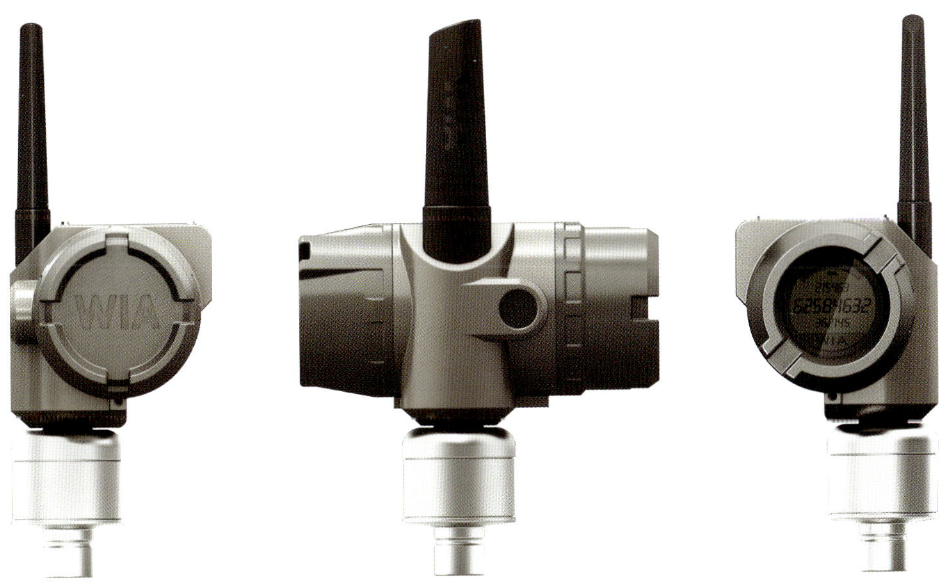

诺基亚西门子通讯三扇区信号基站
Lumina Pico Base–station

生产 / 诺基亚西门子通信
设计 / 深圳市融一工业设计有限公司

Manufacture / Nokia siemens network
Design / Shenzhen RONE Industrial Design Co.,Ltd

这是一款面向室内公共场所应用市场，以时尚、简约、科技感的设计风格，能很好地融入各种公众场合，既有品味，又不失亲和力。

This product is mainly for the application market of indoor public places with design style of fashion, simplicity, sense of technology. It can be well integrated into a variety of public places with both taste and affinity.

流动式三维扫描仪
Floating 3D Scanner

生产 / 北京博维恒信科技发展有限公司
设计 / 中国农业大学工学院

Manufacture / 3D CaMega Co., Ltd
Design / College of Engineering, China Agricultural University

这是一款具有国际先进双光投影功能，内部镜头可水平调节，双侧镜头盖板可互换，1套外壳可实现全部功能，造型小巧轻量，便于携带，可手持使用；扫描方式灵活，可多角度的自由扫描，弹式镜头盖板使用方便，能有效地保护镜头。

Its internal lens can be horizontally adjusted and its bilateral lens covers are interchangeable. This floating 3D scanner is small and lightweight, portable, and can be easily hand-held use. The scanning method is flexible, so it can scan multi-directional and multi-angle objects. The spring lens cover is easy to use, which can effectively protect the lens.

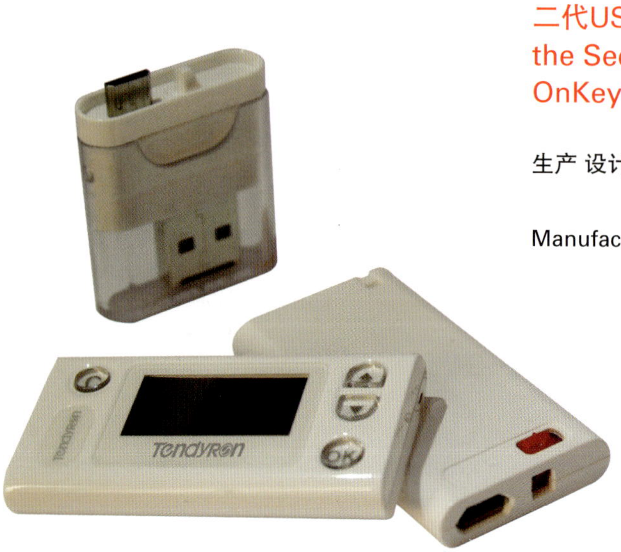

二代USBKey OnKey193D
the Second Generation USBKey OnKey193D

生产 设计 / 天地融科技股份有限公司

Manufacture Design / Tendyron Corporation

通过外接模块化设计，OnKey193D显示型USBKey变身成为一个功能平台，根据业务或技术需要可以外接不同的功能模块，增加了屏幕和按键；产品壳体材料使用高韧性、高抗冲性能的优质塑胶，所有零部件均可回收循环利用；水晶按键使用“防弹玻璃”材质。

With the modular design, the USBKey is turned into a multifunctional platform. According to technical or business needs it can connect with different functional modules such as sound-code module that supports mobile banking. All the components can be reused and recycled. All the parts like PCB board and case are made of echo-friendly materials.

警用执法仪
Law Enforcement recorder police camera

生产 / 深圳市高斯贝尔家居智能电子有限公司
设计 / 深圳汉合产品设计有限公司

Manufacture / Shenzhen Gospell Smarthome Electronic Co., Ltd.
Design / RamarkDesign Co., Ltd.

出音孔设计改变以往的碰穿式设计，改良为X型结构，既能更有效地防水又保证了声音的输出。模块化升级让产品在功能上更丰富，体积更小，组装简易并具有良好的防水功能。本产品经质量检测中心检测，通过国家警用摄像设备产品标准认证。

X-pattern resonator is unprecedentedly adopted to replace through-hole resonator, which provides better water-proof effect and sound quality and ensures 100% yield in mass production. Modular design of the product enables richer functions within smaller size, easy assembly and sound water-proof feature.

太阳能车载警示器
solar car warning device

生产 / 河南天恩太阳能科技有限公司
设计 / 孙合会、陈仕斌

Manufacture / Henan TE Solar Energy Technology Co.,Ltd
Design / Sun Hehui, Chen Shibin

将太阳能转化成电能，给无线设备充电的车载警示器，用于交通、路面、建筑、桥梁、机场、银行、大型国有公司标识警示等。

This is a vehicle warning device that can transfer solar energy into electricity and charing the wireless devices. It is used for traffic, road, buildings, bridges, airports, banks, large state-owned companies.

手持金属探测仪
Hand hcld Mctal Detector

生产 / 成都昂讯电子有限公司
设计 / 成都意町工业产品设计有限公司

Manufacture / Chengdu Angxun electric Co.,Ltd
Design / Chengdu IDing industrial design Co.,Ltd

具备高灵敏度、高效节能、携带方便、高分贝报警、告警灯提示等功能，结构合理，成本低，适用于各种重要场合的安检；外壳采用ABS工程塑料，可回收再利用，手柄被仿皮质的橡胶包裹，用户操作舒适；外观一改传统方正呆板的造型，采用曲面过渡。

The product is with high sensitive, rapid detective, energy efficient, portable and recyclable, high-db alarm and lights prompt. Using ABS plastic shell and rechargeable battery. The handle is covered with imitation leather soft rubber; providing a sense of security and confidence to be detected.

自动果蔬面膜机
Automatic Fruit Vegetables Facial Mask Machine

生产 设计 / 北京东西创新工业设计有限公司

Manufacture Design / East&West Industrial Design Co.,Ltd

将新鲜果蔬直接转化为面膜的原材料的面膜机采用日本高端的MAKA负离子强效融碎技术，可有效保留将新鲜果蔬中的营养成分。蓝光负离子处理过的面膜，营养成分更易被肌肤吸收。造型上运用点线面的有机结合，使产品具有柔性美、时尚美。

This product lets users easily change fresh fruit and vegetables into mask directly from raw materials. Face film machine adopts the Japanese high MAKA anion strong effect melts broken technology, which can effectively keep the nutrients in the fresh fruit and vegetables. Blu-ray anion processed face film, the nourishment composition are more likely for skin to absorb. On modelling using organic combination of point, line, and make products with flexible beauty, fashionable beauty.

LED深紫外便携式隐形眼镜消毒盒
Led Deep Uv Disinfection Box of Portable Contact Lenses

生产 / 青岛杰生电气有限公司
设计 / 北京东西创新工业设计有限公司

Manufacture / Qingdao Jason Electric CO.,Ltd
Design / East&West Industrial Design Co.,Ltd

以先进的UV消毒方式，消除产品和环境中致病微生物的消毒装置，以使人们的身体和生活环境更加健康。造型上将圆润的弧面与柔和的曲线有机结合，时尚又具有亲和力。白色、银色与蓝色照相呼应，展现出个人护理产品的清洁感与科技感。

This is a way to advanced UV disinfection, eliminate products and environment of pathogenic microorganisms sterilization equipment, in order to make people´s body and the living environment more healthy. Modelling draw will round with downy curve organic union, fashion and sociable. White, silver and blue photographic echo, show a personal care products and technology are clean feeling.

LED深紫外便携式消毒牙刷盒
Led Deep Uv Disinfection Portable Toothbrush Box

生产 / 青岛杰生电气有限公司
设计 / 北京东西创新工业设计有限公司

Manufacture / Qingdao Jason Electric CO.,Ltd
Design / East&West Industrial Design Co.,Ltd

这是一款以先进的UV消毒方式消除产品和环境中致病微生物的消毒装置。采用亮度可调节设计，在低温环境下也可发挥高效率，表面采用性价比较高的ABS+PC，有效控制产品成本。耗电量少，奏效迅速。采用先进的深紫外LED杀菌灯，无汞、无毒、无残留。

This is a way to advanced UV disinfection, eliminate products and environment of pathogenic microorganisms sterilization equipment. The adjustable brightness design can play a high efficiency in the low temperature environment. The surface of the high cost performance ABS + PC, effective control of the product cost. Less power consumption and work quickly. The use of advanced deep uv LED the sterilization lamp, no mercury, non-toxic, no residue.

安卓智能高清电视棒 PCTV01
Android Smart HDTV Stick PCTV01

生产 / 韩国三星电子有限公司
设计 / 想象力产品策划有限公司

Manufacture / Samsung Electronics Co., Ltd
Design / Imagination Design Co.,Ltd.

产品实现了家庭多媒体环境智能化，运行Andriod操作系统，HDMI接口，可以随时分享用户拍的照片、录像。智能电视棒用电视连通鼠标代替了显示屏。采用高光镜面模具成型工艺，低碳、可回收的材质和普通PC素材注塑，避免有毒涂料对环境的污染。

This product realizes the multimedia environment in intelligent home; PCTV runs the Andriod operating system, with a HDMI interface can make users usually travel photos, video. With the common flat compared to the computer, intelligent TV stick save display, touch screen, and was replaced by TV and the common mouse. Using of low-carbon, recyclable materials and ordinary PC material injection molding, avoidance of toxic environmental pollution.

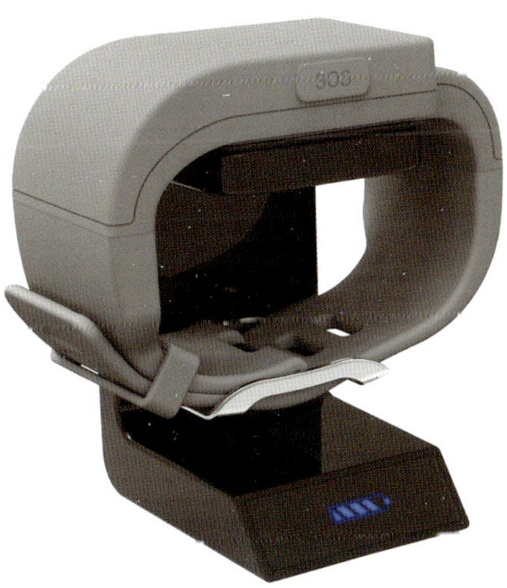

博思泰克牵手腕带
Pulsetech Hand-in-hand Wristband

生产 / 无锡博思泰克科技有限公司
设计 / 洛可可设计集团

Manufacture / Wuxi Pulsetech Co,.Ltd
Design / LKK Design

产品为特殊人群提供更多的帮助，包括痴呆症患者、残障患者、自闭症患者及户外极限运动爱好者等。在户外活动中佩戴使用，产品能够自动发出GPS定位信号，发送到指定监护人的手机终端中，实时掌握他的位置信息，全身防水设计，专用充电座使用便捷。

This wristwatch provides great help and support for specific population groups, such as Alzheimer´s patients, disabled patients, autistics as well as outdoor extreme sports lovers. The wristwatch will automatically send GPS messages to their custodians´ mobiles. And the ´SOS´ button is at the back layout in order to prevent users from carelessly touching it.

快乐童声儿童点读笔
Point to Read Pen

生产 / 湖南快乐童声教育科技发展有限公司
设计 / 深圳市群创工业设计有限公司

Manufacture / Hunan Kuailetongsheng Education Technology Co.,Ltd.
Design / Shenzhen Qunchuang Industrial design Co.,Ltd

这是一款针对儿童的教育产品，造型是在蜗牛的形态上进行抽象与提炼，寓教于乐。利用先进的技术使其真人发音不失真，并大大提高产品的反应速度。采用卡通形象，激发儿童对产品的喜爱，使得儿童在玩的同时达到学习的目的。产品累计销量已达7万台。

It´s an education product targeted at children and this design takes snail as inspiration. With the help of latest technology, it possesses a more realistic human voice feature and a much fast reaction speed. The use of cartoon image inspires the children´s fondness for learning during playing. The sales have reached over 70,000 pieces since it hit the market on Sep.

Transphone

生产 / 华移联科（沈阳）技术有限公司
设计 / 北京致翔创新

Manufacture / China Mobile Internet Technologies Inc.
Design / Aestech Design

创造性地将手机与PAD结合，完美地统一成一件高科技娱乐平板电脑，同时具有手机和pad的功能，价格只比普通手机稍高。主要使用ABS+PC的工程材料，可回收，局部金属材料同样便于回收。整体造型简洁时尚，采用时尚的包裹设计语言，降低视觉厚度。

Creatively combined mobile phone to PAD, perfectly united to one piece of high-tech entertaining Tablet PC. It simultaneously has function of cell phone and PAD with a price a little bit higher than cell phone. The use of ABS and PC engineering material can be recyled, metal material in part can also be recyled. The design is simple and fashionable and it uses wrap-around language and decreased the visual thickness.

航天信息加密移动硬盘
Password Encryption Hard Disk

生产 设计 / 航天信息股份有限公司

Manufacture Design / Aisino Corporation

国内率先使用密码算法和密码芯片，具有安全、周密的身份认证机制和直观、人性化的登录方式；采用高强度复合材料，抗震防冲击，内衬缓冲材料，具有漏电保护和过压过流保护；外壳装饰件为电镀工艺，易抛光、耐高温，具有很好的化学安定性。

The product is using cryptographic algorithms and password chip. It has a safe and careful authentication mechanism, using intuitive, humanized way to login. The professional & precise structural design is lined with cushioning material which prevents leakage and over-voltage or over-current.

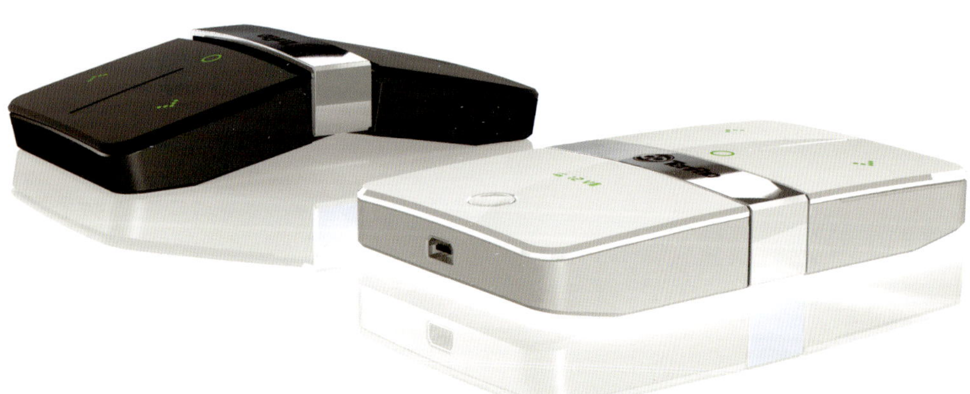

TP移动电源2
TP-Power2

生产 / 天宝国际兴业有限公司
设计 / 谭迪明、洪鸿莹

Manufacture / Ten Pao International Ltd.
Design / Daniel Tan, Tim Hung

将移动充电适配器与无线鼠标的巧妙结合，采用国际环保标准加工，具有可回收循环利用性。

The product is a clever combination of mobile charging adapter and wireless mouse. It adopts international environmental standards and processing, with recyclable materials.

航天标准19寸机柜
Space Standard 19 Inch Of Cabinets

生产 / 航天恒星科技有限公司
设计 / 北京东西创新工业设计有限公司

Manufacture / Space Star Technology Co.,Ltd
Design / East&West Industrial Design Co.,Ltd

利用覆面理念，双层门板的散热设计，有利于对机器进行散热，提高内部机器稳定性，多个机柜可组合使用。钣金的使用令其有优良的防磁防辐射性能，还可彻底防止噪音。以黑白灰为主色调突出产品的工业感、科技感，局部使用亮色，增加产品可识别性。

This product uses innovative surface concept, the double door plank cooling design, give full air circulation inside box, to slow down the ageing of the component speed. The use of sheet metal cabinet to the high and magnetic radiation prevention performance, and can also completely prevent noise. With black and white give priority to color to highlight the product´s industrial feeling and feeling of science and technology which increase the products of identification.

飞利浦 PicoPix 笔记本电脑投影仪
Philips PicoPix Notebook Projector

生产 / Sagemcom
设计 / 飞利浦设计

Manufacture / Sagemcom
Design / Philips Design

该投影仪专门用于笔记本电脑和上网本。仅包含一条USB 电缆，可充电、接收信号。产品机身上没有旋钮或按钮。机形本身显得小巧、坚固，实际占用空间少。拉丝金属和金属铬细节，营造出典雅、优质、精确的外观和感觉。外露区域降至最低，并且关注所有细节。

A very compact projector optimized for notebook and netbook usage. It includes only one USB cable providing both power and signal. No knobs or buttons on the product itself. The product appears small and strong, and it takes a little space. Brushed metal and metal chrome details achieve an elegant, high quality, precision look and feel. The exposed area down to the lowest, and it pays attention to all details.

寰烁PC投影一体机
United PC Projection Machine Electronic Instrument

生产 / 山西寰烁科技有限公司
设计 / 洛可可设计集团

Manufacture / ShanXiHuanShuo
Design / LKK Design

产品结合了投影机、PC、电子白板于一体，将高概率同时使用的会议仪器多合为一的设计，有效解决了多件器械操作与携带的烦恼；造型以产品核心——眼，为辐射原点向外发散设计元素，重点强调“眼”的视觉冲击，在投影设计领域上引领着最新趋势。

This product combines the projector, PC, electronic board all in one which will be more efficiency when having the meeting, it´s easy to operate and carry. The main design feature is the ´eye´. Keep the ´eye´ as a key word and storming other design features of this product.

机械翻转屏
Mechanical Flip Screen

生产 设计 / 北京闪图科技有限公司

Manufacture Design / Beijing Bright Vision Digital Technology Co,.Ltd

由N*3个显示单元组成的多层旋转运动拼接系统，通过机械控制和多媒体技术的结合，实现机械、广告艺术的完美呈现。三转屏系统可以根据要求定制多种层次、多种尺寸，液晶显示单元使用寿命可达3-5万单元，整体设备维护成本低。

N*3 display unit composed of multi-layer rotary motion splicing system, through a combination of mechanical control and multimedia technologies realize the mechanical and advertising art of the perfect appearance. Three-screen system can be customized according to customer demand or video showing the effect of a variety of levels, a variety of sizes. Liquid crystal display unit life can reach 30000-50000 unit, the overall equipment maintenance cost is low.

美臀电踏机
Meitun Electric Stepping Machine

生产 / 广州飞达运动按摩器材有限公司
设计 / 深圳市畅为工业设计有限公司

Manufacture / Guangzhou Feida Exercise & Massager Equipment Co., Ltd
Design / Shenzhen Municipal Industrial Design Company Limited

改变了传统机械式的运动方式，运动幅度和效果大幅增大，健腹、束腹、美腿、提臀，有塑形美体之功效，可减缓压力，减轻疲劳，对腰肌劳损、肩关节、膝关节、腰椎、脊椎、颈椎等有保健康复作用，亦可针对腿部受伤的患者进行康复训练，使运动伤害降至最低。

This product has changed the way of traditional mechanical movement and with the larger of movement range is, the body reconstruction can be better. It can help patients to recover and reduce the damage as soon as possible.

现磨全自动咖啡机
Full Automatic Coffee Machine

生产 / 苏州工业园区咖乐美电器有限公司
设计 / 无锡迪可工业设计有限公司

Manufacture / Suzhou Industry Park Kalerm Electric Appliances Co.,Ltd
Design / Wuxi DEEK Industry Design Co.Ltd

这是一款全自动现磨咖啡机。外观现代、科技，界面采用最先进的触控技术；原料为咖啡豆等，免除手动操作，整个操作过程精准控制，全新体验；平价体验星巴克咖啡，制作工艺环保；产品外观模具成型，采用金属亮面与黑色磨砂塑料材质，现代感与科技感完美结合。

A full-automatic coffee machine, using the mos advanced touch technology. The whole process avoid manual operation and to achieve precise control The craftmanship presents the idea of environmenta protection. Appearance by molding which adopts bright-surface and black matte plastic material.

和锦胶囊咖啡机
Hejin Coffee Machine

生产 / 上海和锦咖啡科技有限公司
设计 / 上海木马工业产品设计有限公司

Manufacture / Shanghai Hejin Coffee Technology Co., Ltd
Design / Shanghai Moma Industrial Product Design Co., Ltd

采用世界最严格的标准制程，通过国际专利的太空舱技术包装咖啡并填入氮气的革命性系统。完全密封充氮气包装的保护，能有效地保持咖啡的新鲜，防止氧化，使保存期长达2年之久。自动化填压，可以保证每杯咖啡的品质稳定。

Not remove packaging is placed directly into the machine, after they are cooked or facilitate the recovery Completely sealed under the protection of nitrogen-filled packaging, it can effectively keep the coffee fresh prevent oxidation, keep for 2 years of its quality and stability.

7天滴漏式咖啡机
7 Days Drip Coffee Maker

生产 / 广东美的精品电器制造有限公司
设计 / 广州易用设计有限公司

Manufacture / GD Midea Premium Appliances Mfg. Co.,Ltd.
Design / EASE Design Guangzhou Co.,Ltd

通过对温度、融合度、过滤度进行科学控制，全封闭的底板承热，保持咖啡的最佳口味，解决长期饮用速溶咖啡或外卖咖啡对身体有害或错过最佳口味等问题；采用国家食品级塑料，产品所有零部件中对人体有害的重金属物质全部被控制在安全范围内。

Through scientific control of temperature, blend and filtering fineness, it creates the best conditions to brew coffee. The totally-enclosed baseboard can keep the perfect taste of coffee. This product has achieved ROHS CE GS UL SGS TüV 3C and other international certification.

“慢生活”饼式咖啡机
"Slow Life" Soft pad Coffee Machine

生产 / 广东美的精品电器制造有限公司
设计 / 广州易用设计有限公司

Manufacture / GD Midea Premium Appliances Mfg. Co.,Ltd.
Design / EASE Design Guangzhou Co.,Ltd

这款饼式咖啡机简化了咖啡的制作流程，缩短了制作时间，采用自主研发的single-serve酿造系统，无需前期耗时的准备，配合独立包装的咖啡饼包，即酿即饮，使制作咖啡变得非常容易，让普通消费者也能轻松地品尝到专业优质的咖啡。

With the self-developed brewing system ´single-serve´, the product simplifies the coffee brewing process which highly reduces the waiting time and provides the best user experience.

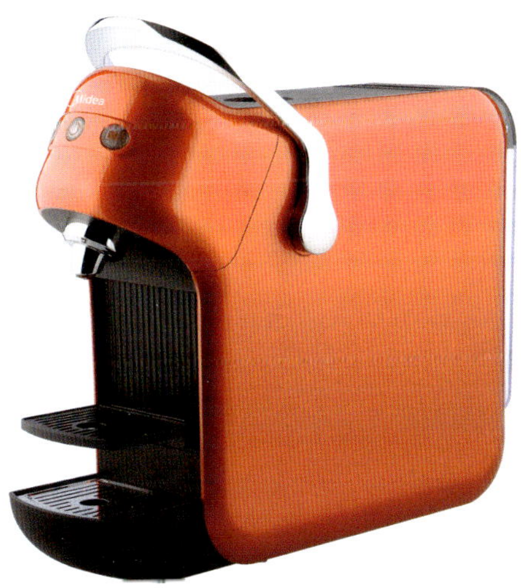

“Emotion”胶囊式咖啡机
"Emotion" Capsule Coffee Machine

生产 / 广东美的精品电器制造有限公司
设计 / 广州易用设计有限公司

Manufacture / GD Midea Premium Appliances Mfg. Co.,Ltd.
Design / EASE Design Guangzhou Co.,Ltd

这是一款新型高压意式浓缩咖啡机，自主研发的酿造系统，配合专用咖啡胶囊（塑料外壳内填装咖啡粉末），让消费者在家中就可以享用到与咖啡馆里素质相当的咖啡饮品。这款咖啡机使用便捷，酿造出的咖啡纯正，打破国际品牌对高端咖啡机市场的垄断。

"Emotion" Capsule Coffee Machine is a new-type high-pressure espresso coffee machine working with special coffee capsules (the plastic shell filled with coffee powder). It makes consumers enjoy coffee as same quality as coffee shop serves.

智能即热式开水机
Intelligent & Fast Water Machine

生产 / 宁波清清环保电器有限公司
设计 / 宁波柯怡工业设计有限公司

Manufacture / QingQing Environmental Protection Electrical Co.,Ltd.
Design / CO-YES industrial design Co.,Ltd.

整合了二合一滤芯全方位滤效技术，带净水滤芯，可以用自来水作为水源。只要3-5分钟，开水就能源源不断地供出，是铝制、不锈钢制的电热水壶的400倍，快速电热水壶（开水煲）的70倍。配有童锁，安全可靠。采用液晶显示屏，时尚的外观，大面积的镀铬饰件，彰显档次。

Intelligent & fast water machine integrates the filter technology and can be the resources of water. It just spends 3 to 5 minutes to boil water and save more time than other equipments. Equipped with safety components and reflects its high class manufacturing.

智能化自动升降厨具机
Intelligent Kitchen Machine

生产 设计 / 宁波柯怡工业设计有限公司

Manufacture Design / CO–YES industrial design Co.,Ltd.

智能厨具机迎合现代厨房理念，善用人们忽略的空间，结合人体工程学，利用高科技解决了传统厨房在电炉布线、料理流程、储藏收纳格局等方面的不合理与混乱状况，同时呼应节能、健康的设计诉求，将现代生活的优雅内涵发挥到极致。

The smart kitchen caters to the modern concept of kitchen to make good use of neglected space, combined with high technology to solve the problem of the electric furnace wiring, cooking and so on, meanwhile, it saves the energy conservation to make life become better and better.

天际智能型隔水炖盅
Intellectual-controlled stewpot

生产 / 广东天际电器股份有限公司
设计 / 佛山市顺德区潜龙工业设计有限公司

Manufacture / Guangdong Tonze Electric Co., Ltd
Design / Chinno Industrial Design Co.,Ltd

可对滋补、家常、甜品3大领域共49个品类进行专业烹饪；将炖、蒸、煮多种烹饪方式集合在该产品中实现；100℃“隔水优炖”采用精准加热技术，以水为媒介对容器中的食物进行烹饪，使容器内食物处于在恒定、亚沸腾状态；保存食物营养最佳和原始滋味。

The product is professional in cooking, nourishing, homemade desserts three major areas for a total of 49 categories. Set a variety of cooking methods like stewing, steaming, cook in the product. The Innovative point is to apply for the impermeable excellent stew at 100 ℃. Precision heating technology, using water as a medium of cooking food in the container, make food at a constant sub-boiling. Save the best and original taste of food and nutrition.

艾美特2.8L电压力锅
Airmate 2.8L electric pressure cooker

生产 / 艾美特电器有限公司
设计 / 佛山市顺德区潜龙工业设计有限公司

Manufacture / Airmate Electrical (Shenzhen) Co., Ltd.
Design / Chinno Industrial Design Co., Ltd.

设有独特的“电量查询”功能；“蒸鱼”、“煲粥”等8个常用功能的同时增设“电量查询”、“蛋糕”、“营养糊”新功能；一锅多用，2.8L容量，满足两口之家、三口之家的基本使用需求；采用高温高压烹饪，缩短烹饪的时间，从而节省用电量，符合现代社会的低碳生活趋势。

User can check how much power is used by pressing the unique button of ′check the power′. 8 common functions are set to meet the basic need of most family. Additional function such as ′check the power′, ′cake′, ′ cereal porridge′ is design for young people. It shortens the cooking time with high temperature and pressure which reduces the power-consumption.

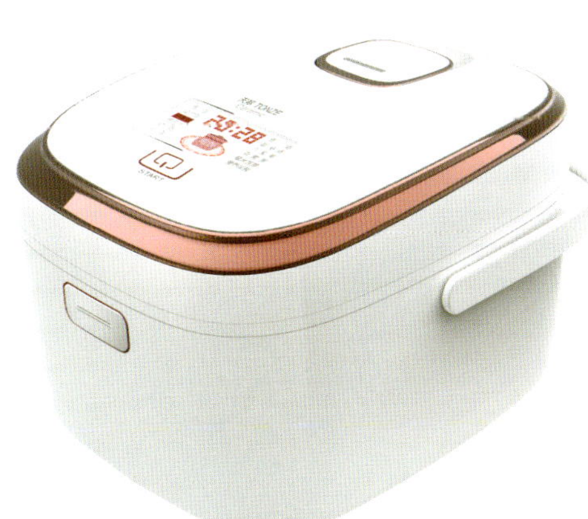

天际陶瓷饭煲
Tonze ceramic rice cooker

生产 / 广东天际电器有限公司
设计 / 佛山市顺德区潜龙工业设计有限公司

Manufacture / Guangdong Tonze Electric Co., Ltd
Design / Chinno Industrial Design Co.,Ltd

内胆以天然陶土烧制，以全程智能探测温度，实现“健康·营养八步烹饪曲线”；内胆没有化学涂层，做饭不粘，保全米粒营养结构，米饭更加营养。采用美味优质控制技术；可对稀饭、煲汤、米粥、五谷饭、白米饭、煲仔饭、八宝粥等常用食物进行针对性烹饪。

Temperature control to the whole intelligent detection, to achieve ′health, nutrition eight-step cooking curve′; the liner is truly no chemical coating, cooking non-stick; preservation of the structure of a grain of rice nutrition rice more nutritious delicious; the use of modern technology combined with traditional ceramic, play to local advantages.

便携式电热锅
Portable Steamer

生产 / 浙江苏泊尔股份有限公司
设计 / 杭州金瑞工业产品设计有限公司

Manufacture / Zhejiang Supor Co.,Ltd
Design / Hangzhou Canew Industrial Design co.,Ltd

采用强化玻璃，钢复合锅盖，强度高，可直接观察锅内食物，采用0.6mm厚度的304加厚不锈钢一次冲压成型，久用不变型。独有性专利叠放收藏设计整体造型简洁大方，普适性强。

With glass steel composite lid of high strength, the use can directly observe the food in the steamer. The steame adopts the material of 304-thick stainless steel of 0.6mn thickness, mentally forming. It is of high precision, hig strength and high duration. With the unique paten stacking design, its overall shape is simple, generou and widely applicable.

苏泊尔电蒸锅
Supor Tainless Steamer

生产 / 浙江苏泊尔家电制造有限公司
设计 / 和硕设计

Manufacture / Zhejiang Supor Electrical Appliances Manufacturing Co.Ltd
Design / Pega Design &Engineering

主体可压缩收纳，节省40%储物空间；底部隐藏式把手方便移动与堆栈收纳。性价比高，人性化功能设计；结合实用、易用的结构设计与美观的圆弧造型。不锈钢及光面塑料材质形成对比，大方且易于接受。为符合中国人蒸食的习惯，特地选择中国传统蒸笼的圆形。

We not only considered practicality of western life style and healthy concept but also improves new products along with the contrast between stainless steel and smooth plastic, gives the electric steamer a friendly and fashionable feelings.

便捷系列电蒸锅
Convenient Series Electric Steamer

生产 / 浙江苏泊尔家电制造有限公司
设计 / 马汉、成凯

Manufacture / Zhejiang Supor Electrical Appliances Manufacting Co.,Ltd.
Design / Vincent Ma, Ck

该电蒸锅蒸笼倒扣后可节省40%收纳空间；涡轮增压蒸汽系统，12秒快速产生大量蒸汽，定时响铃，火力可调，节电省电；采用强化玻璃钢复合锅盖，强度高，使用时能观察锅内食物；采用0.6mm厚度的304不锈钢一次冲压成型，底座裙边设计稳重，有层次感。

SUPOR Convenient-series Steamer is convenient to store, it can reduce 40% space after storing the food steamer. It can produce steam fast and fully in 12 seconds by the turbo supercharging system. There is a alarm clock which can prevent drying out and needless to look after. It also uses less electricity. It has high strength cover by the tempered glass and steel. It makes consumer could watch food inside when it´s working. It´s made by 0.6mm thickness 304 steel and punched once, that make it high accuracy, high strength and durable.´It seems steady by the skirt edge design of the base.

多媒体电源播放器
Multimedia Power Strip

生产 / 深圳航嘉驰源电气股份有限公司
设计 / 深圳航嘉工业设计部

Manufacture / Shenzhen Huntkey Electric Co.,Ltd
Design / Shenzhen Huntkey industrial design department

此产品采用排插与音响进行合二为一，转换器设计在音响的后端，采用背部走线，插上电源线之后完全不影响音响外观；标准音频3.5输入方式，USB提供5V/1A的充电电源，可轻松为数码产品充电；整齐的孔位分布还具有集线功能，让桌面更整洁。

This product integrates the power strip and speaker into one. The converter and the wire is at the back of the speaker. When plugged in, it does not influence the appearance of the speaker. It uses the input mode of 3.5 standard audio with USB providing 5V/1A charging power supply, you can easily charge digital products; the neat distribution of the holes at the same time has the function of collecting the wire, making the desktop clean and neat.

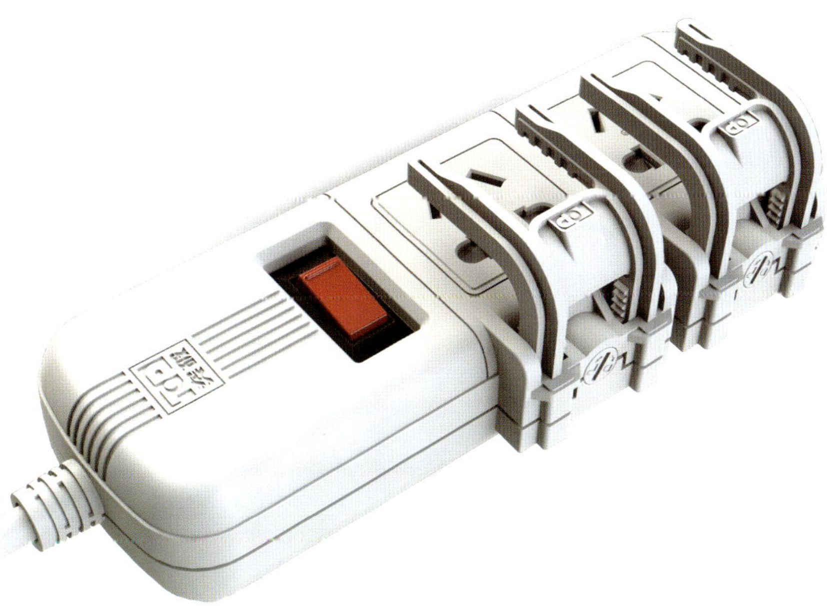

儿童防漏电保护转换器
Children-protective Leakage-preventing Adaptor

生产 / 北京突破电气有限公司
设计 / 杜大勇

Manufacture / Beijing Top Electric Co .,Ltd
Design / Du Dayong

采用专利技术的插头固定锁死机构，有效锁紧插头，不会轻易松脱，避免了插头松动情况的发生，并且操作简便，与高灵敏度的漏电保护插头配合使用，避免儿童触电事故的发生。

This product adopt plug locking mechanism. It is a patented technology for locking the plugs from loosening. The locking mechanism is easy to operate, co-ordinated with the use of highly sensitive leakage-protective plug. The product can effectively avoid electric shock accidents of kids.

原汁机
Slowjuicer

生产 / 浙江苏泊尔家电制造有限公司
设计 / 马汉、杜聪

Manufacture / Zhejiang Supor Electrical Appliances Manufacturing Co.,Ltd.
Design / Vincent Ma, Kevin Du

创新的立式螺旋挤压结构，改变榨汁机的出汁方式，完美呈现水果的原始风味；创新的多滤网设计，为不同的水果量身定做；创新的结构设计，提高水果的出汁率；慢速螺旋挤压，低噪音。产品的外观线条简练，辅以清新配色，彰显轻松乐活的生活体验。

Two kinds of filter are supplied to deal with the specific fruits, to provide more professional using.This kinds of creative structure could provide much higher juice rate than common products. This slow juicer is much lower on working noise. Elegant and concise curves together with the fresh color matches makes a happly-life product, and provide a relax using experience.

家用豆奶机
Household soy milk machine

生产 / 广东东菱电器有限公司
设计 / 宁波市鄞州潜龙工业设计有限公司

Manufacture / Guangdong Dongling Electrical Appliances Co.Ltd
Design / Ningbo Yinzhou Chinaloog Industrial Design Co.Ltd

引进高压系统，发明家用豆奶机，改变商用豆奶机的庞大体积与繁琐操作过程。内锅带把手的实用新型设计增加使用中的便捷与安全，符合国家“中国强制性产品认证制度”要求。外观造型亲和力强，与功能结构和谐统一。

This product created a new product category, it introduced high pressure system and invented the domestic soy milk machine which changes the volume of commercial soy milk machine and tedious operation process. The new design increases the convenience and safety when using it. This product meets the requriment of China Compulsory Certification (3C).

微压豆浆机
Micro-pressure Soymilk

生产 / 中山市美斯特实业有限公司
设计 / 上海跃意工业产品设计有限公司

Manufacture / Zhongshan Mester Industrial Co.,Ltd.
Design / Shanghai YOY Industrial Design Co.,Ltd

采用水平旋合过电方式，相比传统的上下直插式过电结构不容易进水，更安全，而且可以垂直提拿，使用更便捷；采用上置式排气装置，能有效防止蒸汽四溢，减少热量流失。在微压环境中使得制浆温度更高，煮浆过程中泡沫量得到了减少，从而释放出更多的营养物质。

The newly released Soymilk machine changed traditional structure. First, horizontal rotary joint electric way, compared to the top and bottom-line over power structure is not easy to be watered , even more safer, and can be lift vertically which more convenient to be used.

九阳豆浆机-D56SG
Joyoung SoyMilk Marker-D56SG

生产 / 九阳股份有限公司
设计 / 和硕设计

Manufacture / Joyoung Company Limited
Design / PEGA Design &Engineering

这是业内第一个可以收纳顶部把手的豆浆机，方便收纳。另外收纳把手也扩大了操作界面的区域，使用者操作更加直观。针对国内家庭，为1-3人提供营养豆浆。携带方便，无噪音不锈钢杯体、PC材质。人性化设计，美观舒适。

This is the first soya maker with the hidden handle; it´s convenient to accept raw materials and can widen operation areas to realize directly operation. Also according to domestic families it can be carried easily, the PC material shows human nature design, beauty and comfort.

美的凡帝罗滚筒洗衣机
Midea Vandelo Front-loading Washing Machine

生产 / 无锡小天鹅股份有限公司
设计 / 小天鹅工业设计团队

Manufacture / Wuxi Little Swan Company Limited
Design / Little Swan ID team

紧凑控制面板，人性化设计，增高底座，不仅能够储存用具，而且操作舒适，按键开门，即使是孕妇或老人也能轻松开门；创新型“S型提升筋”、“鹅卵石”内筒设计，搓揉加搅拌，使洗衣效果达最佳状态；“8”倾斜鼓设计，易于使用，同时提升和摔打面料。

The compact control panel and the heightening pedestal can even make pregnant women and old people operate easily. Shape of baffles and pebbles cylinder achieve the best wash performance by rubbing and agitating clothes. The 8 tilted cylinder is easy to use while loading and unloading fabrics.

小天鹅迷你机
Little Swan Mini Washing Machine

生产 / 无锡小天鹅股份有限公司
设计 / 小天鹅工业设计团队

Manufacture / Wuxi Little Swan Company Limited
Design / Little Swan ID team

全新的外观设计，钢化玻璃阻尼门盖，承压能力大，耐划伤，不易磨损，滴塑把手，创新使用，PP材料加ABS注塑，既环保又节约成本；LED显示，洗涤过程一目了然；3公斤容量更突出其小容量、大身手，卫生安全，健康杀菌、分类洗涤。

The product uses tempered glass damping door appearance, mini size, compact and convenient, scratch resistance. Cylinder diameter is smaller, uses less water and light weight. Plastic drop handles, innovative use of PP material and ABS injection, echo-friendly and cost savings.

美的凡帝罗波轮全自动洗衣机
Midea Vandelo Top-loading Washing Machine

生产 / 无锡小天鹅股份有限公司
设计 / 小天鹅工业设计团队

Manufacture / Wuxi Little Swan Company Limited
Design / Little Swan ID team

采用自主研发的“intime”技术，可以帮助用户自己定制在规定的时间内的洗涤和用水比例，完美洗净衣服，非常的人性化；创新的“泉涌”水流技术，可以使得衣服在该洗衣机内比常规洗衣机得到更好的清洗，并且衣物不缠绕。

The ´intime´ technology can help users to their own custom settings within the stipulated time washing and water ratio.The innovative ´Spring´ water gush technology can make the clothes better than conventional washing machines, also prevent twist of closhes.

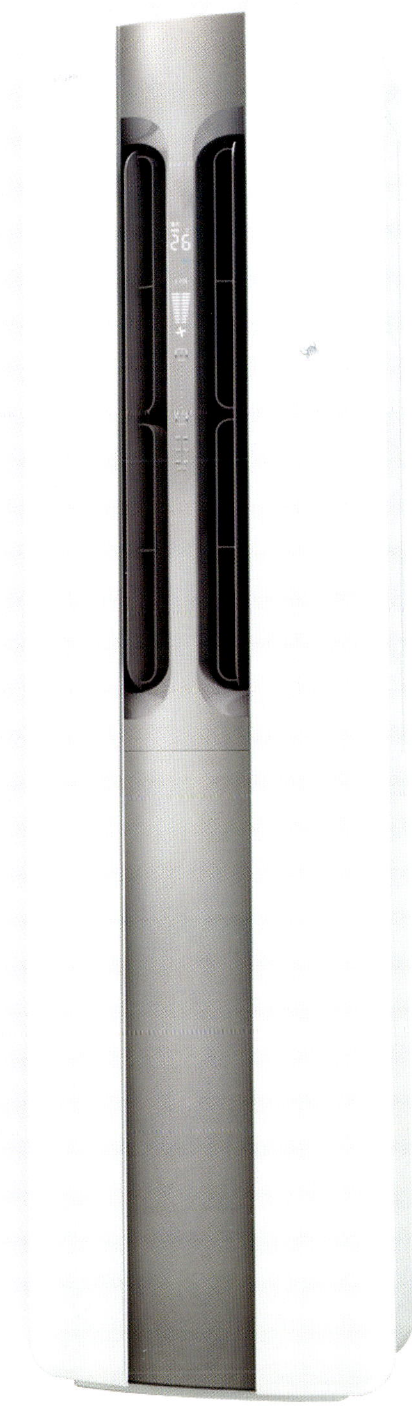

美的KF双贯流柜式空调
Midea KF Air-Conditioning

生产 设计 / 广东美的制冷设备有限公司

Manufacture Design / Gd Midea Air-Conditioning Equipment Co., Ltd.

创新双贯流结构，745mm超长纵向双出风口，上下左右立体送风。在进风格栅处设计两条引导轨道，过滤网可以方便地拆卸与安装。产品能效等级达到国家二级能效标准，更加节能省电。整体风格简洁大方，柔和、光滑的形态设计，赋予这款家电产品感性的、亲和的外观。

The innovative structure of Double Tubular contribute to all side 3D blowing with a super long double direction blowing air outlet, the length of which is 745mm. And it uses a intelligent Sensor Technology which realize the functions of inductive switch and inductive prevention of hand hurt.

家庭植物工厂
The Plant Factory for Family

生产 / 北京京鹏环球科技股份有限公司
设计 / 北京博蓝士科技有限公司

Manufacture / Beijing Kingpeng International Hi-Tech Corporation
Design / IDC design

这套系统不仅能满足家庭对蔬菜安全、卫生、绿色需求，而且通过结构设计，使得植物工厂通过侧面通风孔吸入室内的二氧化碳，释放出氧气，形成与室内环境的空气循环，在带来绿色蔬菜的同时，还能给室内营造良好的空气环境。

The system not only can keep the vegetable of family safety, health, green demand, and also absorb Habitat environment of Carbon dioxide and emit oxygen to create a comfortable environment for families and building office. Also the large area of transparent acrylic material reflects the viewing and technological sense, the overall style attributes of the home appliances product.

新飞BCD-366WV除菌冰箱
Xinfei BCD-366WV Anti-bacteria refrigerator

生产 设计 / 河南新飞电器有限公司

Manufacture Design / Henan Xinfei Electric Co. Ltd

设定了新的立体除菌技术标准，达到国家除菌A级标准，成为行业除菌技术的领路人。低能耗，0.95kw·h/24h，成本低廉，优化的工艺。无CFC/HFC，低噪音。

The product set a new technological standard of three-dimensional sterilization satisfying the national sterilization Class A standard, leading the industry of sterilization technology. It has the advantages of low energy consumption, 0.95kw. h/24h, low cost, the optimizing process, without CFC / HFC and low noise.

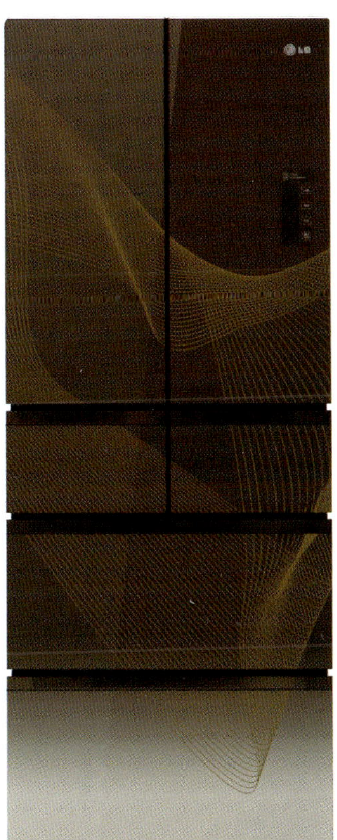

第二代“五星”玻璃面板多门冰箱
Five Star 2.0 Glass Panel Multi-door Refrigerator

生产 / LG电子
设计 / LG电子中国设计中心

Manufacture / LG Electroni
Design / LG Electronics Design China

这是一款无边框、全钢化玻璃面板的冰箱，隐藏式触摸显示屏，内嵌式一体化把手；冷藏室随心空间设计，用户可分开存储不同物品，增加冰箱内部实用性；智能变频技术，高效节能；无霜风冷，持久保鲜；四阶段净味杀菌系统，饮食健康有保证；超白玻璃双面印刷，图案层次分明。

Borderless, full toughened glass panel, hidden display touch screen; embedded type all in one handle, outward concise appearance and prevent being injured. Refrigerator room Hygiene zone design,to help the user to achieve different things, different items separate storage purposes, increasing the practicality of the refrigerator. Smart frequency conversion technology, high efficiency and energy saving. Frostless, cool air and lasting preservation; four-step sterilization system for healthy diets. Ultra white glass with double-sided printing, well arranged design patterns shows glistening impressive feeling.

物联网智控抽油烟机
Networking Intelligent Control Range Hoods

生产 / 万家乐
设计 / 梁智坚、刘诗锋

Manufacture / MACRO
Design / Benie Liang, Liu Shifeng

采用整板设计倒角处理，更加融入家居环境。采用新型的整板钢化玻璃，与拉丝铝型材搭配，减少废料，多重滤网设计，更彻底净化油烟。工艺与材料使用合理，产品品质符合和达到国内外相关质量标准；整体设计简洁大气，与现今消费者的审美观吻合，稳重大气。

Using a new type of the plate glass and brushed aluminum collocation has been adopted for construction to reduce the waste. Technology and theory have been combined to reach the international quality standards also according to modern aesthetic.

莲花灶B809C
Lotus Cook Top B809C

生产 / 中山华帝燃具股份有限公司
设计 / 北京圣宝地工业设计有限公司

Manufacture / Zhongshan Vatti Gas Appliance Stock Co.,Ltd.
Design / CBD Group Corp.

针对用户需求而设计，符合客户品牌的核心价值，增强了品牌竞争力。采用“3D开放式进风技术”，热效率比国家标准高出7%-8%，实现燃烧性的大幅提升，减少了废气的排放。集成和整合的设计，减少了生产流程、开模和安装，易于生产。

This product is designed targeting the user needs in line with core value of a customer brand, enhancing the brand competition. It adopts the 3D open-air intake technology with thermal efficiency of 7-8% higher than the national standard. It greatly improves the burning efficiency and reducing the waste emission. The integral design simplifies the production process, molding and instalment, easy to produce.

德意JZDY(T)-299A灶具
DE&E JZDY(T)-299AStove

生产 / 浙江德意厨具有限公司
设计 / 杭州飞鱼工业设计有限公司

Manufacture / Zhejiang DE&E Kitchen Utensils Co.,Ltd
Design / Hangzhou Feish industrial design Co., Ltd.

“智慧火”以“智燃”技术和“智控”设计，实现660W-2200W功率的6段火力，稳定高效；灶具燃烧所需空气完全从灶具台面上方进入，独立供氧，彻底杜绝燃气灶与电磁炉混合进风、散热的问题；一体钢化玻璃面板搭配电磁灶肖特微晶玻璃，精致典雅。

The ´intellectual fuel´ technology and ´intelligent control´ design are used for the ´Smart Fire´ to realize 660W-2200W power with 6 paragraphs of firepower. Its glass-ceramic appearance is easy too clean and shows dedication and elegance.

红星奖 Excellent Prize

灵劲系列
Dynamica Series

生产 / 中山华帝燃具股份有限公司
设计 / 北京圣宝地工业设计有限公司

Manufacture / Zhongshan Vatti Gas Appliance Stock Co.,Ltd.
Design / CBD Group Corp.

采用“一键自动清洗”的专利技术，解决内部清洁问题；整个套系产品以玻璃材质为主，表面光滑，且金属表面采用特殊处理，易打理。针对中国的高端消费者，将“聚能灶”、“自动清洗”、“智能控制”等核心技术有机地结合在一起，着重于提升使用者的操作体验。

This product uses the patented technology of the onebutton automatic cleaning´ to solve the problem of internal cleaning. The entire series of products is mainly made of glass with smooth surface. The metal surface uses special treatment and easy care. Targeting China´s high-end consumers, it integrates ´shaped kitchen´, automatic cleaning´, ´intelligent control´ and other core technologies into one, focusing on improving the user´s operating experience.

25mm 超薄电磁炉
25mm Ultra Slim IH

生产 / 浙江苏泊尔家电制造有限公司
设计 / 马汉、杜聪

Manufacture / Zhejiang Supor Electrical Appliances Manufacturing Co.,Ltd.
Design / Vincent Ma, Kevin Du

采用创新的结构及风道设计，把电磁炉品类的厚度从55mm减小到25mm，最薄的厚度仅为21.5mm。创新的加热部件及结构设计使得产品热效率更高，用电更少，加热更快。产品小巧易收藏，超大磁板永不褪色。超薄、时尚磁板设计给消费者带来更艺术更时尚的烹饪体验。

The thickness of this product is reduced from more than 55mm normally to 21.5mm thanks to the innovation of structures and air channel, which is the thinnest in the market. The innovation of heating technology make this possible: less electronic cost, less noise, less time. Due to the excellent design for the fixing structure, it can be used longer than before, and never lose color. The ultraslim and pattern design greatly fit the kitchen decoration and shift cooking behaviors from house working to fashion enjoyments.

消毒柜ZTD90B16
Sterilizer ZTD90B16

生产 设计 / 宁波欧琳厨具有限公司

Manufacture Design / Ningbo Oulin Kitchen Utensils Co., Ltd

该产品采用独创旋转独立式开关加液晶LCD显示控制系统设计，满足各种食具的放置要求。臭氧、紫外线双重消毒；高效光波热循环烘干系统；拥有制动锁、门开关、过热过电流保护三重保护。

This product uses the original rotation independent switch and the design of LCD display control system meeting the placement of a variety of utensils. The duel disinfection of ozone and ultraviolet; efficient light wave thermal cycle drying system; triple protection of brake lock, door switch and overheating-overcurrent protection.

i-FIVE 集成灶
i-FIVE Integrated Environmental Kitchen

生产 / 浙江奥田电器有限公司
设计 / 杭州金瑞工业产品设计有限公司

Manufacture / Zhejiang Aotin Electric Appliances Co.,Ltd
Design / Hangzhou Canew Industrial Design co.,Ltd

将油烟机、燃气灶、蒸汽炉、烤箱、拉篮五位一体，采用无缝隙电磁升降风门，集成化设计，碳晶玻璃整体切割，搭配进口304不锈钢，燃烧器采用德国IBG技术特氟龙喷涂。一体式设计理念，玻璃不锈钢完美比例搭配，整机大气干净。

This product integrates range hood, gas stoves, boilers and furnaces, ovens, baskets into one. It adopts seamless electromagnetic lift throttle and integrated design. The panel imports of carbon cut crystal glass as a whole, combined with imported 304 stainless steel. Burner is sprayed Teflon of German IBG technology Teflon. Integrated design concept, glass in perfect proportion with stainless steel makes the whole atmosphere is clean.

ROBAM-812

生产 / 杭州老板电器股份有限公司
设计 / 王强

Manufacture / Hangzhou ROBAM Appliances CO.,LTD
Design / Wang Qiang

创新的回形闭合杀菌技术，实现真正360度全方位杀菌。采用晶钻光感技术，多重反射杀菌，净化无味。

This product innovatively adopts back to front closed sterilization technology to achieve true 360-degree sterilization. It adopts crystal diamond light sensing technology, realizing multiple reflective sterilization, tasteless purification.

水滴石LED电视
Constant Dropping Wears The Stone Led TV

生产 / 深圳创维——RGB电子有限公司
设计 / 创维创新设计中心

Manufacture / Skyworth–Rgb Electronics Co.,Ltd
Design / Skyworth–Rgb Electronics Co.,Ltd

设计灵感源于中国成语“水滴石穿”。主体装饰条像一滴水滴入下边的圆盘，圆盘内置电路板、整套音响系统和主体通过无线连接技术进行传输。框式的金属支架固定住电视主体，用底部圆盘来做配重。电视和下方圆盘之间射出一条光线，使用者可通过阻隔光线来开关机。

It is based on the Chinese idiom: constant dropping wears the stone. The main–body decoration strip looks like a drop of water dropping into the disc below, which is internally installed with the electric circuit and sound system and connected with the main body by wireless connection technology. The main body is fixed by the metal frame, the disc below could well weight balance the whole. There is light between the main body and the disc, which could control the on and off of the TV.

K91

生产 / 联想（北京）有限公司
设计 / 联想创新设计中心

Manufacture / Lenovo
Design / Lenovo Innovation Design Centre

使用方式从被动变成了主动操控，内置摄像头面部识别，充当应用程序锁定安全功能。配有3副3D眼镜和1副夹片式3D眼镜，实现2D与3D的轻松切换。“沉稳和写意”的设计风格。流畅的线条则像极了中国水墨画里写意的手法，让它的外观里多了一份灵动。

The Lenovo′s first smart TV– K91 transfers users from passive view to active administration. Equipped with 3 pairs of 3D glasses and 1 pair of clamping 3D glasses, the TV can meet the needs of a family to watch 3D programming and achieve switch between 2D and 3D easily.

"都看"阅读器
Doucon Reader

生产 / 北京当当科文电子商务有限公司
设计 / 洛可可设计集团

Manufacture / Beijing Dangdang Kewen E-commerce Co., Ltd.
Design / LKK Design

依托于当当的图书平台，设计的一款方便快捷的显示设备，机身两侧的翘边设计很好地解决了电子书持握手感不好和单手持握易掉的问题，同时支持红外感应，还原人们纸质书的阅读体验；方便快捷的获取当当的图书资源，同时获得良好的阅读体验。

This product is designed based on Dang Dang Online. The two curved edge were designed for slide-proof and improve the feeling of touch.IR device is designed to reappear the original reading experience. It is easy to get the book resources and better reading experience form Dang-Dang book store.

Asus Padfone Series A66/P02

生产 / 华硕电脑（上海）有限公司
设计 / 华硕电脑设计中心

Manufacture / Asustek Computer, Inc.
Design / Asus Design Center

这是一款手机与平板产业相结合的突破性产品。配有Android 冰淇淋三明治操作系统；Padfone Station能让使用者享受手机与平板电脑各自的优点，加入SIM卡，就能拥有手机的便利性与平板大屏幕的双重享受；锂电池能维持高达63小时的通话时间，节能环保。

Asus Padfone is a breakthrough product for the mobile phone/tablet industry. Users will only need to carry one SIM card but with unrestrained usage. All data will be stored in one place; there will be no syncing data between devices. They are easy to decompose, recycle and reuse. Batteries can last up to 63 hours of extended talk time.

平板电脑
MID

生产 / 深圳市群创电子有限公司
设计 / 深圳市群创工业设计有限公司

Manufacture / Shenzhen Qunchuang Electronics Co.,Ltd
Design / Shenzhen Qunchuang Industrial design Co.,Ltd

集传统平板电脑功能与通话功能相结合，除具有上网、娱乐、办公等功能外，支持2G、3G视频通话，网络传输等功能。在造型上以"钱包"形态为设计概念的时尚跨界便携式数码通讯产品。产品自2012年4月上市以来，销量已经突破10万台。

It´s a portable digital product which uses purse as inspiration, integrates the function of panel computer and mobile phone. Beside the regular entertaining, games, internet and office utilities, it´s also support 2G and 3G video calls and data transfer with a slim and smart look. The sales have reached over 100,000 pieces since it hit the market in April, 2012.

SKYWORTH-E810 LED TV

生产 / 深圳创维——RGB电子有限公司
设计 / 创维创新设计中心

Manufacture / Skyworth-Rgb Electronics Co.,Ltd
Design / Skyworth-Rgb Electronics Co.,Ltd

该产品采用透明渐变印刷装饰条，高亮不锈钢前壳，磨砂拼接中框。独特的双立人底座，既节省了材料，又增强了整机的稳定性，底座下部空间可以用来摆放DVD等产品。金属折弯拼接，减少开模成本，屏体前壳直接作为外观前壳。整体高亮金属材质体现出极强的奢华感。

It adopts the transparent and gradual changed color of the print decoration strip, with the highlight stainless steel front cover and the dull polish montage middle cover. What's more, the shape of the base could great reduce the cost of the material, but also add to the stability of the TV and the space of the base could well contain the DVD. The technique of bending and split joint of the metal could reduce the cost and the front cover is the screen cover. The overall highlighted metal material reflects the strong sense of luxury.

V6500超窄边3D液晶电视
V6500 Ultra Narrow 3D LED TV

生产 / TCL多媒体科技控股股份有限公司
设计 / TCL多媒体工业设计中心

Manufacture / TCL Multimedia Technology Holdings LTD.
Design / TCL Multimedia Industrial Design Center

极窄包边设计，边框相当于一枚硬币的厚度，极致弱化了电视画面与真实环境的界限的电视，采用第二代不闪式3D技术，支持WIFI无线上网、超级智能云电视、Android4.0平台、语音识别，手势识别，多屏互动等功能属性，充分满足了消费者的多样化需求。

This product has an extremely narrow edge design, the border is equivalent to the thickness of a coin, which weaken TV screen and the limits of real environment. It uses the second generation no-flash type 3d technology, support wi-fi wireless internet, super smart cloud TV, Android4.0 platform, speech recognition, gesture recognition, screen interaction between functional attributes, which fully meet the diverse needs of consumers.

苹果（iPhone 4/4S）专用高容量后备电源
iPhone 4/4S Mobile energy

生产 设计 / 福建考克电子科技有限公司

Manufacture Design / Fujian Kaoke Electronics Science & Technology Co.,Ltd

产品便于携带，无需充电线，就可给苹果手机（iPhone4/4S）供电。设计了灵活的滑杆式结构组件，可上下拉动外壳，不损害手机。当给手机充电时，拨打电话、接听等都无需拆卸。产品电路设计上采用多重电路保护方案，有防止过充、过放、瞬间电流增大等保护。

The product is easy to carry and charge power for iphone 4/4s without charging wire. The slider construction system design can make it prevent from damage. Also multi protection planes have been made to give better safety environments for users.

盲文点读机
Dotty

生产 设计 / 和硕设计

Manufacture Design / PEGA Design &Engineering

设计师设计了卡片般大小的发音器，机身与按键分别使用橡胶与塑料，方便用户清楚分辨按键的位置。仿真盲文字板在背面扎凸点，正面摸读盲文的方式，提供简单而高效的练习方法，背面扎点按键周边倒角斜面设计，按压更加舒适。用高丽的颜色与黑色相结合，提高弱视儿童对盲点的识别率。

Combining the design and technology, the visual impaired children can learn Braille on their own without adult´s assistant on site. We created a pocket sized pronunciation device, with different materials so the users can identify the keys easily. The action of pressing the keys is designed to mimic how the children write dots on paper.

移动电源2900
Mobile power 2900

生产 / 比亚迪精密制造有限公司
设计 / 岳文龙

Manufacture / BYD Precision Manufacture CO.,Ltd
Design / Yue WenLong

UI界面简洁，内置震动感应器件，摇晃后显示电量；小体积大容量，极简方圆体形，有舒适握感和优秀抗压性；优化电源管理技术，提升充电转化效率；高度可回收铝合金机身运用铝挤压成型工艺，不等厚度特殊截面设计，阳极氧化着色工艺使产品色彩更丰富、持久。

UI interface is simple, the built-in vibration induction device, after shaking it can display power. The smallest size for high capacity, extremely brief the body shape. The simple design for eaiser holding and fine resistance to pressure. The optimized power management technology improves charging transformation efficiency. Highly recycling aluminum alloy fuselage use aluminum extrusion forming process, unequal thickness special section design, anodic oxidation coloring process make the product´s color more rich and lasting.

华硕变形平板
ASUS Transformer Series

生产 / 华硕电脑（上海）有限公司
设计 / 华硕电脑设计中心

Manufacture / Asustek Computer, Inc.
Design / Asus Design Center

一款理念领先行业的创新产品，开创了一个全新的产品类型，其独有的可拆卸基座设计完善地为用户提供了移动的灵活性，以其广泛且富弹性的使用模式进一步地满足了用户们多样的需求。运用先进的电子科技提供最长的电力使用时间。华硕变形平板代表着工艺与技术的成就。

Transformer series successfully creates differentiation and opened up a new type product that benefits users from its mobile flexibility by introducing a detachable docking design. It fits with a new perspective of lifestyle on enjoying watching and sharing digital contents anytime and anywhere for instant and intuitive media consumption.

IdeaPad Yoga

生产 / 联想（北京）有限公司
设计 / 联想创新设计中心

Manufacture / Lenovo
Design / Lenovo Innovation Design Centre

通过360° 自由旋转的触控显示屏，提供给消费者从笔记本到平板电脑最为便捷的使用转换路径，从而带来最为顺畅的多模式体用体验；在硬件配置方面，它搭载Intel Ivy Bridge平台的最新的第三代Core i7处理器，即开即用；灵感源自于人练习瑜伽的各种体式，配合烟灰和日光橙两种颜色，优雅时尚而又简洁。

The most outstanding feature is the touch screen and specially designed dual-hinge which can be rotated 360° supports to meet different user scenarios from an ultra book PC to a tablet. With the arrival of mobile Internet era, customers need a portable device that not only meets work requirements but also the entertainment.

太阳能便携式充电器
Portable Solar Charger

生产 设计 / 成都浪尖工业设计有限公司
Manufacture Design / Chengdu ARTOP Industrial Design Co.,Ltd.

以太阳能为发电能源，用户在户外运动时，通过弹性尼龙带，佩戴在肩上或是背包肩带上，在充电器前端有LED灯，能在夜间为用户提供照明；功能实用，生产成本低，标准的外壳，不同容量的电池可任意更换；搭配保护橡胶垫，手感良好，材质与色彩选择恰当。

This product provides charging power supply for outdoor sports lovers in athletic process. It uses solar energy as the power. The users can wear it on the shoulder or backpack shoulder belt by the flexible nylon tape. In athletic process, it can provide power for the equipments. It is with a piece of rechargeable batteries, can store up the surplus energy.

光荣使命游戏显卡
Glorious Mission Game Graphics

生产 / 七彩虹科技发展有限公司
设计 / 张美昭

Manufacture / Colorful Technology and Development CO. Ltd
Design / Amei

该产品的设计灵感来源于德国“豹”IIA6坦克，应用军事风格的机械美学，设计师以精炼的军事元素内涵完美诠释军事游戏的三大精髓，将军事风格的机械美学展现得淋漓尽致。“一键超频按钮”，无需专业繁琐设置，只要轻轻一按，游戏速度立即提升。

This product originates from the Germany IIA6 Tank and use the aesthetic of machinery to perfectly annotate the core part of military games, and widely use the military aesthetic in various parts in manufacturing process.

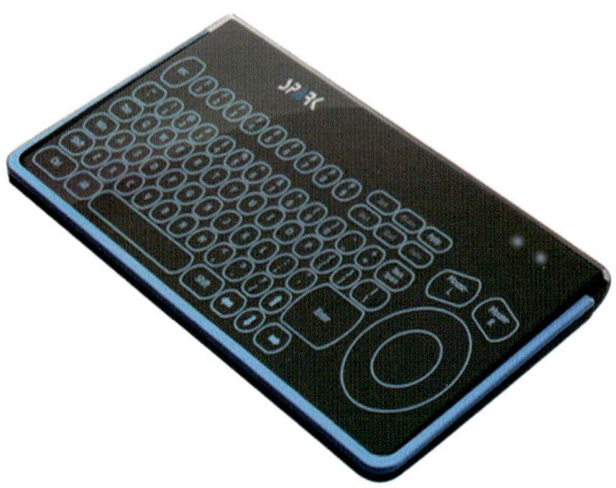

同体点阵鼠标键盘
Lattice Mouse And Keyboard With The Body

生产 / 斯巴科（北京）科技有限公司
设计 / 曲建全、杨哲

Manufacture / SPARK (Beijing) Technology Co., Ltd.
Design / Qu Jianquan, Yang Zhe

在键盘上实现鼠标、滑条等多种功能操作，外形小巧，适合于网络电视遥控鼠标键盘；无菌键盘均由符合医疗器械产品的材料制成，结构上采用防尘、防水、防菌设计，没有死角，细菌没有滋生的空间，防水设计可以任意采用液体、气体、紫外光等方法消毒处理。

The all-in-one product realizes keyboard, mouse, sliders and other operations together, small and portable, giving users a new experience, suitable for network TV remote mouse and keyboard. Sterile keyboard are in line with the material of the medical device products, the structure o a dust-proof, waterproof, anti-bacteria design.

天秦键盘
TianQin Keyboard

生产 / 天秦
设计 / 何峰枫

Manufacture / TIANQIN
Design / VINCENT HE

空格键下沿采用了加长坡度设计，能很好减轻长时间游戏所带来的手腕疲劳，同时在坡上采用了防滑条设计，适当的阻力感很好的提升了操作体验。在防泼溅液体方面，导水槽的设计，当液体泼溅至键盘时，能够从键盘背部迅速排除液体。

The slippery course of the design has been used in this keyboard design to make users feel more convenient when playing games. Also its direction exposure surface treatment can keep this keyboard preventing from water and remove liquid smoothly.

功能充电防盗支架FU系列
Multifunctional and Theftproof Electrical Source Bracket – FU Series

生产 / 天津市雅铁科贸有限公司
设计 / 洛可可设计集团

Manufacture / Tianjin Yatie Techs &Trade Co., Ltd
Design / LKK Design

这是一款在防盗报警的主要功能之外强调了对产品的展示功能，并且以模块化的组合方式针对不同的消费类电子产品进行保护和展示，形成防盗报警器的系列化产品，既节约了成本又提升了防盗报警器在行业中的传统形象，铝合金插接方式及其底座中灯光效果的运用。

Burglar alarm outside the main features highlighted on the product display feature and combinations of modules for a variety of consumer electronics products to protect and display. Thus forming the burglar alarm series products, both cost savings and enhance the traditional image of a burglar alarm in the industry.

电视小贝
Television Set–top Boxes

生产 / 永新视博
设计 / 何峰枫

Manufacture / Vovel Supertv
Design / Vincent He

使用圆形作为机顶盒产品的外观，给了产品以多样化的使用方式，可以立在电视旁边，也可以通过挂绳挂在电视背后。圆形的机顶盒加上古香古色的底座，中国风的融入，多变的使用方式，产品整体焕然一新。所以，它不仅仅是个机顶盒，更像是个摆在家里的工艺品。

The new technology named of Circular shape – unprecedented design which helps to create an aesthetic and auspicious ways to install. Also the product can stand by or hung behind the TV set by a strap. It is not only a set–top box, but also a craft of art in home.

哈曼卡顿 BDS 577
Harman Kardon BDS 577

生产 / Harman International Industries,Incorporated
设计 / 哈曼设计中心

Manufacture / Harman International Industries, Incorporated
Design / Harman Design Centre

第一台具备蓝牙功能的家庭影院系统。整合AirPlay与DLNA并利用iOS/ Android控制Wi–Fi，用户可以毫不费力地分流任何数码内容。符合人体工学的新操控方式简化了用户界面和蓝光功能。

The product is the first Bluetooth–enabled home theater systems. Integration of AirPlay and DLNA and using iOS / Android to control Wi–Fi, users can easily divert any digital content. The ergonomic control simplifies the user interface and Blu–ray function.

网络视频音箱
Sound Bar

生产 / 惠州纳伟仕智能媒体技术集团
设计 / 深圳市柏斯工业设计有限公司

Manufacture / NIVS IntelliMedia Technology Group, Inc
Design / Shenzhen Perth Industrial Design Co.,Ltd.

此款视频音箱一种规格便可广泛地应用于各种品牌和规格的电视机。采用ABS环保型塑料，表面采用纳米镜面喷镀工艺，材料及加工各项数值均符合国际标准。新的结构工艺设计也减少了螺丝的使用，降低了成本，同时也让外观变得更加简洁明快。

This specification of video speaker can be widely used in various brands and specifications of TVs. It uses environmental friendly ABS plastic, the surface of which adopts nano-mirror plating process. The materials and the various processing data are all in line with international standards. The new structure design reduces the use of screws which in turn reduces costs while it also allows the appearance simple and neat.

哈曼卡顿水晶——无线
Harman Kardon SoundSticks Wireless

生产 / Harman International Industries,Incorporated
设计 / 哈曼设计中心

Manufacture / Harman International Industries, Incorporated
Design / Harman Design Centre

机身采用环保材质,可循环再利用。添加了无线蓝牙技术，提高了音效表现。精湛和超现代的工业设计，优雅的黑色基调和明亮的白色LED光效融为一体，被纽约现代艺术博物馆选为永久收藏。

The body of the product uses environmentally friendly materials which can be recycled. Adding Bluetooth wireless technology to improve the sound performance. Superb and ultra-modern industrial design, elegant tone of black and bright white LED light effects are blended. It is selected as the permanent collection of the Museum of Modern Art in New York.

豌豆龙
I-bean

生产 设计 / 幻响神州（北京）科技有限公司

Manufacture Design / I-mu Technology Co., Ltd.

精美时尚的外观足以令粗笨又无设计感的同类产品相形见绌，完全可以满足苹果粉丝的高品味追求。

The appearance of fine fashion enough dwarves the design sense of similar products. It fully meets the high taste of the pursuit of Apple fans.

梅薇思蓝牙音箱
Mavis Bluetooth Speaker

生产 / 西西艾
设计 / 陈波、黄小龙

Manufacture / CCA
Design / Chen bo, bruce-huang

这是一款2.1声道家居音箱，采用蓝牙连接的方式，主体外壳采用PVD(真空环保电镀)工艺进行表面处理。配合特殊的造型能很自然与室内装饰融为一体，进一步提升家居品位。

The product is a 2.1-channel home speaker with Bluetooth connectivity. The main shell adopts PVD (vacuum environmental plating) process for surface treatment accompanied with the special shape which naturally blends with the interior decoration, further enhancing the home grade.

K-BOX不插电音响
K-BOX

生产 / 康佳集团通信科技有限公司
设计 / 龚晟宇、卫波

Manufacture / Shenzhen Konka Telecommunications Technology Co.,Ltd
Design / Gong Shengyu, Wei Bo

利用独特的声音扩大原理，不需要外部电力的零功耗音响，机械原理扩音，效果非常明显；纯塑胶注塑，与包装做在一起节省资源，搭配多种色彩，简洁时尚，是手机很好的配件。

The zero-power audio applies unique amplify principle which needs not any external power. Mechanical principles application shows an obvious effect. Plastic injection molding together with the packaging saves resources. It is concise and fashionable, can be good mobile accessories.

飞利浦桌面对接扬声器 DS6200
Philips Desktop Docking Speaker DS6200

生产 / 荷兰皇家飞利浦电子公司
设计 / 飞利浦设计

Manufacture / Royal Philips Electronics
Design / Philips Design

连接个人电脑 / iPod / iPhone 播放高保真音乐，同时与 iPod / iPhone 同步并为其充电。DS6200 提供真正的立体声扬声器，体积纤细，适合放在桌面上。它是保持工作台整洁的完美解决方案。对接扬声器的设计结构提升了声音性能，尽情展露音质。

The product delivers high fidelity music from your PC/ iPod/iPhone and syncs and charges your iPod/iPhone at the same time. The DS6200 offers true stereo speakers, shrunk to fit on your desktop. It´s a perfect solution for a clutter free workstation. The docking speaker´s architecture enhances sound performance and radiates sound quality.

飞利浦 Soundbar 家庭影院 HTS7111
Philips Soundbar Home Theatre HTS7111

生产 / 荷兰皇家飞利浦电子公司
设计 / 飞利浦设计

Manufacture / Royal Philips Electronics
Design / Philips Design

利用 Ambisound 技术，营造完全身临其境般的家庭影院体验，可与任何平板电视搭配。最薄、最纤细的条形音箱设计，搭配采用 Ambisound 技术、享有专利保护的全角度扬声器。独特的设计元素包括拉丝金属饰面、无缝显示、曲线形扬声器网罩和镀铬驱动器环。

This product uses Ambisound technology. A fully immersive home theater experience with Ambisound technology in a single stunning thin and slim bar that´s a perfect match for any flat screen TV. The thinnest and slimmest soundbar design which incorporates the patented angled speakers of Ambisound technology. Exclusive design elements include touch controls, brushed metal finishing, a leading edge seamless display, curved metal speaker grille and chrome-plated driver rings which help to communicate the sound story.

蓝牙小音箱
Portable Bluetooth Speaker

生产 / 深圳市钜弘科技有限公司
设计 / 想象力产品策划有限公司

Manufacture / Shenzhen Joyhong Technology Co.,Ltd
Design / Imagination Design Co.Ltd

此款音箱利用蓝牙技术和内置锂电池供电；提供便携无线的音乐体验。设计简单易用，随时随地可以使用，设计理念延续包豪斯抽象的几何设计风格，在极致简洁的设计下实现产品的所具有的功能和美感，涂装高档金属漆以代替铝合金对蓝牙信号的干扰，却保持铝合金的质感。

This product uses bluetooth technology and a built-in lithium battery and it provides a portable wireless music experience. The product design is simple and easy to use. Exquisite workmanship, elegant appearance, in the extreme simplicity of the design to achieve the product with the function and beauty. Coating of high-grade metal paint to replace aluminum alloy for Bluetooth signal interference, but keep the aluminum alloy texture.

JBL贴耳式耳机 J55i
JBL On-ear Headphone

生产 / Harman International Industries,Incorporated
设计 / 哈曼设计中心

Manufacture / Harman International Industries, Incorporated
Design / Harman Design Centre

该产品拥有强大的40毫米直径的喇叭，强劲低音和震撼音效。耳罩采用180° 可旋转设计，降低外部噪音和突出低音效果。

The product has a 40 mm diameter speaker, strong bass and powerful sound. Earmuffs adopts the design of 180 ° rotating to reduce external noise and outstanding bass.

Antilope

生产 / 浙江魔杰电子股份有限公司
设计 / MOGIC ID TEAM

Manufacture / Zhejiang Mogic Electronic Co., ltd
Design / MOGIC ID TEAM

采用压耳式设计，耳罩能隔离城市噪音，柔软海绵耳罩和独特的高保真喇叭设计，保证了独享专业音质的舒适性；该产品所采用的ABS塑料，属于可循环使用材料，头带使用高强度抗裂材料，具有强延展纤巧头箍设计；可与任何音源设备连接，方便使用。

The product is made in ABS plastic which is recyclable and could be reused. On-ear isolating cushions block out the city´s noise. Soft foam cushions guarantees long-listening comfort. Superior speakers deliver high performance sound. Headband used with high stress crack resistant with high flexibility.

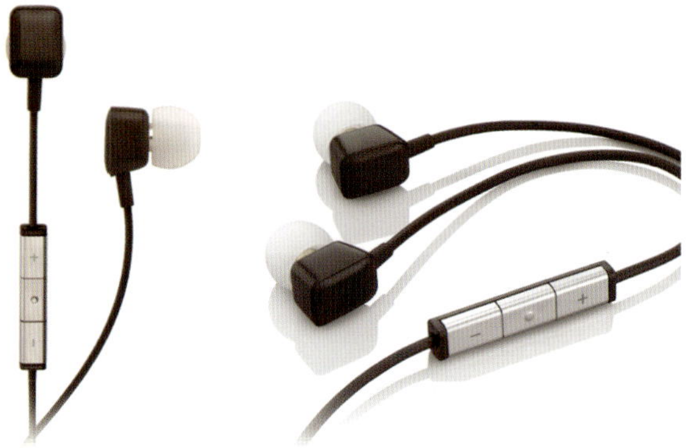

哈曼卡顿NI&AE入耳式耳机
Harman / Kardon NI & AE In Ear Headphones

生产 / Harman International Industries,Incorporated
设计 / 哈曼设计中心

Manufacture / Harman International Industries, Incorporated
Design / Harman Design Centre

这是一款在消噪的设计上使用户在较低的音量清晰地听到音乐的耳机。3.5mm插头为镀金处理。与众不同的长方形入耳式耳机，呼应苹果设备的外观设计。

The product enables users to clearly appreaciate the music at a lower volume. The 3.5mm plug is gilded. The distinctive rectangular headphones, echoing the design of the Apple device.

骨传导助听耳机
Bone conduction hearing aid system

生产 / 北京美尔斯通科技发展股份有限公司
设计 / 洛可可设计集团

Manufacture / Melst Technology co., ltd, Beijing
Design / LKK Design

利用骨质震动传导到听觉神经，让有一丝听觉神经的聋哑人能与正常人一样交流，让聋哑儿童开口说话。产品从儿童角度关注人机使用，符合儿童头部长时间舒适佩戴；让医疗性质产品数码时尚化，让助听医疗产品给儿童的心里感受转向装饰、时尚的心里感受。

The Melst hearing aid system uses bone vibration conduction auditory nerve, so as long as there is a little effectiveness of their auditory nerve, the deaf children can begin to hear and speak. Focus on the human engineering theory of kids, the system suits the child´s head even for long time wearing. The product was designed to make the medical instrument more fashion as well.

便携式老人音箱
Portable elderly speaker

生产 / 惠州纳伟仕智能媒体技术集团
设计 / 深圳市柏斯工业设计有限公司

Manufacture / NIVS IntelliMedia Technology Group, Inc.
Design / Shenzhen Perth Industrial Design Co.,Ltd.

针对中老年人设计的关爱性产品—mini便携式音箱，根据中老年人的生理特点和使用需求，音箱配备了FM/AM收音机、照明、求助、超长待机、SD卡和U盘直读播放等功能，操作简易，贴心使用，并且提供了高标准的音质。

This is a product designed for caring for the elderly–mini portable speakers. According to physiological characteristics and use needs of the elderly, the speaker is equipped with functions such a FM / AM radio, lighting, help devices, long standby capacity, SD card and U disk directly reading, which is easy and intimate in use, and provide a high standard of sound quality.

折线桌面音箱
Line desktop speakers

生产 / 惠州纳伟仕智能媒体技术集团
设计 / 深圳市柏斯工业设计有限公司

Manufacture / Nivs Intellimedia Technology Group, Inc.
Design / Shenzhen Perth Industrial Design Co.,Ltd.

巧妙地将屏幕和按键区域“折出”最舒适的观看和使用角度，符合欧盟RoHS标准，采用ABS环保型塑料，产品内外包装均采用可回收纸张和塑料，表面采用无铅印刷工艺。

The product skillfully produces the most comfortable viewing angle between the screen and key areas, in line with RoHS standards. It adopts environmentally friendly ABS plastic. The packages inside and outside of the product adopt recyclable paper and plastic. The surface adopts lead–free printing process.

“Grande”系列无尘袋吸尘器
"Grande" Series Bagless Vacuum Cleaner

生产 / LG电子
设计 / LG电子中国设计中心

Manufacture / LG Electronics
Design / LG Electronics Design China

超大容量集尘桶减少垃圾倾倒次数；双排口变速气旋系统，尘气分离，保护电机。经过简化的设计方便倾倒和清洗，无滤芯设计，易清洁使用无需二次消费。能够过滤掉99.95%的微小灰尘，使家居始终保持洁净健康。实现集尘桶超大容量的同时保持外形紧凑感。

Bucket with high-capacity can be less dumping, double air vent with variable speed cyclone system can protect the motor. Easy to empty dust canister due to it´s simple design. Easy and convenient to maintain. No filter design, easy to clean without cost again and it can leach 99.95% tiny dust which can keep the home clean and health. It realizes dust barrel super capacity at the same time it keeps appearance compact feeling.

蒸汽式挂烫机
Garment Steamer

生产 / 江苏松桥电器有限公司
设计 / 苏宁电器股份有限公司

Manufacture / Jiangsu Mazuba Co.,Ltd
Design / Suning Appliance Co.,Ltd

精确温控，底盘可360° 旋转，使用便利。具有自动断电防干烧功能，双层壶身，使用中可防止烫手。采用不锈钢发热盘，加热均匀，提高加热效率，减少能源的消耗。采用不锈钢加塑料双层壶身，部件配合紧密。经典白色壶身，时尚典雅。

Precise temperature control, the chassis can be rotated 360° , ease to use. Also with the functions of automatic power-off, anti-dry feature, double expensive, which can prevent a high heating efficiency. Its classic white, plastic and stainless steel shows stylish and elegant.

手持式电动吸奶器
Electronic Breast Pump

生产 / 佛山市顺德区美诺电器科技有限公司
设计 / 佛山市尚致设计有限公司

Manufacture / MyCarol Electric Technologies Co.Ltd
Design / Foshan BOB DESIGN Co.,Ltd

模仿婴儿吸奶的周期动作，可自动调整吸力及吸奶频率，以适应不同使用人的具体吸奶效果，减少母亲哺乳时的乳房酸痛麻的副作用。结合先进的生产工艺，保证了产品的可靠性。材料主体为ABS，奶瓶为PP，奶罩为硅胶，外观简洁、清新。

By mimicking the baby breast pump suction technology cycle action as well as the suction and discharge time of free control to adapt to different people use the specific effect of additional breast pump and reduced when lactating breast ache hemp side effects. Let mother no longer on lactation of psychological stress. The products used in precision technology. The combination of advanced production technology to ensure product reliability. Material main body is ABS, bottle PP, silica gel bra. This product appearance simple, fresh, generous.

臻尚剃须刀
Vogue-wit Shaver

生产 / 上海奔腾电工有限公司
设计 / 龙域设计

Manufacture / Shanghai POVOS Electric Works Co.,Ltd.
Design / LOE DESIGN

18mm的超薄机身，圆润的形态，航空级铝合金材质及圆形拉丝的电镀装饰件，卓越的耐磨性能；轻触式开关配以幽蓝背光灯，USB充电方式，轻巧灵动，携带方便，该剃须刀采用了磁吸触点式USB的充电方式，更加节能。

The design emphasizes the slimness and comfort of the product. With the ultra-thin body of 18mm, aviation-grade aluminum material, excellent wear-resisting property, it highlights the simple and stylist sense of the product. The charging mode with USB tends to be light, smart and portable.

家用理发剪
family electric hair device

生产 / 上海奔腾电工有限公司
设计 / 龙域设计

Manufacture / Shanghai POVOS Electric Works Co.,Ltd.
Design / LOE DESIGN

灵感来自于生物身上流畅曲线的家用理发剪，运用亲和饱满的形态，强调了手握产品的舒适性；理发剪刀头附近的黑色透明件背面有肌理效果，突出产品精致的细节；产品主体为高亮珍珠白，按键采用了轻触式开关，产品在未开启电源时，仍然是一整块黑色透明件，突显产品的整体感。

The design inspiration comes from the smooth curve of the creature body. The design stresses on the handling comfort of product by with full and graceful shape. The button adopts the touching switchgear. When being switched on, it keeps being a black transparent part as a whole to highlight the integral feeling of products.

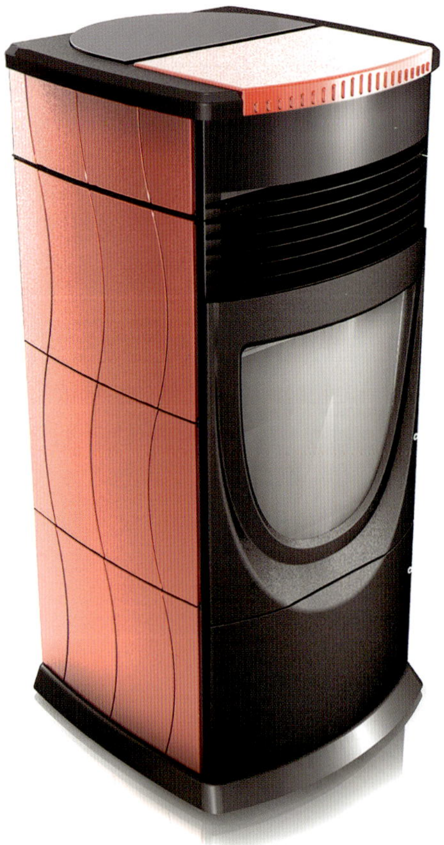

模块化欧式颗粒火炉系列（模块化拆装DIY自由组合）
European Pellet Stoves (Modular combinations & DIY)

生产 设计 / 宁波柯怡工业设计有限公司

Manufacture Design / CO-YES Industrial Design Co., Ltd.

满足不同客户对不同颗粒炉容积的需要，随意自由增加容量，也满足了消费者挑选喜欢的陶瓷颜色自由组合搭配的需求。这是该产品区别于其他同类产品特有的气质和显著特征，表现出了对人的关爱和体贴。

This product can meet the needs of different customers on different particles of furnace volume at liberty to increase capacity. It reflects the utility function and brings special consideration to users.

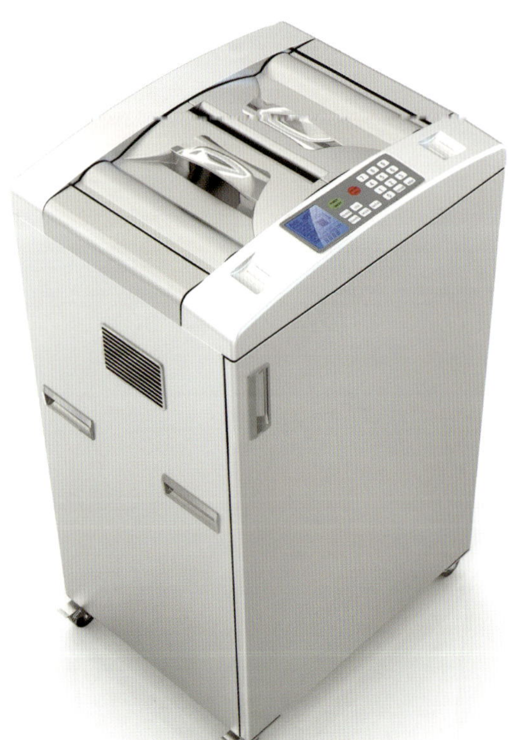

自动进纸碎纸机AF650
AF650 Auto Feed Paper Shredder

生产 设计 / 东莞福泰电子有限公司

Manufacture Design / Dongguan Forta Electronics Company Limited

该碎纸机设有开创性的内建式自动碎纸及个人密码锁装置，30分钟内无操作机器即自动断电，大大减少待机电源消耗；采用德国工艺设计，配有一体钢刀 LCD显示屏钢结构碎纸桶及滑轮。

The product has a groundbreaking built-in automatic shredding and personal password locking devices. The machine will automatically cut the power if no operation is done within 30 minutes greatly reducing the standby power consumption. It adopts the German engineering design, equipped with one steel blades, LCD display, steelstructure shredding drums and pulleys.

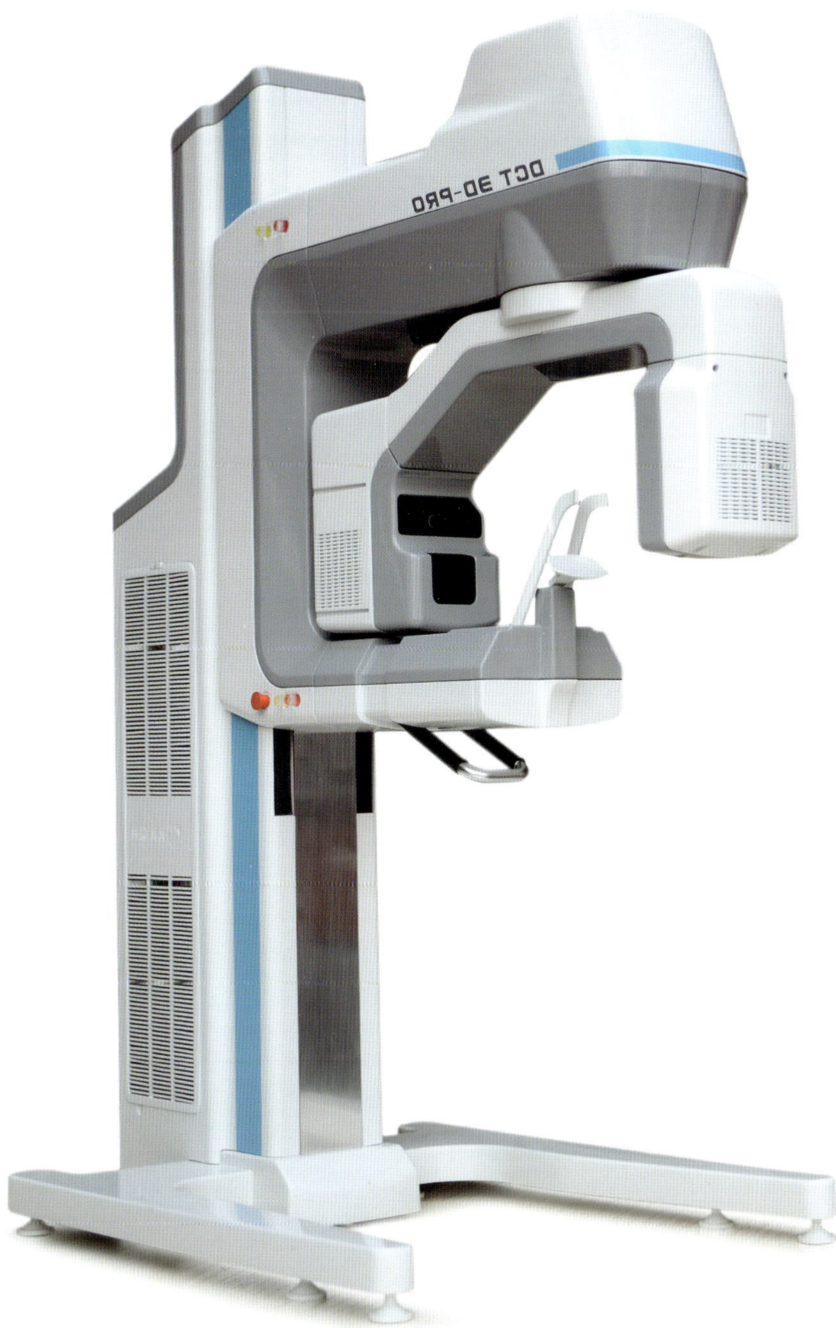

口腔CT成像系统
Oral Cavity CT Block Diagram System

生产 / 四川九九瑞迪数字成像技术有限责任公司
设计 / 成都嘉兰图设计有限公司

Manufacture / Sichuan DNDR Digital Radiography Co., Ltd.
Design / Chengdu Newplan Design Co., Ltd.

为口腔进行全方位检测，三维立体图形成像，多角度转动检测。紧凑机身设计，可适用各种治疗环境，360° 立体调节无死角，局部小范围检测，降低医疗成本。ABS工程塑胶壳体，全钢骨架机身。造型圆润，亲和力强，色彩搭配轻盈明快，减少患者心理压力。

This product can deliver a comprehensive detection for oral cavity by rotating from multiple angles, and the images are formed as three-dimensional blockdiagram. It is suitable for all kinds of therapeutic environments for its compact body.The machine can be regulated by 360 stereoscopically without any blind angle.The cost of medical care can be reduced for the local detection. The machine uses ABS engineering plastic shell which makes it strengrh and toughness.It also has a steel skeleton body which is stable and firm. Strong affinity is showed for its round modeling. Patients´ pressure can be reduced as the color collocation is light vivid.

多功能数码保健盒
Multi-functional Digital Health Box

生产 / 广州市原子工业产品科技发展有限公司
设计 / 广州市沅子工业产品设计有限公司

Manufacture / Atomic Industrial Product Technology Development Co., Ltd.
Design / Atom Industrial Design Co., Ltd.

一种可以在家庭和旅途中自助使用的多功能数码保健盒。包括带LED灯的微型摄像头、手柄、连接线、液晶显示屏、锂电池、电路板、电源开关、耳腔体温传感器、充电插口、数据插口、塑料盒等十一部分，其特征在于保健盒内安装有带LED灯的微型摄像头的手柄与耳腔体温传感器。

The multi-function digital health box can be self-help use in the home and on the road. With led light´s miniature camera, handle, cable, LCD, lithium batteries, circuit boards, power switch, ear cavity temperature sensor, charging jack, data jack, and plastic boxes and so on and 11 parts in total.

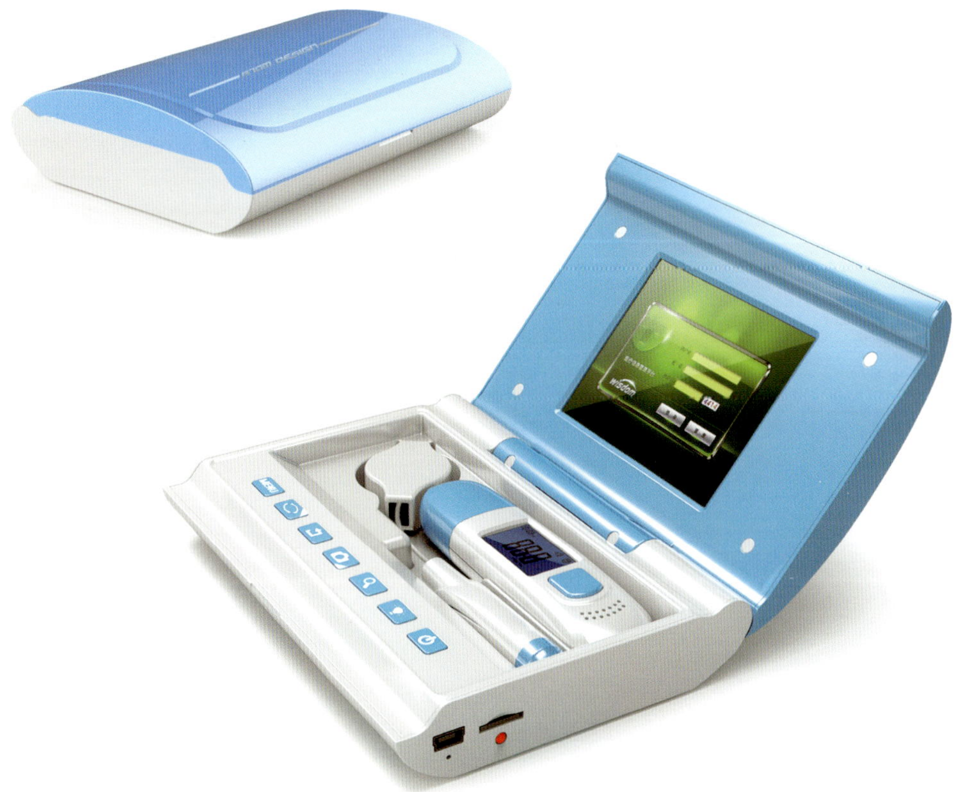

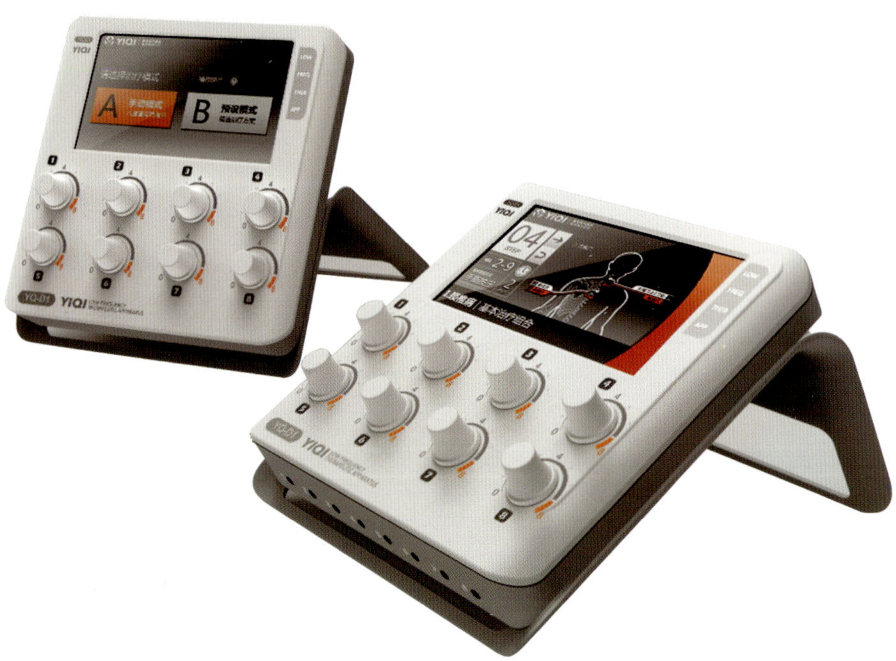

易奇糖尿病治疗仪
YiQi Diabetes Treatment Instrument

生产 / 河南易奇生物科技有限公司
设计 / 罗琦

Manufacture / Henan YiQi Biotechnology Co., Ltd.
Design / Luo Qi

将现代电子技术与传统中医治疗紧密结合，采用脉冲磁场对患者进行物理治疗。创新之处在于其独创的八通道设计——外接八组探头，同时对人体的八处穴位进行治疗并分别调整强度，解决了单穴位治疗效率低、用时长的问题。八处穴位对应八组探头、八个插孔、八个调节旋钮，提升操作的灵活性和易用性。

The product joins modern electronic technology and traditional acupuncture together closely by physical therapy of pulse magnetic field. The innovation comes from its unique eight-Channel design-with outer eight pairs of silica gel flakes, it can simultaneously act on eight body points and adjust intensity separately.

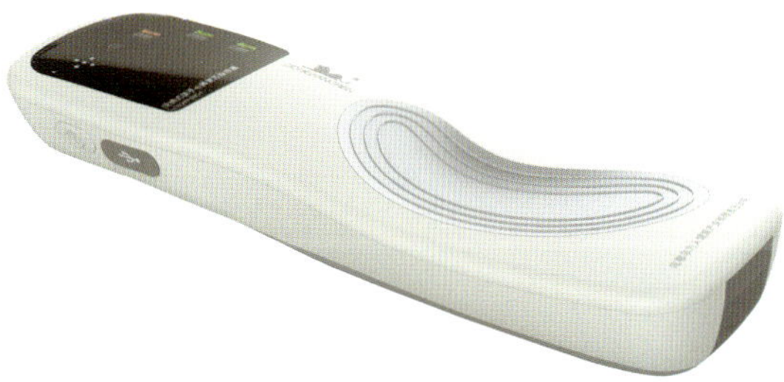

便携式徒手心肺复苏指导器
Portable Unarmed CPR Guidance Device

生产 / 成都东方人健康产业有限责任公司
设计 / 成都意町工业产品设计有限公司

Manufacture / Chengdu DFR Health Property Industrial Co., Ltd.
Design / Chengdu IDing industrial design Co., Ltd.

使用极为简单方便，极大地提高心肺复苏术的准确率与成功率；方便携带，使用简单，结构合理，成本低，适用于医疗救护人员或者受过训练的人员实行急救；外壳采用高强度工程塑料，可回收再利用；人性化操作为依托，创造全新的产品形象。

The Portable unarmed CPR guidance device is the instrument used to guide the medical staff operating on patients cardiopulmonary resuscitation. It is portable, with reasonable structure design. There is a soft gum can reduce the substantial and high–frequency compression injury on the patient´s body and ease the medical staff operating fatigue.

个人剂量计
Personal Dosimeter

生产 / 成都麦特斯科技有限公司
设计 / 成都意町工业产品设计有限公司

Manufacture / Chengdu Memory Test Technology Co., Ltd.
Design / Chengdu IDing industrial design Co., Ltd.

具有同时测量剂量率与累积剂量，防护报警时自动存储测量数据，以便查看，自动保存累积剂量及累积起始日期；配有独特的LED灯，反映出射线强弱，断电后累积剂量可长时间保存，方便携带，使用简单；结构合理，成本低，外壳采用高强度工程塑料，可回收再利用。

The instrument can measure the dose rate and cumulative dose at the same time. When it alarms, the product can automatically store the measured data for future viewing. It has unique LED lights, and can tell the strength of the rays by changing the LED blink rate. The shell is made of high strength plastic, recyclable.

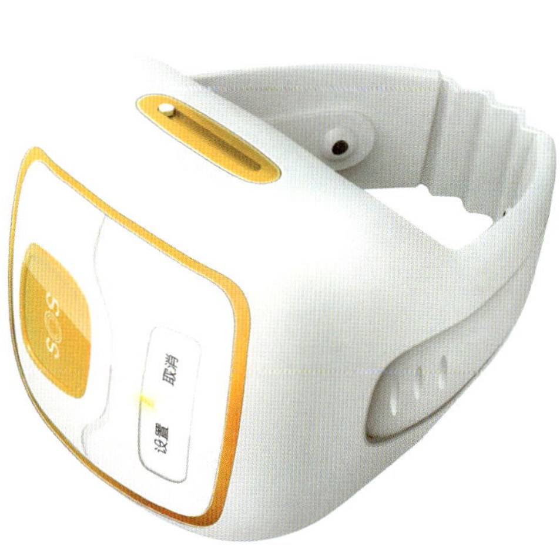

智能小护士
Intelllgent Nurse

生产 / 北京盈科通达信息技术有限公司
设计 / 北京智加问道科技有限公司

Manufacture / Beijing Full–tech Way Information Technology Co., Ltd.
Design / ZCO Design Co., Ltd.

这是一款用于独居、有心脏病史、需要实时监护的老人的小型医疗仪器产品。产品在采集到老人异常心跳数据后可自动报警，即刻自动发送短信至监护人，争取宝贵的营救时间。以科技创新与人文关怀为老龄化社会提供实用型产品及信息化解决方案。

This product is for the old man who lives alone, has heart disease and needs for real–time monitoring. When the device gathers the data of heart problems, it will give an alarm automatically. Meanwhile, it can gain further time to rescue the patients with sending messages to the custody automatically. Basing on the technological innovation and humanity in the aging society, the intelligent nurse offers practical product and informational solution.

公牛墙壁开关
Gongniu Decorative Switches

生产 / 公牛集团
设计 / 浩汉工业产品设计（上海）有限公司

Manufacture / Gongniu Group
Design / Nova Design (Shanghai) Ltd.

独创“专利悬摆技术”，使开关能够连续开、关8000次，使用寿命超出国家标准3倍。外观形态简练柔和，造型百搭，以IMR技术创造炫丽色彩与花样。多样的选择无论家居风格是现代简约，还是清新田园，无论要装修客厅、主卧或书房，皆能随家装需求完美搭配。

Bull´s world first IMR decoration wall switch design breaks the common perception of white colored wall switches, giving consumers an option to pick suitable trims for dif errant interior decoration needs. With the fast rising living standard and the ever changing home decoration styles, traditional wall switches no longer satisfy the needs of home enthusiast.

音乐花园
Music Garden

生产 设计 / 创意生活（北京）科技发展有限公司

Manufacture Design / Creatife Corporation

将种植、照明、音乐播放以及储物收纳的各项功能完美地结合在了一起。播放器的设计兼容了收音机、外放、闹铃以及为IPHONE、ITOUCH、IPOD充电的功能；具备较好的音质，性价比颇高；音乐花园的设计造型可以轻易地融入各种居家、办公环境。

Music Garden is a fine product that combines gardening, illumination, music play and storage functions together perfectly. The design of Music Garden also includes different functions of radio, alarm and charge battery for IPHONE, ITOUCH and IPOD. The full usage of Music Garden´s own light represents its concept of environmental protection and concerns of life.

直流折叠式台地扇(FSZ-3006Cg7)
DC Folding Wall and Desk Fan

生产 设计 / 格力电器（中山）小家电制造有限公司

Manufacture Design / GREE (Zhongshan) Small Home Appliances Co., Ltd.

采用折叠式拆装和触摸式操控，减少了室内空间的占用，收纳简单，拆装便捷。还可以自由调整送风角度，使电风扇拥有了新的工作方式。新型直流式电机更省电更节能，经久耐用。

The product uses a folding disassembly and touch control which reduces the interior space. It is easy for storage and convenient disassembly. It is also free to adjust the air supply angle, so that the fans have a new way of working. The more energy-efficient new DC motor is more energy efficient and durable.

加湿暖风机NTJ20–12S
Heater with Humidifying Function NTJ20–12S

生产 设计 / 广东美的环境电器制造有限公司

Manufacture Design / Gd Midea Environment Appliances Mfg. Co., Ltd.

采用PTC陶瓷发热体，安全节能热效高；并配置进风口过滤网，具有电热加湿功能，取暖不干燥。采用环保ABS材料，符合低碳、环保的发展趋势。整机造型饱满、圆润、富有亲和力。深咖啡色与黑色搭配，凸显产品高品质感。

The product uses PTC ceramic heating element with high thermal efficiency, safe and energy conservative. It is configured with the air inlet filter, having the function of electric humidification function, heating but not dry. It uses environmentally friendly ABS material, in line with the environment trend of low–carbon. The whole shape is full and mellow with rich affinity. Dark brown accompnied with black highlights the sense of high quality.

滑动门式直流冷风扇(KSZ–0801RCgL)
Sliding Door DC Cooling Air Fan

生产 设计 / 格力电器（中山）小家电制造有限公司

Manufacture Design / GREE (Zhongshan) Small Home Appliances Co., Ltd.

该产品采用古典水车取水加湿，无水泵设计，节能更安全，送风更清爽，自动导风叶片，风向操控方便。低碳节能环保新主张，新型直流电机耗电更少，效率更高。

This product uses the classical waterwheel water humidifier, without a pump, which is more secure and energy conservative. The air is more refreshing. It automatically direct the blades easy to control the wind direction. It advocates the new low–carbon energy saving and environmental protection. The the new DC motor is more power efficient.

无叶风扇
Air Multiplier

生产 / 深圳市艾克派特科技开发有限公司
设计 / 想象力产品策划有限公司

Manufacture / Shenzhen Accipiter Gentilis Technology Co., Ltd.
Design / Imagination Design Co., Ltd.

无叶风扇是电风扇市场的一次革命，取代了普通有扇叶风扇。它响应节能环保，舒适又省电。ABS注塑，银色和白色搭配，简洁而不失设计品位，沿用了简约设计风格，同“日蚀”这一全新的概念有机地结合，使功能同造型以及设计概念合二为一。

No fan electric fan market is a revolution, it replaces the common fan blade fan. It responses the energy saving and environmental protection, no fan comfort and energy saving. ABS injection, silver and white collocation, simple yet design grade. The product design idea comes from the concept of "Eclipse" and it also happens to meet the product definition, it follows a simple design style, with this new concept of organic union, make the function of the same shape, as well as the design concept becomes concise fashion and generous.

飞雨Select 150手持花洒
Raindance Select Shower

生产 / 汉斯格雅欧洲股份有限公司
设计 / 凤凰设计室

Manufacture / Hansgrohe SE
Design / Phoenix Design

Easy Select一键式选择功能，可自由切换花洒出水；Airpower空气注入技术在水中注入大量空气带来舒适柔和的淋浴体验，同时又起到节水的效果。

The Easy Select one-button selection function can b free to switch the shower water; the Airpower air injectio technique injects a lot of air in the water which bring people soft and comfortable shower experience and a the same time saves water.

恒温淋浴器
Thermostatic Shower

生产 / 佛山市安蒙建材科技有限公司
设计 / 唐小平

Manufacture / ABM BUILDING MATERIALS TECHNOLOGY CO., LTD.
Design / Xiaoping Tang

采用进口恒温阀芯，温度误差在0.5℃以内。龙头把手和置物板运用了环保材质，耐腐蚀，硬度大，绿色环保可回收利用。造型独特新颖，且简约时尚，把手和主体设计协调完美，轻盈犹如“飞”，动感十足。

The product adopts imported thermostatic valve core controlling the temperature error within 0.5 ℃. The fauce handle and the compartment plate use environmentally friendly materials, corrosion resistance, high hardness and green recyclability. The modeling is unique, simple and stylish. Handle and the main body is designed perfectly, light like ´flying´.

时光
Time

生产 / 福建中宇建材集团有限公司
设计 / 李春山

Manufacture / Joyou Group Building Materials Co., Ltd.
Design / Chunshan Li

创意龙头时钟，采用先进电镀工艺，表面质量高，耐磨性好，产品艺术性强，销售卖点突出，经济效益可观；采用低铅环保材料，绿色环保，洁净健康;采用瑞士进口低压铸造工艺加工，良品率高；由电子触摸控制出水温度与流量， LED灯时钟的设计，营造一种温馨的氛围。

It uses advanced electroplating process and high abrasion resistance with low lead echo-friendly material. The Swiss import low pressure casting process. The digital touch panel controls the water temperature and flow.

智享未来
ntelligent Future

生产 / 佛山百德嘉卫浴科技有限公司
设计 / 郑文凯

Manufacture / Foshan BDC Sanitary Ware Technology Co., Ltd.
Design / Kevin Zheng

该产品设计线条简洁明快，体现“少中见多”的设计理念，现代科技感十足。智能三挡水流控制，按需选择，精确温控，断电保护，瀑布出水体验别样的水流感受，有智能化的温度感应触控。无铅，符合环保、健康概念。铸造工艺成熟，抛光电镀工艺性好。

The clean and simple lines of the product reflects the design concept of ´less is more´ and with a strong sense of modern science and technolgy. Intelligent control, precise temperature control, power protection, temperature display, safe and reliable, waterfall brings a different kind pf feeling of water flow, the three level water-falling control makes the products more intelligent and energy saving. Comply with lead-free requirements, harmless to the human body, in line with environmental protection and healthiness. Eclectic design, simple and elegant, reflects the designer´s fine mind and a bold innovation.

IDEAS创想面盆龙头
Ideas Basin Faucet

生产 / 辉煌水暖集团有限公司
设计 / 李建民

Manufacture / Huihuang Plumbing Group Co., Ltd.
Design / Jianmin Lee

设置两种出水体验，独创龙头分水结构，将起泡出水、瀑布出水融为一体，使其带给使用者不同的生活体验。起泡器可以随意调节出水角度，满足使用者不同的用水需求，更能避免水资源的浪费。产品由无铅铜精铸而成，健康环保，可回收利用。

Two kinds of water discharing experience and the original distributive water structure blend bubbling water with waterfall water, which gives the user a different life experience. The bubbler is free to adjust in any aspect of water discharge, which meets users´ different demand for water and also can avoid the waste of water.Product Casts from lead-free copper, which is environmental, healthy, harmless to human body and recyclable.

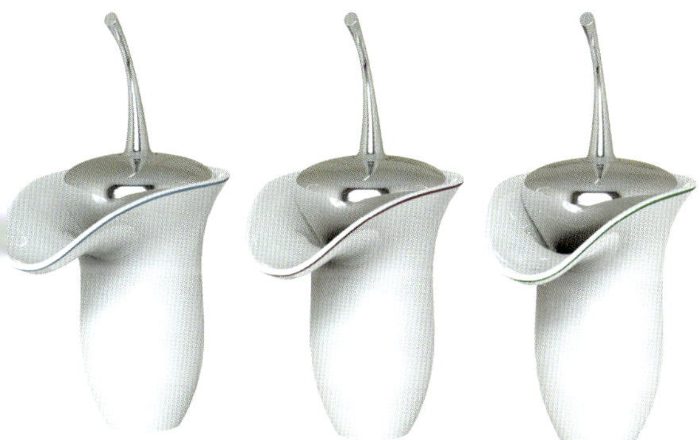

“清源”单柄双控面盆龙头
"Pure Source" Single Handle Double Control Basin Mixer

生产 / 辉煌水暖集团有限公司
设计 / 孙瑞

Manufacture / Huihuang Plumbing Group Co., Ltd.
Design / Sun Rui

使用陶瓷材料，水质更加纯净，健康，将水龙头材质朝着更加环保健康的方向发展，让资源合理利用。突破了一般的出水嘴与阀芯相融合的结构，两者相互独立，相互依托。

This product uses ceramic materials in it, of lead-free. The use of ceramic materials, make water quality more pure and healthy. This make the faucet material go to more environment friendly and healthy direction and let the recource has a more reasonable use. It breaks the structure of integration the spout with the cartridge, both independent of each other, relying on each other.

“谦·影”面盆水龙头
"Modest Shape Series" Basin Faucet

生产 / 辉煌水暖集团有限公司
设计 / 刘建南

Manufacture / Huihuang Plumbing Group Co., Ltd.
Design / Liu Jiannan

该产品使用不同材料和不同表面处理的嵌入式立体搭配，把手细节层次感设计更立体更人性化，产品操作手感好，更简便。用更经济更环保的新材料来镶嵌，让环保材料发挥到淋漓尽致。简洁沉稳的造型与色调的搭配，高贵典雅。

Different materials and surface treatment are embedded with stereoscopic match. The layering design of handle´s details is more stereoscopic and more human. The user-friendly operation of the product feels easier. Inlay more economical and environmentally-friendly new materials to the design and make environmentally-friendly materials to the fullest. The concise and calm style and color match gives peple a feeling of elegance and grace.

“金樽玉宴”触碰面盆龙头
Golden Grail and Jade Feast Smart Touch Basin Faucet

生产 / 辉煌水暖集团有限公司
设计 / 江镇林

Manufacture / Huihuang Plumbing Group Co., Ltd.
Design / Jiang Zhenlin

采用触碰式控制方式，更加方便及人性化。水利发电方式也起到节能减排的效果。突破分色生产技术及半透明球体内置LED灯的结构限制。采用中国传统文化元素“樽”，结合现代简约设计思想，塑造优美大方的造型及清新自然的色彩搭配。

It used the intelligent touch operation makes operation more convenient and humanization. The convenient operating shortened the distance of use and control, and reduce unnecessary waste at the same time. It breakthrough the colour separation produce technology and the structure limit of LED lights build-in the frosted translucence sphere. It uses the Chinese traditional culture elements (The drinking cup in ancient is named "ZUN"), and combine with the design of contemporary and contracted. It was fashioned graceful and easy molding and fresh and natural colour collocation.

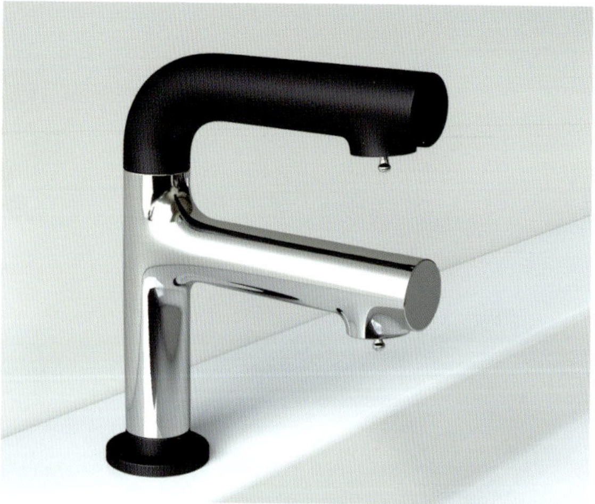

“轻色”面盆龙头
"Nature Color" Basin Faucet

生产 / 辉煌水暖集团有限公司
设计 / 陈文芳

Manufacture / Huihuang Plumbing Group Co., Ltd.
Design / Chen Wenfang

以低碳生活为设计理念，左右旋转间掌控水的动态，释放空间。把手与主体融为一体，90° 的直角设计更有利于开关的控制。采用精湛的金属烤漆工艺，配备高品质的进口起泡器七层过滤装置，防喷溅防噪音，节水20%以上。

The product with low-carbon life as the design concept, and the left and right rotation to control the dynamic of the water, and to release the space. Integrate the handle and the body, 90° right angle design is more conducive to the switch control. It adopts exquisite metal painting process, with high-quality imported seven layer filtration devices, anti-splash and noise abatement, water saving for more than 20%.

Double-F 两人用单冷面盆龙头
Double-F Single Cold Basin Faucet with Two People

生产 / 佛山市日丰企业有限公司
设计 / 彭江明、黄建元

Manufacture / Foshan Rifeng Enterprise Co., Ltd.
Design / Peng Jiangming, Huang Jianyuan

这是一款可供两人同时使用（单人也可以用）的单冷面盆龙头，突破现有龙头单人使用的状态，实现绝对的创新。节省了一般龙头上的把手操控部件，降低了铜材消耗，节能环保。

The product is single cold basin water-tap available for 2 people at the same time breaking the state of the existing water-tap for only 1 people. It realizes absolute innovation omitting the hand manipulating units on the general faucet, reduces the consumption of copper and realizes energy saving and environmental protection.

RF-9117TP面盆混合龙头
RF-9117TP Basin Mixer Faucet

生产 / 佛山市日丰企业有限公司
设计 / 蔡增熠、钱星宇

Manufacture / Foshan Rifeng Enterprise Co., Ltd.
Design / Cai Zengyi, Qian Xingyu

采用优质低铅铜材，耐腐蚀可杀菌，健康安全无毒性。引进先进环保的电镀工艺，对电镀废水进行循环利用。

The product uses high-quality low-lead copper of corrosion resistance and sterilization, healthy, safe and non-toxic. Introducing the advanced plating process, it can recycle the waster water from the plating process.

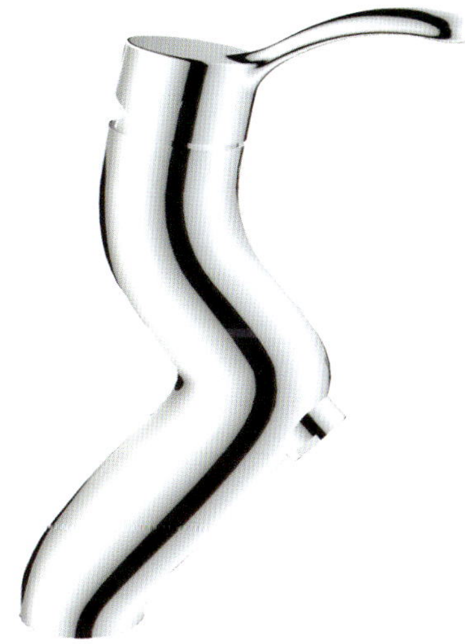

灵石
Pebble

生产 / 申鹭达股份有限公司
设计 / 杨黎明

Manufacture / Sunlot Shares Co., Ltd.
Design / Yang Liming

功能结构完全符合国际标准，适合各种面盆，结构简单，成本低廉，材料可回收利用。

The functional structure of the product in full compliance with international standards for a variety of basins with cimple structure, low cost It is made with recyclabe materials.

亚马逊系列面盆水龙头
Amazon Series Faucet

生产 / 珠海威锦卫浴设备有限公司
设计 / 新约设计工作室

Manufacture / Zhuhai weijin Bathroom Equipment Co., Ltd.
Design / New Testament Design Studio

以功能得以实现的最小尺寸、最普通加工方式、最大量使用通用件的原则设计，节省材料，节约成本。材料选用中采用国标59无铅黄铜，加工余料回收利用。

With the smallest size, ordinary processing method that is able to realize the function, this product is designed to use the common parts to the greates degree. It saves materials and costs. It adopts the materials GB 59 lead-free brass. The remaining materials can be recycled.

天歌面盆龙头
Tiange-Basin Faucet

生产 设计 / 九牧厨卫股份有限公司

Manufacture Design / Jomoo Kitchen & Bathroom Appliances Co., Ltd.

设计前置调节开关，方便用户操作；可识别的水温颜色，防止误操作。采用新型阀芯，较传统阀芯有很高的性价比。采用无铅铜铸造，安全环保无污染；内置水力发电机，为产品色彩显示源源不断地提供绿色能源。圆润且流畅的外形，符合重力铸造的高良品质要求。

A new valve core installed in the front-end outlet and easy for user to use. According to water color to effectively prevent wrong operation. This product is equipped with the new valve core, the cost of which is higher than the traditional one. Lead-free copper casting, safety and environmental protection; built-in hydro-electric machine can provide green energy for a steady stream of the product color display. Round and smooth appearance conformed to the requirements of high production rate of gravity casting product.

蝶恋
Butterfly–Loving

生产 / 惠达卫浴股份有限公司
设计 / 孙辉

Manufacture / Huida Sanitay Ware Co., Ltd.
Design / Sun Hui

使用脲醛盖板为可降解材料。独有的纳米自洁釉技术，其制作成本较低，相当于国外厂家开发成本的1/4，节水座便器实现了3/4升超强节水功能。

The urea–formaldehyde cover this product uses is biodegradable. The unique technology of nano self–cleaning glaze is cheap to process equivalent to 1/4 of the cost of foreign manufacturers. The water–saving toilet realizes the super water–saving function of 3/4 liter.

圆融
Integrate Harmony Without Obstruction

生产 / 惠达卫浴股份有限公司
设计 / 许月娥

Manufacture / Huida Sanitay Ware Co., Ltd.
Design / Xu Yue´e

独有“高平滑底釉+自洁釉”双层施釉工艺，持久洁净。产品品质符合国标及国外相关标准，适合批量生产制造。流动的线条，回环的结构，悠然的气韵。视觉上的美感，优雅但不张扬。

The product´s unique ´highly smooth glaze at the bottom + self–cleaning glaze´ double glazing processes, lasting clean. Product quality is in line with domestic and foreign relevant standards, suitable for mass manufacturing. This product possesses flowing lines, a looping structure and leisurely charm giving people visual sense of beauty, elegant but not exaggerating.

“尊尚” 连体座便器
"Honour Fashion" One–piece Toilet

生产 / 辉煌水暖集团有限公司
设计 / 江镇林

Manufacture / Huihuang Plumbing Group Co., Ltd.
Design / Jiang Zhenlin

利用水箱的独特造型体现时尚品味，便盖与座便器的完美结合提升产品的整体性，恰到好处的金边装饰设计提升了产品的气质。采用3/4.5升的冲水量，更加节水。此款产品线条简洁流畅的，形态饱满，时尚的元素，整体的形象凸显其与众不同的气质。

The molding of the water tank reflects the fashionable taste. The perfect collocation of the toilet´s cover and body promoted the integrity of the products and the proper gold line decoration design promote the temperament of the products. With the 3/4.5 litres of water flush makes water save. This product uses concise and fluent line, the full form, generous shape, fashionableelement and the overall image, which highlights itsdistinctive temperament.

“霞姿月韵”浴缸 "Afterlight Beauty & Moon Elegance" Bathtub

生产 / 辉煌水暖集团有限公司
设计 / 刘建南

Manufacture / Huihuang Plumbing Group Co., Ltd.
Design / Liu Jiannan

打破封闭式浴缸，把镂空式理念带入浴室，与传统固定浴缸不同，可根据需求随时改变位置。用新型高档亚克力材料制作，表面更加亮丽，材料可回收，环保性更强。一体式成型，分色表面处理。一体的人性化曲面设计，整体性强。

The product breaks the traditional enclosed bathtub concept, and bring hollow-type concept into the bathroom. Product changes the traditional fixed bathtub, and it is available to change the location upon the requests at any time. It adopts new and high-grade acrylic material, which make the product surface more beautiful, the materials are recyclable and more environmentally friendly. The integrated humane curving design is more integrated and color contract is striking, which make the product simple, stylish and mighty.

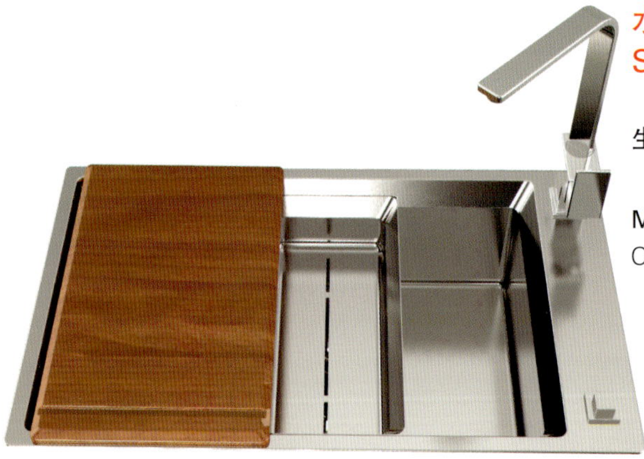

水槽OLVA8105
Sink OLVA8105

生产 设计 / 宁波欧琳厨具有限公司

Manufacture Design / Ningbo Oulin Kitchen Utensils Co., Ltd.

采用独特的大单槽设计，镜面与拉丝双重表面处理，国家首创的60度斜面的挡水边设计，可以防止水花飞溅。搭配优质304不锈钢材质龙头，环保健康。下水系统采用高密度PP材料，银离子抗菌技术，营造厨房环境持久洁净空间。

It adopts the original design of large single-slot and the dual-surface treatment mirror and wiredrawing 60-degree inclined water-retaining edge design is an initiative in this industry which is advantageous to the prevention of water from splashing. The high-quality 304 stainless steel faucet is envirmentally healthy. The sewer system adopts the high-density PP material and silver-ion antimicrobial technology, creating a kitchen environment with lasting cleanness and freshness.

水槽OLSP5203
Sink OLSP5203

生产 设计 / 宁波欧琳厨具有限公司

Manufacture Design / Ningbo Oulin Kitchen Utensils Co., Ltd.

该产品采用双层超大提笼，全不锈钢内胆，新型大口径下水系统，畅排无忧。精细表面处理工艺和脱磁工艺，使表面更光洁。水槽背面的反渗技术，防止冷凝水，保护橱柜不受侵蚀。

This product uses the double-layer enhanced cage and full stainless steel liner. Its new large diameter sewer system gurantees smooth draining. The crafts of fine surface treatment and demagnetization making the surface more smooth. The reverse osmosis technology adopted on the back of the sink prevents condensation of water to protect the cabinet from erosion.

集成水槽
Integrated Sink

生产 设计 / 嵊州爱尔卡厨卫科技有限公司

Manufacture Design / Shengzhou Aier Ka kitchen and Technology Co., Ltd.

集水槽、厨房龙头、食物垃圾处理器、净水器、小厨宝热水器、直饮龙头、刀架、砧板、皂液器、挂架系统等多项功能于一身。235毫米超深水槽垂直盆壁，R10黄金半径，更大释放水槽空间，更适合中国家庭使用。

The product posses a variety of functions such as a set of sinks, kitchen faucets, food waste disposers, water purifier, Kitchen Po water heaters, drinking fauct, cutting boards, soap dispenser, rack system. It has 235 mm ultra-deep water tank and vertical pelvic wall, R10 Gold radius, the greatly releasing the sink space and more suitable for Chinese families.

四合一多功能安全锤
Four in One Multi-function Safety Hammer

生产 / 杭州易舍工业产品设计有限公司
设计 / 孙惠兵、庄振华

Manufacture / Hangzhou Yes Industrial & Products Design Co., Ltd.
Design / Titan Sun, Jevin Zhuang

这是一款具备私家车安全、照明、警示、逃生等多种功能，适用于各种突发环境时使用；智能芯片超长使用时间；以啄木鸟曲线为元素完全创新设计；多功能、必须性组合；LED长寿命、超省电性能，方便实用；原色注塑，抗磨损性高；防弹玻璃灯罩、高强玻璃透镜片具有很高的抗摔性。

A product is used for private car security, lighting, warning, escape from unexpected dangerous environment. Also used as torch light, LED strobe warning distress. The product has a high abrasion resistance, bullet-proof glass shade, high strength glass lenses provide excellent resistance to fall.

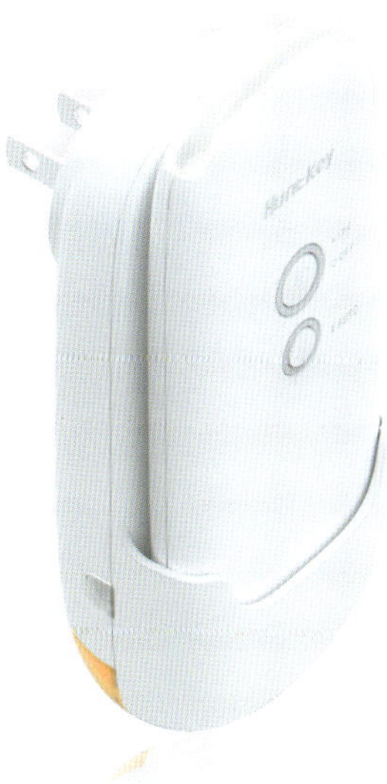

智能无线充手电
The Smart Wireless Rechargeable Flashlight

生产 / 深圳航嘉驰源电气股份有限公司
设计 / 深圳航嘉工业设计部

Manufacture / Shenzhen Huntkey Electric Co., Ltd.
Design / Shenzhen Huntkey Industrial Design Department

采用五颗高亮聚光LED灯，可自动应急断电，高质量的可循环充电锂电池，光敏感应，自动调节小夜灯，工艺精巧，外观小巧，手电筒可以直接放入口袋。

The product uses five highlight condenser LED lights. It can automatically provides emergency power with high-quality rechargeable lithium batteries, the photosensitive sensor which can automatically adjust the night light. It is designed with sophisticated technology and can be directly put in the pocket.

维易（显示器支架）
Victoria Easily (Monitor Stand)

生产 / 大连三维广界数字科技有限公司
设计 / 初龙梅

Manufacture / Extensive World 3D Technology Co., Ltd.
Design / Chu Longmei

采用亚克力制作，具有可弯折性和可粘合无缝隙性，材料可循环使用；配有键盘灯，可减少电能浪费。造型简洁、大气、时尚，使西方极简主义外形与东方古典回字纹结构有机结合，是中西方文化的代表。

The product is made of acrylic. It can be bent and seamless pasted. The material can be recycled. Keyboard lights can reduce energy waste. The modeling is simple, fashionable. It's the organic combination of the western minimalist and oriental classical herringbone structure perfectly representing the Chinese and Western culture.

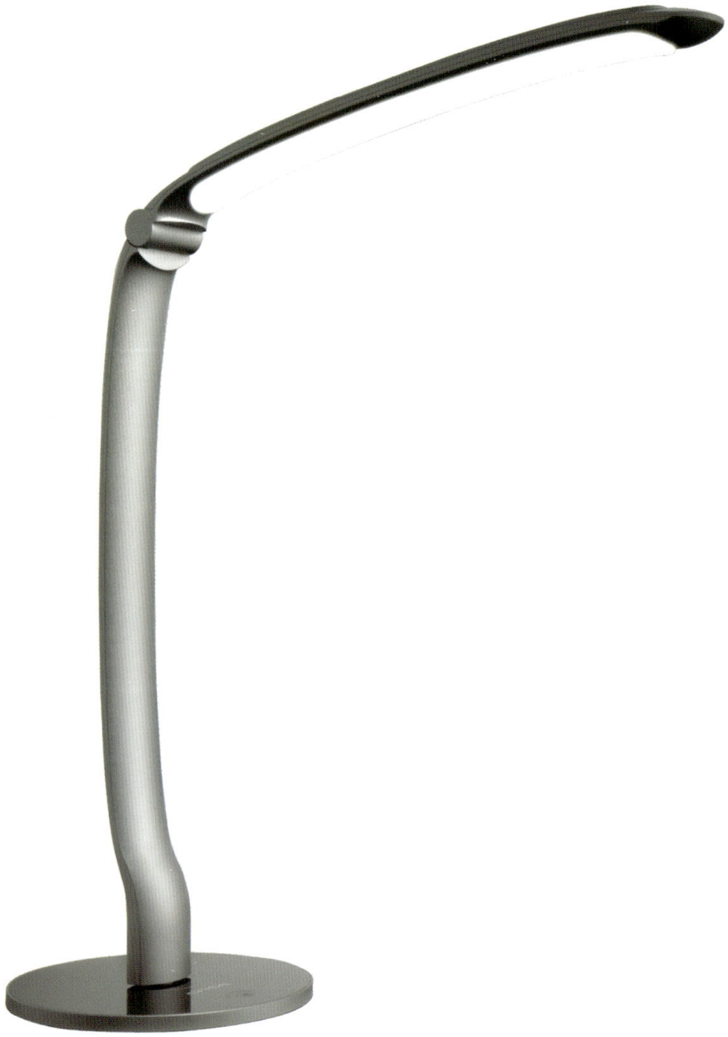

一树光阴
Nature Light

生产 / 鹤山市明可达实业有限公司
设计 / 广州易用设计有限公司

Manufacture / Mingkeda Industries Co., Ltd.
Design / EASE Design Guangzhou Co., Ltd.

应用饱含生命力的形态设计，使用时如植物开合般优美地旋转；采用触摸滑动式调光，实现无级调光，可针对不同场景光感做出任意调整，用较低的耗能产生较高的亮度效率，工作寿命可达48000小时以上。

The Nature Light Table lamp has a shape full of vitality. It can be unfolded like a vine gracefully spreads. And the step-less touch-slide dimmer makes it very smart to meet your need.

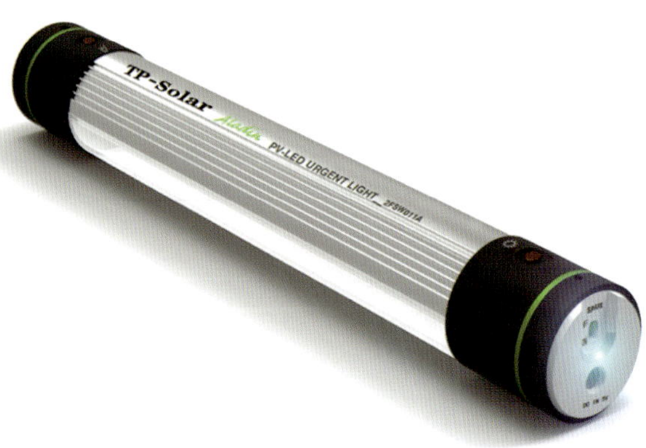

太阳能多功能LED一体灯
Solar Multifunctional Intergration LED Lights

生产 / 厦门冠宇科技有限公司
设计 / 高广德、朱有淋

Manufacture / Xiamen Topunive Technology Co., Ltd.
Design / Gao Guangde, Zhu Youlin

一体式环保设计，产品功能多样化，操作形式方便合理，实用性强，LED新光源、太阳能供电，工艺精湛，质感突出。造型简洁、大方、合理。

This product adopts the design of integrated environmental protection with a variety of functions, convenient and reasonable operation. It is practical with LED light source, solar power and exquisite workmanship. Its shape is generous and reasonable.

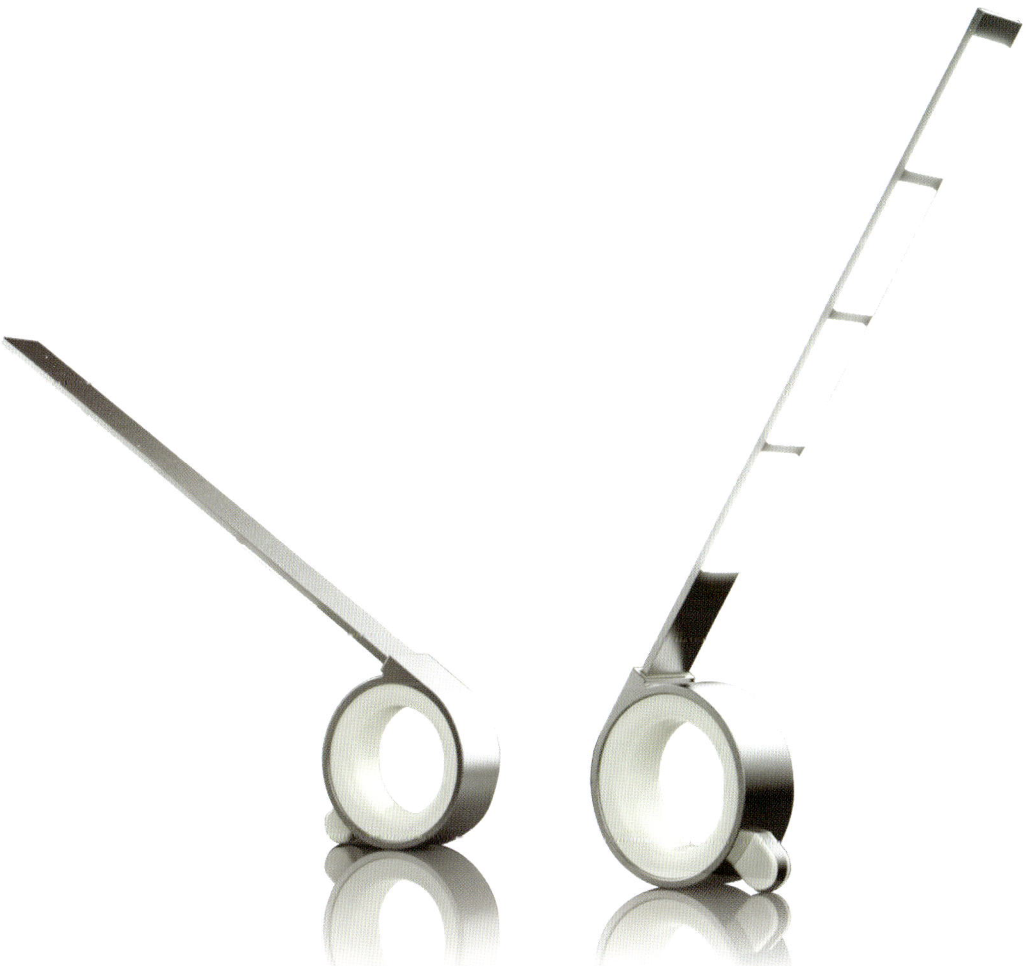

“Q”系列OLED台灯
"Q" Series OLED Desk Lamp

生产 设计 / 南京第壹有机光电有限公司

Manufacture Design / First O–Lite, Inc.

Q系列外观简洁活泼，采用了多种色彩搭配。四片发光板的光照强度比较适宜人们在阅读时使用。考虑到包装的便利性，设计师将底座和发光板设计成可拆卸式。底角的磁性材料，不仅保持了台灯的平衡和外观的美观，还可以用来调节光照的角度，是本款设计的点睛之笔。

The base and lighting slab are designed removable by the designers. The magnetic material has been used at the bottom is not only keep the balance of the desk lamp and appearance beauty, but also it can be used to adjust the Angle of light.

便携系列台灯
Portable Series Lamp

生产 设计 / 南京第壹有机光电有限公司

Manufacture Design / First O–Lite, Inc.

OLED照明技术主要由其及薄的发光片来发出柔美的光线，散热少，质轻。即针对这些特点设计这款台灯主要由6片发光片和金属外壳组成，以其极简的设计特点来说明其使用特色。人们可以在出外旅行、办公等特殊环境中使用，其所占空间小，便于携带。

OLED illumination technology becomes a disruptive innovation for human lighting technology with its characteristic of light weight, thinness, environment protection and soft beautiful light, which has a deep impact to improving our environment. The product is simple in operation and easy to carry and suitable for use at home, in office, while travelling or in outdoor environment.

迷你影院
Mini Cinema

生产 设计 / 北京丹方科技开发有限公司

Manufacture Design / Doon Design

这是一款利用物理及环保手段达到扩音和屏幕放大效果的产品，可以在完全不插电的情况下为iPhone扩音15分贝，为屏幕放大图像2.5倍，绿色环保；本品源自经典留声机形象，并用现代化设计语言进行重新诠释，简洁大方，符合现代生活。

The product can amplify 15 dB in sound and 2.5 times in view without energy support. It can serve as either horizontal or vertical stand for iPhone4/4S to play music, watch film and use facetime. Gramophone retrodesign makes it a desk decoration as well.

通士达LED PAR30 射灯
TOPSTAR LED PAR30 Reflector Lamp

生产 / 厦门通士达照明有限公司
设计 / 洛可可设计集团

Manufacture / Xiamen Topstar lighting Co., Ltd.
Design / LKK Design

充分发挥了LED照明设计优势，让光源不再是光源，而更像是灯饰，良好光学设计，混色均匀无光斑，色空间一致性好；高功率因数、低谐波、照明效率高、绿色照明光源、使用寿命长、节能环保；以即将绽放的鲜花造型为灵感来源，简洁、美观、大方，赋予产品时尚的元素。

This project is aimed to use the design to change the LED lamp´s role which becomes more like decorations rather than equipment. Highlights of the LED PAR30 lamp are simple shape, easy installation and a professional optical design. The concept comes from the shape of upcoming blooming flower which indicates a simple, beautiful, elegant image.

玉兰花传说
Magnolia Legend

生产 / 霍尼韦尔 朗能
设计 / 朱创艺、刘诗锋

Manufacture / Honeywell
Design / Powell Zhu, Liu Shifeng

ABS导热新材料，环保节能。配光技术使LED点光源扩展为面光源，增大发光面，升华视觉效果。无频闪，纯直流工作，消除了传统光源频闪引起的视觉疲劳。节能环保，损坏后抛弃自然界，对环境几乎不会造成任何污染，符合新社会理念。寿命长，管理方便，更换频率低。

The heat conductive ABS new material is environmental protection, also equipped with LED light contents to widen light areas. The LED lamp is 50000h while Halogen tungsten lamp is 2000h, also its Simple and generous appearance.

ED蝴蝶导轨灯
ED Butterflaire Track Light

生产 / 佛山市凯西欧灯饰有限公司
设计 / 吴育林

Manufacture / Foshan Cosio Lighting Co., Ltd.
Design / Yulin Wu

采用灯具轴套模式，灯片与驱动器的连接采用可分离式设计，在驱动器报废的情况下能及时更换，以配合原有的发光灯片持续使用，有效降低了更换成本。采用灵巧的内部卡扣结构设计，组装方便，结构安全。

The product uses lamp sleeve mode. The linkage between the light and driver is designed seperatable, so that the driver can be timely replaced when it is broken to continue using the original lights. In the way, it effectively reduces the cost. It uses the design of internal smart buckle, easy to assemble and structurally safe.

可旋转式LED灯管
LED Dimmable Rotatable Tube

生产 / 立碁电子工业股份有限公司
设计 / 李逸启、张哲玮

Manufacture / Ligitek Electronics Co., Ltd.
Design / Yi-Chi Li, Che-Wei Chang

可旋转改变照明的方向，有效利用光源，减少浪费。LED节能灯可减少能源消耗，延长使用寿命，生态友好、无紫外线、红外线、汞等物质。易于安装和维护、无闪烁及阻燃干扰、启动不延迟，安装方式与传统灯管相同，以铝挤散热，灯管不烫手更安全。

It also could be rotatable to change the direction of lighting, effectively use the light and decrease the waste. The LED energy-saving light can reduce the energy consumption, it has a long service life, eco-friendly, it has no harmful substance like ultraviolet and infrared mercury. It easy to install and maintain. The way of installation is the same with the traditional tube, with the extruded aluminum radiator, tube not hot and more safety.

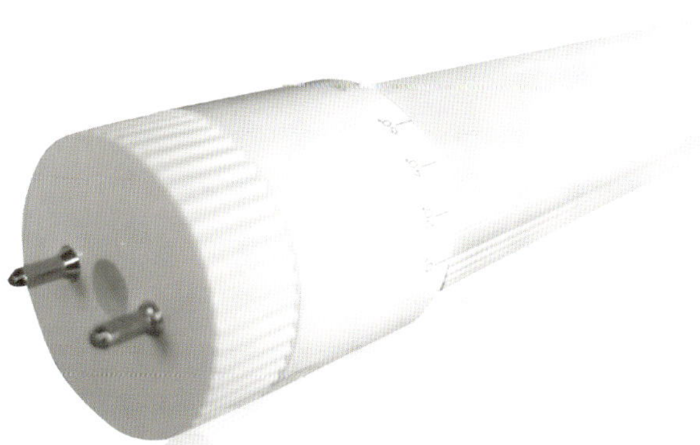

飞利浦Arcitone 洗墙灯
Philips Arcitone Wall Washer

生产 / 荷兰皇家飞利浦电子公司
设计 / 飞利浦设计

Manufacture / Royal Philips Electronics
Design / Philips Design

Arcitone 是一系列建筑风格的照明装置，适合家居使用。这款 LED 碟式灯具系列专注于解构主义建筑风格，采用不对称的造型设计，令其独树一帜，并根据位置的设置，营造出重复、混沌或对称感。设计师隐匿所有人为的技术痕迹，令这款壁灯与建筑风格丝丝入扣。

The Arcitone collection is a range of architectural-style lighting fixtures for domestic use. This LED disc family tops the collection. This product focuses on deconstructivism as an architectural style. The asymmetric shape of the wall light allows it to be distinctively placed in a space, creating a sense of repetition, chaos or symmetry according to the placement. A great amount of effort has been put in to hide all technical artefacts, to make the wall light an extension of the architecture.

快速充气帐篷
ast Inflatable Base Camp Sleeping Tent

产 设计 / 福建哥仑步户外用品有限公司

Manufacture Design / Fujian Kolumb Outdoor quipment Co., Ltd.

采用空气作为支撑材料，产品整体重量降低，且单人一分钟内即可完成两人帐的充气工作，放气收纳也更加简单方便。防水热压TPU膜支撑杆，轻质且防水抗风能力强。高密封性能的气嘴设计，一个双向阀门既可充气也可放气，尼龙帐面采用超轻30D防水涂层处理。

Using air as the support material, the entire weight is redused and you can use mouth to blow it up within 1 minute. It´s more convenient and easy to deflate and storage. The TPU pole supported, light, waterproof and strong wind resistance. High sealing performance of the air valve design, inflating and deflating quickly. 30D waterproot nylon flysheet.

李宁轻云跑鞋
Li-Ning Cloud Running Shoes

生产 / 李宁（中国）体育用品有限公司
设计 / 刘铮

Manufacture / Li-Ning (China) Sports Goods Co., Ltd.
Design / Axis Liu

这款产品分为冬季版和夏季版。冬季版采用传统的绗缝技术，解决多层材料的复合问题，减少胶水的使用。夏季版采用一片式薄膜工艺；鞋底超轻EVA发泡材料，较传统材料重量轻30% – 40%。

The winter version of the product uses traditional quilting techniques to solve the composite multilayer materials reducing the use of glue. The summer version adopts the craftsmanship a thin film; the sole uses ultralight EVA foam material, 30–40% lighter than the traditional materials.

K-FIT全方位保护登山鞋
K-Fit Multifunction Protection Hiking Shoes

生产 设计 / 福建哥仑步户外用品有限公司

Manufacture Design / Fujian Kolumb Outdoor Equipment Co., Ltd.

采用DESMA工艺，3D灌注一体成型大底，全方位保护系统。底身导泥槽设计能将附着于鞋底凹槽内的顽固淤泥迅速排出，内置SYSMPY-TEX防水透气袜套，外底双密度橡胶，硬质密度橡胶可强力抓地，软质密度橡胶可强力止滑。不使用溶剂胶粘剂，无毒，阻燃。

This product uses DESMA process, 3d perfusion mono-assembly outsole and protection system. Bottom mud tank design can be attached to the sole slots in the stubbornness of the silt rapid discharge, built-in SYSMPY – TEX waterproof breathable socks, outer bottom double density rubber, hard density rubber can be strong grasp, soft density rubber can be powerful slide. No glue, non-toxic, non-combustibilit.

皮佐越野跑鞋
The Pizzo Trail Running Shoes

生产 / 南京边城体育用品股份有限公司
设计 / 左智越

Manufacture / Nanjing B.C. SPORTS Products Co., Ltd.
Design / LORENZO

运用蜥蜴爪子的仿生学原理设计的鞋底大大提高了抓地力；鞋面仅由八片部件构成，降低了成本，提高材料的使用率，减少加工环节；鞋面采用防泼水网布，将服装用防水拉链突破运用在鞋面，保证鞋面的可透气调节和防水性；大面积采用3m反光材料，增加户外运动的安全性。

The trail running shoes structure can regulate the temperature of the shoes according to environment. Lizard claws bionics outsole improves the grip of the soles. The product uses only eight components on the whole vamp, and a large area of 3M reflective material to increase the safety outdoors.

共工60升背包
GongGong 60L Backpack

生产 设计 / 北京探路者户外用品股份有限公司

Manufacture Design / Beijing Toread Outdoor Products Co., Ltd.

将中国传统医学与人体工学相结合，背负系统选取特殊高分子材料，运动时进行穴位按摩，缓解疲劳。背包面料采用Toread可再生纤维面料和环保高分子材料，超轻环保适合长途旅行。功能性突出，是户外背包的发展方向。产品品质符合QB/T 2155–2004。

This product combines the traditional Chinese medicine and ergonomics, it applied the advanced polymer material into the backpack design. Acupoint massage technique helps to accelerate blood circulation and relieve body tiredness. In addition to all the function of traditional outdoor backpack, Toread fabrics offer the ideal combination of lightweight, durability and environment protecting. The unique design and the environmental friendly materials in this product improve the economic value added that it is the development direction of outdoor backpack. The product quality meets the industry standard QB/T 2155–2004.

探路者TiEF SKIN超轻外套
Toread Tief Skin Ultra–Light Coat

生产 设计 / 北京探路者户外用品股份有限公司

Manufacture Design / Beijing Toread Outdoor Products Co., Ltd.

采用TIEF SKIN面料，T字型胸袋设计和可拆卸设计；下摆有超轻止滑带，肩部有反光印花，提高产品安全性能。从人体工学角度设计，良好的防风透湿性可有效控制人体湿热平衡，穿着轻盈剔透、内里干爽无粘连，符合户外休闲运动的需求。

Adopting TiEF SKIN fabrics that possess superior protection performance. This product is with T–shaped breast pocket design and detachable design. TiEF SKIN fabrics have the capabilities of wind–resistant, waterproof, uv–resistant and ultra–light to balance human body´s humidity and heat effectively that meet the needs of the outdoor sports. Appling advanced materials into product to highlight the comfort and quality. Elegant formal expression, simple and natural.

无缝线衬衫
Seamless Shirt

生产 设计 / 鲁泰纺织股份有限公司

Manufacture Design / Luthai Textile Co., Ltd.

该产品彻底突破传统用机针、缝纫线缝合衣片的观念，提出无缝制衣理论，并创造性地研制出新型高强环保粘合材料，形成无缝线粘合制衣技术，首创无缝线纯棉衬衫，实现了从有缝线到无缝线的跨越，堪称世界制衣史上的一次技术革命。无缝线制衣项目开发填补国内外空白，是目前世界上最先进的全棉面料，具有抗皱、免烫功能的服装制作技术。

The product breaks through the traditional idea of sewing shirt pieces with machine needles and sewing threads thoroughly, creatively develop the new echo–friendly polymer adhesive material and real seamless adhesive garment technique. The development of seamless project fills the blank home and abroad, and it is the world´s most advanced manufacturing technology of wrinkle–resistant and non–ironing cotton apparel.

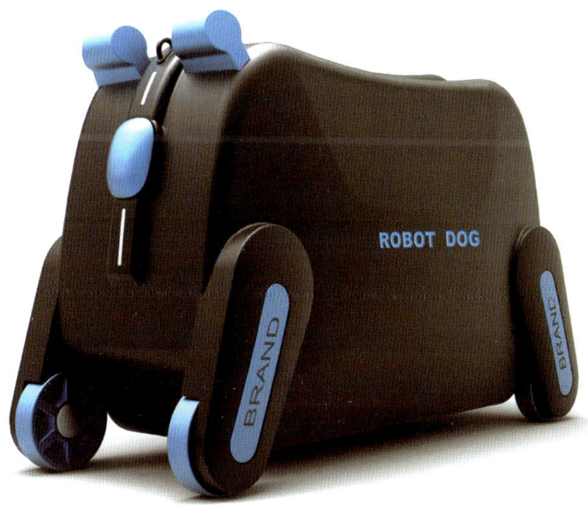

儿童箱包
Children´s Suitcase

生产 / 浙江步步乐箱包有限公司
设计 / 天津市易诺威工业产品策划有限公司

Manufacture / Zhejiang Ppluggage Co., Ltd.
Design / Innova Industrial Product Planning Co., Ltd.

将玩具与箱包结合，具有双重功能，机器狗形态，小孩可以骑在上面当做玩具。准确切入市场需求点，为客户带来很好的市场收益。整体造型圆润饱满，具有科幻感，表面可以喷涂不同图案衍生出多款产品。

It is a combination of toy and luggage. The box is shaped like a dog robot which kids can ride on played as a toy. It accurately targets market demand point, providing customers with a good market gains. The shape is rounded and full, with a sci–fi sense. The surface can be sprayed into different patterns.

江航家用制氧机
Oxygen Concentrator Recommend

生产 / 江苏江航医疗设备有限公司
设计 / 洛可可设计集团

Manufacture / Jiangsu Jianghang Medical Equipment Co., Ltd.
Design / LKK Design

利用简单的操作方式满足老年人使用者的吸氧需求，简单的实体按键式操作，符合人机的把手与底轮设计，移动便捷；利用分子筛物理吸附和解吸技术，在加压时分离空气的氧气与氮气，经过净化处理后成为高纯度的氧气，具有噪音小、节能等优点。

A simple physical push–button operation, fully meet the operating habits of the aged; in line with the handle and bottom of the man machine wheel design, to meet the mobility needs of the home space; simple operation is good to meet the oxygen demands of the aged.

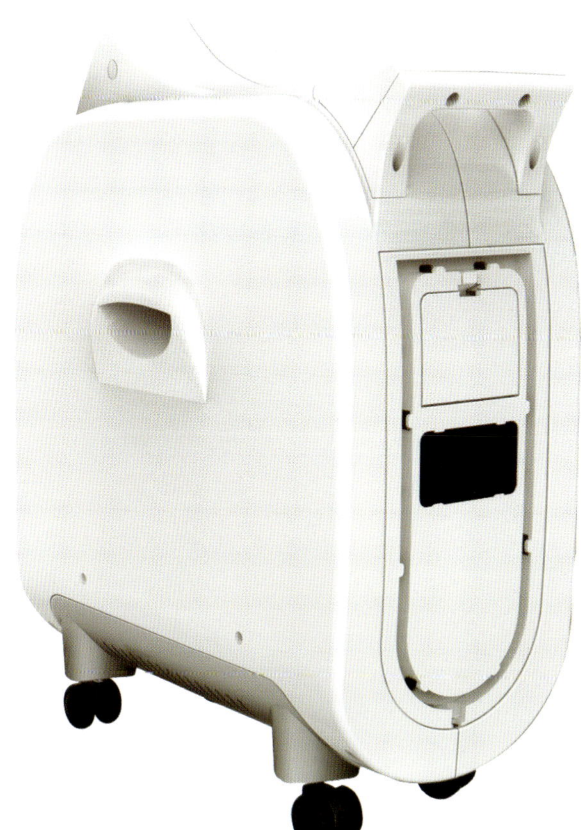

阿拉丁挑战者旅行壶
Aladdin Challenger

生产 / 奔迈(上海)国际贸易有限公司
设计 / 上海木马工业产品设计有限公司

Manufacture / Pacific Market International, LLC(´PMI´) LEGAL NOTICE
Design / Shanghai Moma Industrial Product Design Co., Ltd.

具有特有的双杯盖设计，配合大容量的储水量，给使用者带来很大便利。保温壶底部配有茶叶盒，旋盖的方式和壶身一体化，方便携带，内层加盖，不会泄漏，特别适合长途旅行。主色调为中性的白灰调，还有不锈钢原色和黑色的搭配方式，充满力量感，手握舒适。

The product is accepted by the majority of consumers of all ages and equipped with large amount of water capacity to make more convenient for users. The double cover design realize long distant travel also its color intergradations shows comfortable life and quality.

旋风卷发器
Hair Curler

生产 / 肯威专业美发用品有限公司
设计 / 深圳市鼎典工业产品设计有限公司

Manufacture / Guangzhou Yuexiu District Canway Trading Firm
Design / Shenzhen Designdo Industrial Design Co., Ltd.

此产品打破了以往复杂的卷发工艺，利用结构的变换，便利地吹出一头美丽的卷发。方便、快捷、安全、成本低、易加工，耐高温为126℃；在每一个细节都能体会到人性化操作，高效地完成美发的同时更宣导了一种健康、愉悦、时尚、潮流、节能的生活方式。

The hair curler´s design uses arc skillfully. The product uses plastic parts for the ABS, AS materials, thermostability reaches 126℃. The designer use vividly molded in the hairdressing as a design inspiration. It fully meets the design function.

超声波清洗机CE–7200A
Ultrasonic Cleaner CE–7200A

生产 / 东莞市洁康超声波设备有限公司
设计 / 想象力产品策划有限公司

Manufacture / Jeken Ultrasonic Cleaner Limited
Design / Imagination Design Co., Ltd.

以液体做介质作用于污物，无需洗涤剂无污染，可反复使用，对机器本身无损耗。内胆采用铝缸可回收循环材料，外壳采用ABS塑胶，盖了采用半透明亚克力，都是无污染原料。素材抛光，工艺简单，成本低。遵从包豪斯现代主义简约的外观风格设计,外观遵从简约设计。

This product uses liquid as the medium on dirt, without detergent and pollution, which can be reused and there is no any loss to the product. It uses Aluminum cylinder liner of recyclable material and ABS plastic in shell, translucent acrylic lid are pollution–free raw materials. Polishing material, simple process, low cost. Follow the Bauhaus modern minimalist style design, appearance with simple design.

特百惠旋风切剁器
Tupperware Speedy Chopper

生产 设计 / 特百惠（中国）有限公司

Manufacture Design / Tupperware Brands Corporation

创新的盒盖T型拉绳装置，切剁省时省力。无论是左右使用或者大小手掌均适合使用；底部特别设计防滑软胶片，无需用电，节省使用成本。制作过程和产品原料安全无污染。产品材料可回收和再生循环使用。模具制作精细，各主要部件均可拆卸清洁，保持卫生健康。

Innovative lid T rope device, when cutting it saves time and effort. It is suitable for right and left hand use as well as for those with smaller or larger hands. The anti–skid material used for the base ensures that Speedy Chopper is very stable on the countertop and does not slide when in use.It doesn´t use electricity, which can lower the cost. The production process and materials are environment–friendly. All materials are recyclable. All fine spare parts can be disassembled and cleaned completely.

百贴记事叮
The Wall

生产 设计 / P.S.L LTD.

Manufacture Design / P.S.L LTD.

本产品可贴在不同平面上，硅胶壳可以安配不同功能如倒计时或计时温度器，有时间、温度、倒数等实用功能。硅胶是环保物料，产品本身也提供留言位置，减少用纸数量，利用硅胶壳软度特性，方便更换功能和清洗，上下组物层次分明，容易使用且外观简约。

This product could stick on any flat surface by anti-slip. It also fit different features of module like temperature clock or timer clock, it has practise features as timer , alarm clock and temperature. The silicone rubber is environment material and it provide a board to write down some notes instead of use many paper. It uses soft silicone material to fit module and easy to take out for wash. Clean layout to show the function and the board , the button easy to read and the shaped keep simple.

螺钉瓶塞
Screw Bottle Cork

生产 设计 / 麦基格瑞（北京）产品设计开发有限公司

Manufacture Design / Magic Graphic Product Developing Co., Ltd. Beijing. China

利用硅胶的特性，完美保持酒水的本味，比塑料塞耐用安全，无软木、金属塞的异味；使用简便，密封牢靠，适用酒水、饮料及大部分挥发性液体的保存；环保低碳，清洗简便，可反复使用，通过国家质量标准以及美国FDA标准；多色彩的螺钉样式造型，幽默有趣。

Using nano silicon, it keeps original taste of red wine. Safer than plastic plug and has no abnormal taste of cork or metal plug. Easy to use and safe seal properties apply to the preservation of different kinds of drinks. It is low-carbon, easy to clean and can be used repeatedly. Certified by the national quality standard and American FDA standard test.

康多多PRO多雅畚斗附盖
DustPan with Lid

生产 / 福州山崎实业有限公司
设计 / 奥田朋义、土井健史

Manufacture / Fuzhou Yamazaki Industry Co., Ltd.
Design / Okuda Tomoyoshi, Doi Takeshi

在柄上附加了固定扫把的定扣，可以自由角度设定放置。畚斗的容量是一般的1.5倍，可以很便利地清洁垃圾。材料采用热可塑性树脂和铝合金，可循环回收利用。

The handle of the product is attached fixed buckle to fix the broom which is easily place with any angles. The bucket capacity is 1.5 times that of the general ones. It is convenient to clean garbages. Its material is thermoplastic resin and aluminum which is recyclable.

康多多PRO双球除尘掸
Two head– Electrostatic Duster

生产 / 福州山崎实业有限公司
设计 / 奥田朋义、土井健史

Manufacture / Fuzhou Yamazaki Industry Co., Ltd.
Design / Okuda Tomoyoshi, Doi Takeshi

该产品的主体毛绒清洁球是以PP撕裂膜网状纤维材料制作的，手柄可拆卸，包装效率高，输送效率高。产品的主体使用的材料是热可塑性树脂，可循环回收利用。

The main plush clean ball is the reticular fibers of PP tearing film material. The handle is removable. It is with high packing efficiency and transmission efficiency. The main body of the products uses thermoplastic resin which is recyclable.

绿伞品牌洗衣液系列设计
Brand And Product Design of Lv San

生产 / 北京绿伞化学股份有限公司
设计 / 北京光彩无限管理咨询有限公司

Manufacture / Green Umbrella Chemical Co., Ltd.
Design / Shine Design Consultation Center

零配件标准化，符合流水线生产要求，瓶侧结构受力平衡，垂直导入罐装设计，瓶体采用抗压结构设计，优化仓储管理，方便运输分装，降低了运输消耗，设计人性化的重心位置，通过色彩区分产品特性。使用高压HDPE材料，不仅美化瓶体外观，而且节约成本。

Structural design parts standardization meets production line requirements. The structure of the bottles side by the force balance perpendicular to import canned design, appropriate height of the bottle, to simplify the production cycle. Bottle compressive structural design optimize warehouse management, and is convenient to transport and packing which reduce the transportation consumption. The humane design of the center of gravity position and the use of high-pressure HDPE material, not only to beautify the appearance of the bottle, and also reduce the cost.

智能防暴锁
Smart Anti riot Lock

生产 / 湖南泓达科技有限公司
设计 / 深圳市鼎典工业产品设计有限公司

Manufacture / Hunan Hongda Technology Co., Ltd.
Design / Shenzhen Designdo Industrial Design Co., Ltd.

使用全球独创多路独立备份纯电子开启方式，以双备份作为保障，确保电子锁稳定运行，彻底摒弃了安全度低的机械锁备份方式；多种开启方式：指纹开启、密码开启、遥控（选配）开启；多种应急功能：密码备份应急开启方式、应急电池功能、低压报警功能。

It has smart hot copy and manual cold copy to make sure the lock operates regularly. It completely abandons mechanical lock mode of low-safety, and creates a really safe and reliable electronic lock with no keyhole. There are kinds of open mode: fingerprint mode, password mode, remote control (optional) mode, emergency mode.

广铝碰锁
GAL's Latch Series

生产 / 广铝集团有限公司
设计 / 吴志勇

Manufacture / Galuminium Group Co., Ltd.
Design / GAVIN

采用面板无螺丝设计，上下卡紧的安装方式，使产品可快速安装。铝合金材料，可循环使用，回收再造。采用日本牌号ADC12铝合金，具有超强的防断性能；通过原版古钱币图片的直译，使产品的美观性直达我们内心。

Panels made with no screws, upper parts are wedged to bottom parts for fast installation. Aluminium raw materials can be recycled and reused. The Japanese ADC12 aluminium alloy is to have super anti-breaking performance. The beauty of Ancient Chinese coins spirit permeates our inner life.

专玺
Reviving

生产 设计 / 惠州季昶五金制品有限公司

Manufacture Design / Genius Champion Enterprises Co., Ltd.

该产品首创可由消费者自行更换面料的办公椅，采用塑料和钢管的结合作为主体，可回收材料占95%以上，使成本大大降低。

This is an original design that enables the consumers to change the fabric of the chair by themselves. Its main body is the combination of plastic and steel pipe. The recyclable materials takes up more than 95%, which greatly reduces the cost.

君子如意椅
The gentleman you chair

生产 / 北京清美玉尧艺术设计中心
设计 / 杨玉尧

Manufacture / Beijing Kiyomi Yu Yao art and Design Center
Design / Yang Yuyao

该产品是传统与现代的组合，比例符合人体力学，材料用量少，采用天然材质，传统的榫卯结构，扶手椅背手法夸张。

This product is the combination of the tradition and modern. The proportion is in accord with human body mechanics. It is made with natural materials with lower material consumption, traditional mortise structure and exaggerated back and handrail techniques.

椅刚柔
Chair Gang Rou

生产 / 北京清庭文创文化发展有限公司
设计 / 石大宇

Manufacture / Dragonfly Design Center
Design / Shi Dayu

由长度及厚度各异的竹条构成，运用竹的弹性与韧性调节各位置的软硬度，竹条间隙透气，显著提升传统圈椅的舒适度，以坚实的材料达到柔软填充座垫的效果；改良明清时期圈椅尺寸太大、过重的缺点，同时又精简设计，运用榫卯结构，使之符合现代生活家居的特点。

With the faith of passing down Chinese cultural heritage and making innovative application, the designer takes the classic chair design ′horseshoe armchair′as the starting point. Also highlights the principles of sustainability, environmental protection, minimal carbon emission, contemporary practicality and aesthetics.

魔方组合家具
KROS

生产 / 富尔曼（北京）艺术设计中心
设计 / 高强

Manufacture / Form (Beijing) Art & Design
Design / Gao Qiang

KROS的设计概念来自于儿童时代的智力积木玩具。它可以任意组合、插接，可作为具有储藏功能的小型餐桌。分散成独立单元的时候，又可独立成为坐具，同时，还可以组成茶几、储藏柜等。可立于地面，也可以安装在墙面。

KROS originates from the toy bricks. It serves as a coffee table, a small size cabinet & a sitting-ware of various size and forms. It can be simply put on the floor or hung on the wall. It provides some challenging fun and personal creation of a cheerful atmosphere. It can be simply put on the floor or hung on the wall. It provides some challenging fun and personal creation of a cheerful atmosphere.

多功能儿童学习桌B
Multifunctional Desk B

生产 / 北京绿茵天地科技开发有限公司
设计 / 北京智加问道科技有限公司

Manufacture / Beijing Green World Sports Industry Incorporated
Design / ZCO Design CO., Ltd.

这是一款为4-15岁儿童设计的多功能课桌椅，应用1+N模块化设计理念，可根据孩子的爱好进行组合。它应用麻塑材料，桌面可以翻转便于阅读，桌腿可以调整高度以适应不同客户群的需求，还有配套的储物柜、展架、黑板和带有抽屉的凳子，丰富了儿童的生活，节约了空间。

The multifunctional desk and chair can be used at home for the family, adopts the ´1+N´ modularization design, which can assemble base on children´s interest. Moreover, its plastic and gunny mixed material can construct an ecological environment that agrees well with the theory of business.

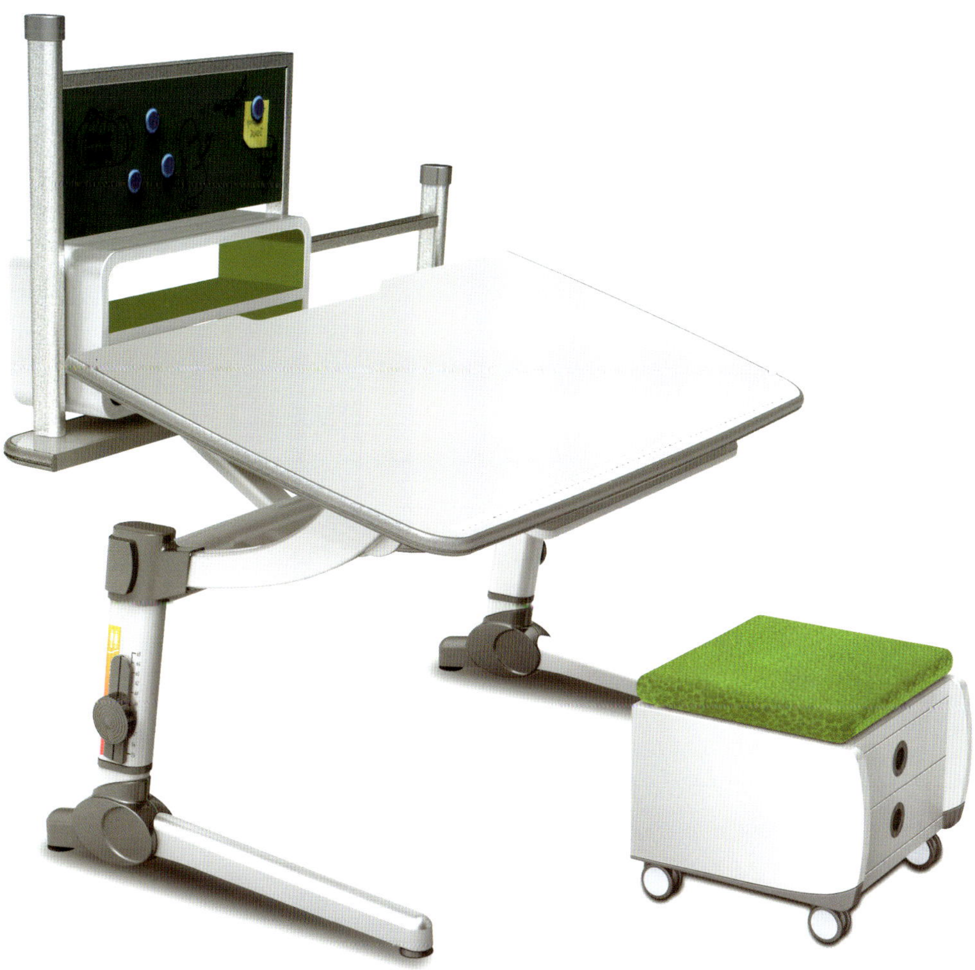

Cleaf

生产 设计 / 震旦（中国）有限公司

Manufacture Design / Aurora (China) Co., Ltd.

Cleaf的创新之处在于，产品之间不需任何连接件，只需通过自身就可实现丰富连接。无论是商业空间还是办公空间，cleaf都可与空间完美结合，在区隔空间的同时将环境装饰得更丰富、更具美力。材质为天然羊毛，安全环保。丰富的色彩可适合各类空间的布置。

Cleaf shows an innovative design that product can be attached randomly to other leaves flat on surface or in three-dimensional manner without any accessories. Cleaf can be connected with space perfectly whether in a commercial display space or in an office space and make surrounding environmental decoration more pretty. Cleaf is made of natural wool, it´s safe and environmentally friendly. Rich color can be suitable for all kinds of space arrangement.

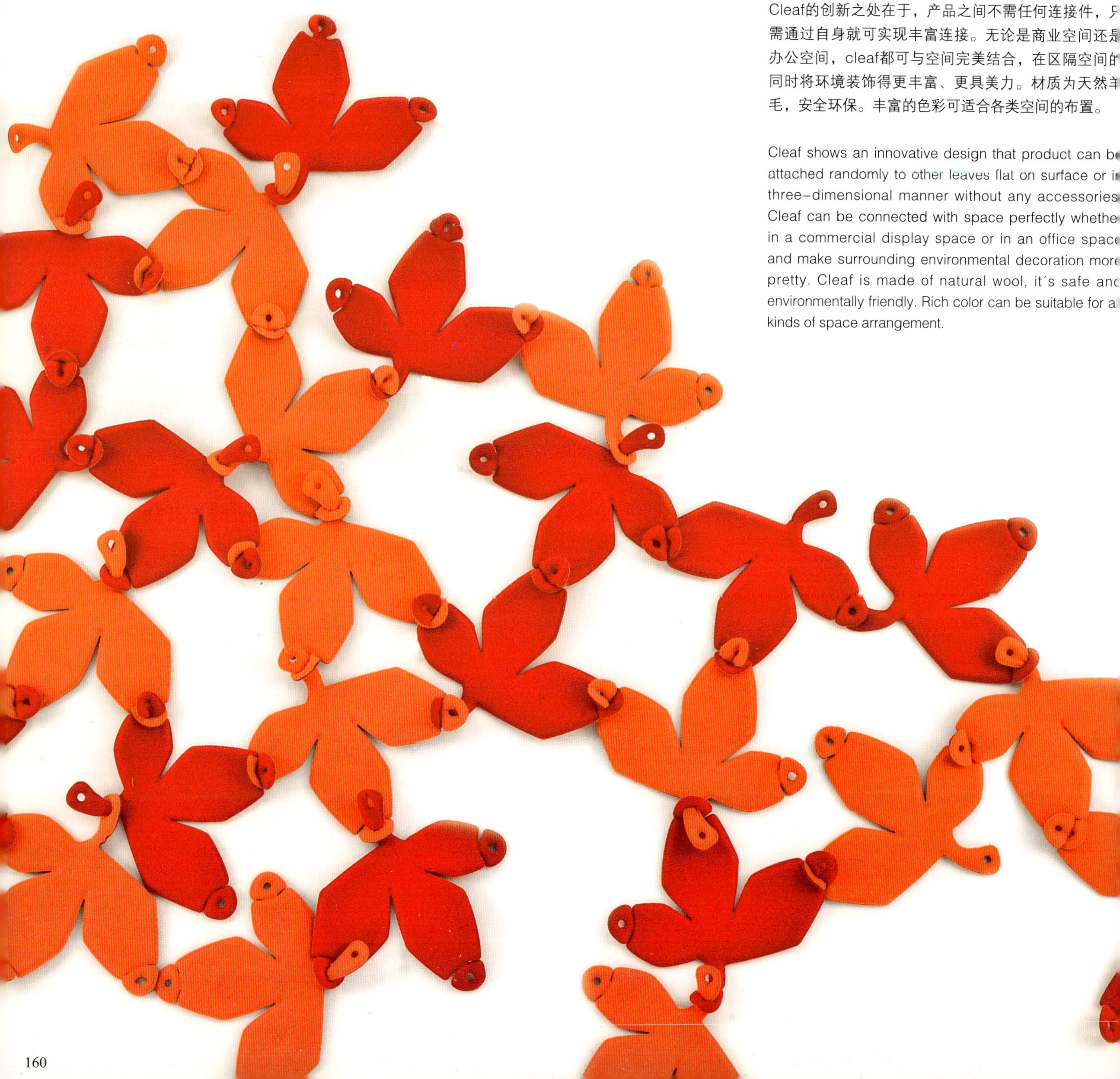

儿童身高树
Children Height Tree

生产 / 源聚德实业有限公司
设计 / 广东华南工业设计院

Manufacture / Sunnyworld Industrial Co., Ltd.
Design / Guangdong South China Institute Of Industrial Design

创意性地将儿童身高尺、墙角防撞条、亲子相册、防寒脚垫、装饰美化等多个功能巧妙结合，技术上采用了高粘合度双面魔术贴，让产品使用起来更加的方便舒心。风格清新自然，充满童话色彩，温馨而具有亲和力。形象采用成长中的小树，让成长中的宝宝像小树一样健康，充满生机。

It combines the children feet tall, corner crash bar, Family Album, cold floor mats, decorative landscaping and other features uniquely and creatively. Also use unique self-invention patents - high adhesion double-sided Velcro that make it become more comfortable.

动物系列木拼玩具
Wood Spell Toy Animal Series

生产 / 搜主意网
设计 / 曲建全

Manufacture / www.soidea.net
Design / Qu Jianquan

通过榫卯方式将看似杂乱的木条拼装成形态各异的动物，而每个动物都有一个部分可以活动；采用自然生长的木材为原料，不加入任何化工处理，保证了儿童玩具本身的安全性；这套玩具可以帮助儿童认识动物和身体的组成部分，锻炼孩子的耐心和动手能力。

A tenon looks like messy strips of wood assembled into different patterns of animal models; each animal has a movable part to assemble. The natural growth of wood as raw material, cutting, polished, without any chemical processing, and ensures children´s safety while playing.

幸符、梦享
LUCKY SYMBOL, FANCY DREAM

生产 设计 / 依波精品（深圳）有限公司

Manufacture Design / Ebohr Luxuries International Co.,Ltd.

将施华洛世奇天然宝石，镶嵌彩色天然宝石，传统贵金属加工工艺与现代精密机械加工合二为一，将珠宝贵金属的雍容华贵和手表的精密计时完美结合。荟萃国际流行时尚的最新发现，为卡纳注入了极致的艺术品性和时尚美感。

The product uses Swarovski natural stones inlaid with natural gemstones. Perfectly integrating the traditional precious metals processing technology with modern precise timing. It perfectly combines the elegance of the gems and precious metals with the precise timing of watches. It aggregates the new findings of the international fashion, injecting the ultimate work of art and fashion aesthetics into Qana.

飞亚达摄影师女表四叶草LA8362
Fiyta Photographer Female Watch with Clover LA8362

生产 设计 / 飞亚达（集团）股份有限公司

Manufacture Design / Fiyta Holdings Ltd.

手表盘面采用抽象的四叶草造型结合进口镂空机械机芯，底盖沿用透明透底工艺，一方面通过透底方式看到机芯背面摆锤效果，一方面赋予了含有洞察生活的寓意。四叶草款式既有着女性追求一生幸福的寓意，又贴近女性内心对美的需求。

The working of rotor can be witnessed through transparent bottom, which implies tracing the temperament and interest of life like photographers observe life through camera lens. Besides, the sapphire crystal covered by red coating film is filled with special charm of female.

洞天福地
Heavenly Place of Good Fortune

生产 设计 / 北京前门文化有限公司

Manufacture Design / Beijing Qianmen Culture Co., Ltd.

造型取自恭王府西洋建筑风格的汉白玉拱形石门，将中国传统元素融入到茶具中，突显茗茶之香醇。传统一壶四杯茶具，将现代设计融入百姓生活。环保材料，易于清洗、消毒。1300度高温烧制。

Blend traditional Chinese elements and the Western-style architectural elements of Prince Gong´s Mansion into the tea service. It is good at showing the fragrance and purity of the tea. The traditional set of one teapot with four cups blends modern design with common people´s lives.

便携式多功能支架
Portable Multi Function Support

生产 / 余姚艾度影视器材有限公司
设计 / 成都浪尖工业设计有限公司

Manufacture / Yuyao IDO Photographic Equipment Co., Ltd.
Design / Chengdu ARTOP Industrial Design Co., Ltd.

这款支架满足卡片机、平板电脑、上网本等数码产品的支撑需求。可以任意调整角度，适应不同环境的使用，可以收拢使之折叠起来，便于携带，利于包装运输；功能多样，趣味性强，市场潜力大；设计中尽量减轻产品重量，缩小体积，降低生产、运输等各个环节成本。

It can compatible the requirements the digital products offer such as the CARDS machines, the tablet computer and the net book. The angle of every bone can be adjusted in order to be used in different environments. Meanwhile, the bones can be folded which is benefit for taking, packaging and transportation.

宝马MINI礼品深度开发
BMW MINI Gift Depth Customization

生产 / 宝马中国汽车贸易有限公司
设计 / 北京华新意创工业设计有限公司

Manufacture / BMW (China) Trading Co., Ltd.
Design / IDEAS DESIGN CO., LTD. CHINA

打破了以往国际汽车品牌礼品制作的“奢华”路线，巧妙的设计与材料合理搭配。低碳环保理念，用再生纸制作包装、说明书，简约中体现产品的品味。同时，礼品的整体表现也有效表现出了MINI品牌在全球汽车领域所倡导的低耗、节能理念，使环保意识深入人心。

The specific innovation performance to give full consideration to ways of thinking, the concept of consumption and cognitive habits of domestic consumers, and then through the gift people can easily understand and accurately convey the theme of foreign car brands.

首饰盒
Jewellery Box

生产 设计 / 北京故宫宫苑文化发展有限公司

Manufacture Design / Beijing Imperial Court Culture Development Company Ltd.

首饰盒采用分层设计或以合页形式打开，可以放置首饰，可盛放香料。制作精美，又是极好的陈列工艺品，可用来装饰家居。选用环保原材料，采用手工彩绘、镶嵌钻石的制作方法，成为家居收纳、装饰中既具传统设计特色又具现代家居实用性的工艺摆件。

The jewelry boxes launched by Imperial Court carried forward the elegance of imperial design as well as the understanding of China Imperial Culture. All of the four jewelry boxes are designed with multi-drawers and can be opened like hinges. The design used in imperial palace means happiness and longevity, for the pronunciation of the word ´bat´ is the same as the ´happiness´ in Chinese.

《邮票上的书画艺术——感悟之美》
Beauty of Enlightenment – Calligraphy and Painting on Stamp

生产 / 北京雅昌彩色印刷有限公司
设计 / 北京雅昌设计中心

Manufacture / Beijing Artron Colour Printing Co., Ltd.
Design / Beijing Artron Design Center

这是凝聚中国传统文化和绘画美学的一套精装邮品，通过文化提升邮品价值，成本低、价值高，具有收藏价值和传承文化的作用。书盒主体部分压凹贴片，中英文书名使用烫红工艺，书名使用书法字体，充分体现了中国传统文化和绘画美学。

The whole package is light, scientific and environmental friendly, saving cost and at the same time making it easier for philatelists to carry. Because of the scroll of 87 immortals is the biggest highlight of the whole stamp album, high-quality reproduction technology is adopted to include its duplicate into the stamp album and closely combine philately with collection.

清华大学百年校庆内供酒（高级浓香型）包装设计
Liquor Packaging for Tsinghua University Centenary Celebration(Senior Aroma)

生产 / 中国泸州老窖股份有限公司
设计 / 李淳

Manufacture / Luzhou Laojiao Co., Ltd. China
Design / Li Chun

包装瓶造型独特，立意鲜明，将清华大学著名建筑——“二校门”这一标志性元素加以提炼，巧妙融于酒瓶造型设计。外包装强烈的色彩对比与传统元素的使用，渲染出清华大学百年校庆浓烈、庄重的庆典氛围。酒瓶典雅的造型与玲珑剔透的玻璃材质相结合，极具特色。

The liquor bottle owns special style and Profound meaning, the inspiration comes from the Old Gate, a famous architecture of Tsinghua University. With the contrast colors and traditional elements (patterns, seals, calligraphy), the graphic design of the packaging has distinctive Chinese characteristics and reflects the history of Tsinghua university.

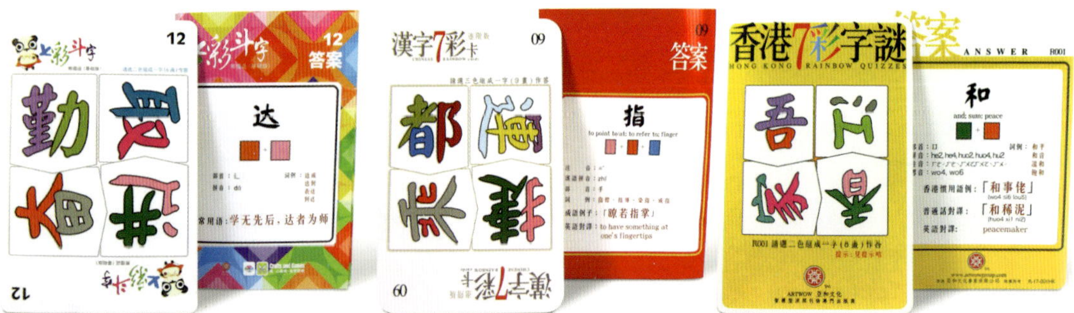

七彩汉字游戏卡系列
Chinese Rainbow Game Cards Series

生产 / 香港亚和文化事业有限公司
设计 / 陈伸

Manufacture / Artwow Group Company Ltd.
Design / Sun Chan

该卡片同时兼备游戏娱乐、IQ锻练、颜色辨认训练、学习与强化汉语等多功能，大小适中，容易携带（整盒或零散），方便随时随地游玩；能因不同的玩家程度，提供提示，并设有进阶玩法；紧遵各地教育部门有关字形、读音、笔顺及部件拆分等标准，也是有效的辅助教育工具。

This product combines the functions of games, IQ exercise, color analysis training and multi-game-play and bilingual card game. It is convenient for different users in different a stage that has become an efficiency auxiliary educational tool.

斗串「汉英」游戏卡系列
Tri/Quad-color Chinese-English Bilingual Game Cards Series

生产 / 香港亚和文化事业有限公司
设计 / 陈伸

Manufacture / Artwow Group Company Ltd.
Design / Sun Chan

兼备游戏娱乐、IQ锻练、颜色辨认训练、学习与强化汉英双语等多功能，使用颜色去标示汉字部件及英文字母，集合以汉字部件猜字、以汉字部件拼字、以英文字母猜字、及以英文字母串字等多玩法。

This product combines the functions of games, IQ exercise, color analysis training and multi-game-play and bilingual card game. Use different colors to mark the Chinese-characters & English-words guessing.

三维纸雕工艺画
Paper Craft Three-Dimensional Art

生产 / 艳丽与美同舞文化发展（北京）有限公司
设计 / 秦艳丽

Manufacture / Gorgeous and Beauty with Dance Culture Development (Beijing) Co., Ltd.
Design / Qin Yanli

采用绘画的远近透视原理，把中国题材的名画做成了栩栩如生的三维纸雕立体画。三维纸雕工艺画装饰性强，艺术效果好，题材广泛、涉及名胜古迹、市井生活、花鸟鱼虫等诸多方面。材料价格低，可以采用半机械化生产，可以量产，能大大地降代成本。

The product adopts the painting distance perspective theory, use Chinese traditional 3D paper carve technology. Also materials are cheap and can be manufactured by machine, can realize volume production which can reduce the cost.

投资币包装设计
A Packaging-design for Investment Coins

生产 / 宝泉钱币投资有限公司
设计 / 程旭锋

Manufacture / Baoquan coin Investment Co., Ltd.
Design / Cheng Xufeng

打破了过去投资币包装功能过于单一的局面，融入国际金融和中国文化气息，既是产品的包装，又是产品展示的一部分。将常用材料进行有效的组合，降低成本；将展示功能附加在包装设计上，性价比高。使用少量桃木，配合亚克力、皮革等无污染的材料，清洁环保。

This product is full of the flavor of international finance and traditional Chinese culture, are not only a outer packaging, but also a part of displayed products. This elegant, readable packaging design can change the situation that there is so little variations for the functions of packaging.

中国创新设计红星原创奖银奖

Silver Award of China Red Star Original Design Award

GRAD LED滑动控制灯
GRAD LED LIGHT

设计 / 单峰

Design / Shan Feng

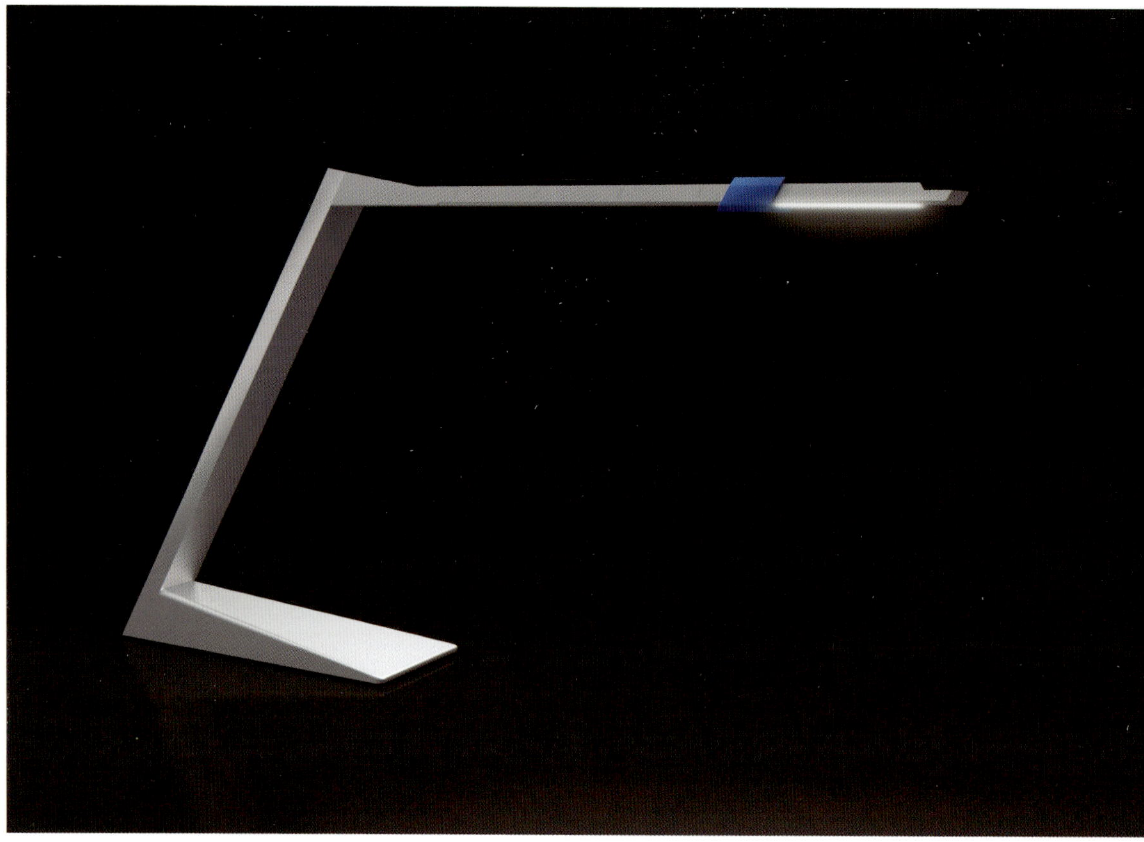

GRAD是一款有着全新控制方式的LED台灯：手拖动滑块移动到哪里，灯就亮到哪里。整条灯带就随着滑块位置的变化而变化，就像是人的手直接抓着光在移动。

GRAD有两层含义：Gradually的缩写，意味着光逐渐地亮起；而Grad(s)有刻度的意思，表示了另一个功能：照度量化。所谓照度的量化就是把照度值分段标注在了灯体上，从50～500lux。使用者在移动过程中，不但可以感性地调整亮度，还可以通过刻度理性地认知照度。此外，灯体还标注了阅读、屏幕、休息三种预设模式，以适应不同的需求。滑动控制的功能依靠单片机实现，可以很容易地扩展为系列化产品。

GRAD最大的意义就在于，相比传统“照亮”的作用，探讨了人与光之间更加丰富的关系。

GRAD is a LED light with brand new control mode. The LEDs will light up one by one as you move the slider. It is like you stretch a light beam back and forth.

GRAD is short for Gradually which represents the way the LEDs light up, while Grad(s) itself means quantification of illumination. Grads from 50lux to 500lux are carved on the body which helps users understand better of light more than bright and dark. There are also three default modes, read, screen and rest to meet different demands.The sliding control mode is realized by a SCM, which is implanted with a program. This makes GRAD easy to be developed into a series of products.

GRAD means more than light itself. It is trying to enrich the relationship between human and light.

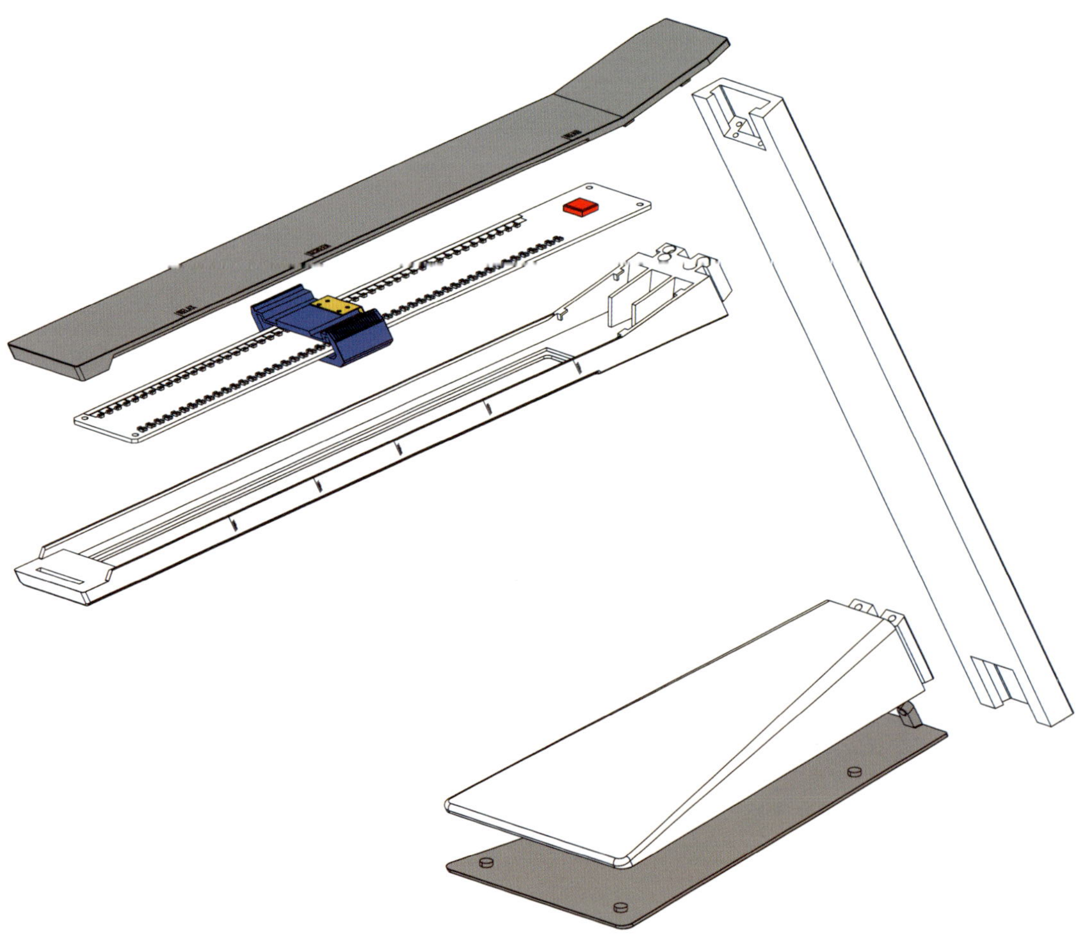

太阳花LED灯
Sun Flower

设计 / LG电子中国设计中心

Design / LG Electronics China Design Branch

太阳花是一个用可再生材料制成的造型简洁又紧凑的太阳能便携式照明灯。用来帮助那些生活在贫困山区的孩子，解决他们在家里、在上下学途中、在教室、宿舍生活和学习时的光线不足。

作品表面为太阳能充电池，通过塑胶外壳的可挤压性使产品与吸附物之间产生真空(吸盘效果)，从而将其吸附于任何光滑的平面上。发光部分采用环保纸张折叠而成，具有透光和漫反射的特点。光源采用LED，具有低温低能耗的特点，更加安全环保。

白天可吸附在窗户上采集阳光，夜晚打开可放置在桌子上或吸附在墙壁上，达到发光照明效果。

感应式花瓣，可以伴随你的触摸改变形态。不同的形态给予人们不同的感受，在你最需要帮助的时候，给你心灵的安慰。

Sun Flower is a simple and compact portable solar energy lighting device which is made of renewable materials. It is designed to help the children who live in the impoverished mountainous regions to solve the lack of light when they are living and studying at home and school. The product surface is solar battery. Vacuum can come in between product and adsorbate (sucker effect) through extrudability of the plastic shell, so that the product can be adsorbed on any smooth surface. The luminous part adopts folding environmental paper design that can reflect lights. The light source adopts low temperature and low energy consumption LED, safer and environmental protection. It adsorbed on windows and collects lights during the day and uses it at night. Induction type petals, can accompany you to touch change form.

空虚时间指示器
VOID TIME INDICATOR

设计 / FABLAB Ltd.
Design / FABLAB Ltd.

设计师希望设计一个能够显示生命隧道的时钟，通过观察仪观察时间如何运行。该作品在中间结构上布置12个嵌入LED的凹槽，每个槽代表一个小时，在前后部都覆盖一个水银镜。夜幕降临时，发光的小时槽将相继发光，直至白昼，此时整个结构呈现为一个三维发光图案。白天这个过程将反向进行，整套装置看起来像一个中间有孔的镜子，正如美学上的二维结构。这种平面与立体的双重性与自然时间指示概念形成鲜明的对比：白天发光，夜间则表示为黑暗。希望用户能够理解时间指示仅仅是人类社会预想的规则，它并非我们相信的那么稳定。设计师希望用户观察时间，并且不会因它流逝的速度而感到恐惧，用户能够拥抱生命的旅程，而不必太在意时间的威胁。

This works uses a centre structure carved with 12 LED embedded grooves, a high reflection mirror is clad over on both front and back. Each of these grooves represents an hour and as night falls, they will illuminate one by one. This process is in reversed during the daytime, the device will seem to be a simple mirror with a hole in the middle, very 2 dimensional in aesthetic. This duality of flatness and volumetric play are in stark contrast with our natural conception of time indication: where daytime is illuminated and night time is in darkness. This concept hopes users to understand time indication is merely a pre-conceived rule and it does not have to be static as most believed. Users observe the time and not be intimidated by its speed and finally they embrace the journey of life and not be too concern with its obsession of time.

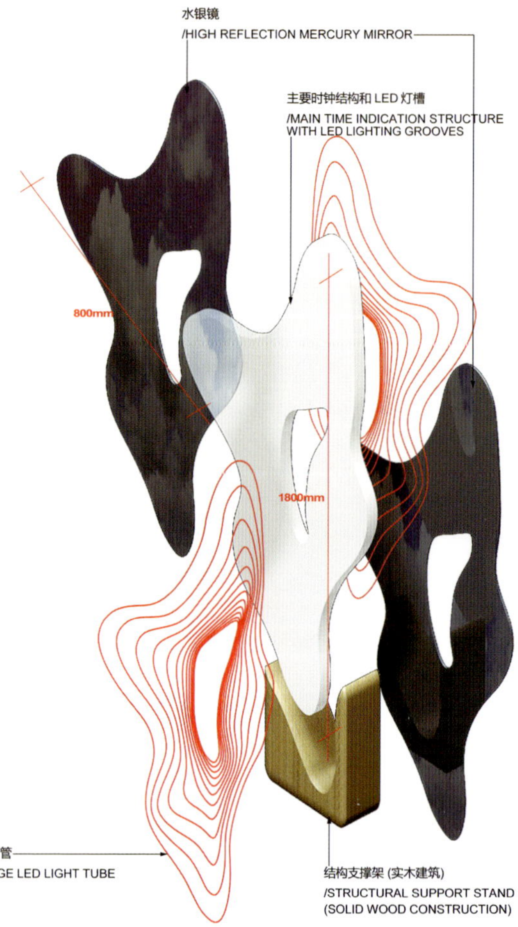

ONEPLUG 可用单手拔的插头
ONEPLUG

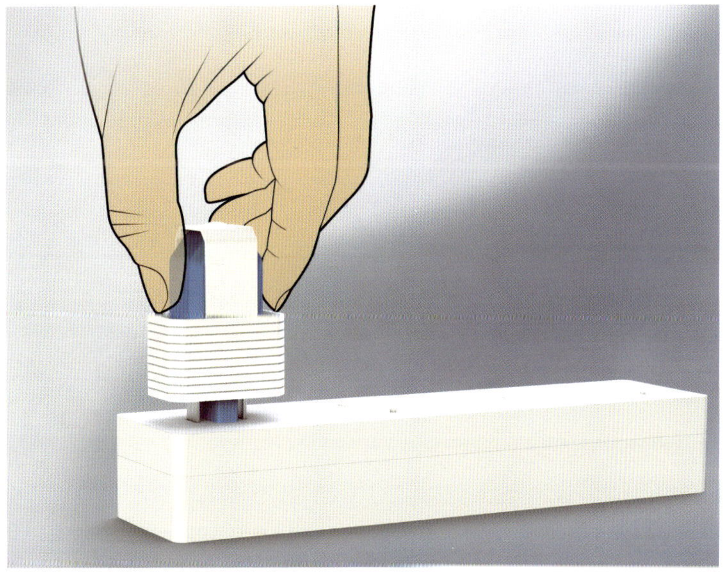

设计 / 单峰

Design / Shan Feng

ONEPLUG是一款可以用单手拔出的插头。
在生活中，人们常常会遇到这种情况：用单手拔插头的时候，由于太紧，插座会被一起拉起来，因此只能用另一只手扶住插座，才得以将插头拔出。尽管这并不是一个复杂的动作，但是却让人感觉不舒服。
ONEPLUG巧妙的解决了这个问题，利用一个伸出机构，以插座为支点，通过两个手指“捏”的简单动作，将插头拔出。由于伸出机构具有弹性，所以动作完成以后，它会自动复位。
ONEPLUG追求的是“一只手，一个动作”的便捷性。某些通过插座来解决这类问题的设计，需要先操作插座，再拾取插头；相比之下，本设计把操作直接转移到插头上，这样“拔出”和“拾取”插头的动作一气呵成。

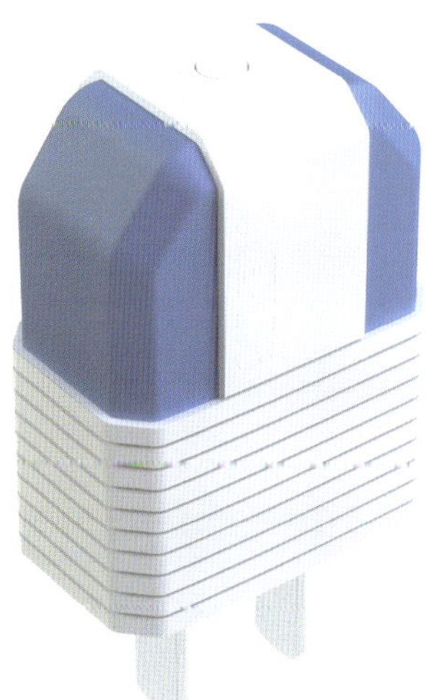

ONEPLUG can be unplugged by one hand.
Such situation is what we often sit through, when you try to pull out a plug by one hand, you pull up the whole socket because they are tightly connected. So you have to hold the socket with the other hand and finish the operation. That feels bad.
ONEPLUG can somehow help you get rid of this feeling. It adopts a simple telescoping system which allows you to use only two fingers to pinch the buttons, and then the plug is lifted up.
ONEPLUG pursues an operation using only one hand, in one move, which maximizes the convenience. At this point, ONEPLUG is better than some socket designs aiming at the same problem, which forces users to deal with the socket first, and then pick up the plug.
Please enjoy ONEPLUG by one hand, in one move.

原创ORIGINAL

优秀设计师奖

Best Designer Award

徐佑荣
Kevin Chu

『一个充满激情的设计师必须坚持设计每一个细节，甚至是每一个螺丝。
A passionate designer should design everything, even down to the last screw.』

1975年出生于香港，在英国留学多年，成为一名建筑师，并于2006年成立K LTD设计工作室。K LTD设计工作室一直致力于原创设计。

他认为，设计作为一门源于艺术的专业，设计师应从不同于非艺术家的角度去发现世界，保留向世界展示另一种现实的渴望。但要进行原创设计，一定要区分灵感和模仿。著名的英国建筑师NORMAN FOSTER说：灵感无处不在，它存在于任何事物和条件。我们可以接受“超级巨星”的启发，但要压制去模仿的愿望。他们之所以成功，是由于一直保持原创。在当前物质的世界里，复制的行为的确可以取得快速成功。但作为设计师，应该为自己的创新能力和开创精神感到自豪。我们需要从每天遇见的平凡事物中去寻找灵感，把几何学作为我们和外界沟通的语言，通过挑战自己对设计的理解，展开充分的想象来完成作品。

Mr. Kevin Chu is an England educated architect born in Hong Kong in 1975 and in 2006 he set up KLTD design studio which has always been "stubborn" at holding true to original design insisting on the original design. He thinks that as a profession that stems from art, all see the world in a different light to most non-artists and retain a desire to show the world our alternative view of reality. To create something original, one has to know the difference between inspiration and imitation. The famous English architect Norman Foster said that inspiration comes from everywhere, everything and every situation. It is ok to be inspired by "superstar designers" in our profession but we should try to suppress our desire to imitate. In this materialistic world and the incentive to succeed quickly will indulge in the act of "copying", but as designers, we should be proud of our creative ability and a sense of pioneering spirit. Always think of geometry as our language to bridge our ideology to the layman. It is important we challenge our understanding of a design brief and truly expand our imagination to tackle issues.

原创ORIGINAL

未来之星奖
Future Star Award

李 菁
Li Jing

『对设计的理解：功能大于形式，一切以使用者的需求为本。
The understanding of design: function is greater than the form, all is based on users needs.』

1991年生于北京，2009年至今就读于北京林业大学工学院工业设计系。在校期间，努力学习，积极参加社会活动并参与、主持了多项设计任务及科研项目。在老师的帮助及指导下，积累了丰富的设计及管理经验，逐渐成长为一名具有一定专业能力的未来工业设计师。

作为2012中国创新设计红星原创奖获奖作品FREE——多功能儿童座椅的主要设计师，作品设计灵感来源于对生活的细致观察。过多的玩具已经成为许多家庭的首要问题，这些玩具不仅造成了资源的浪费，也对居室环境有一定影响。她希望通过对传统玩具的再设计，使简单的玩具可以伴随孩子整个童年。通过对市场现有产品的充分调研研究，秉承一切以使用者需求为首的理念，不断跟进、调整设计方案，最终完成了对传统木马玩具的再设计。该设计突破了传统使用方式，在保持作品造型语言简洁的基础上，衍生出了更多功能，完成了使用属性和娱乐属性的完美结合。

Born in Beijing in 1991, Lijing is a student of Engine-ering Department of industrial design, Beijing Forestry University since 2009. While in school, she is not only engaged in the academic work, but also actively involved in social activities. Through the experience of participating and leading several design and research projects, she has gained plenty practical experience in product design and project management, and gradually grows up as a competent industria designer.

As the awarded works of 2012 China Red Star Origina award, the Free was inspired by the observation of children´s daily life. Possession of too many toys has become a headache of many families, these toys not only the waste of resource, but also affect indoor environment. So she developed this concept to expand the features of traditional toys, making them feasible to accompany children for their entire childhood. Based on the research of existing products in the market and following her philosophy of design, which is to fits customer´s needs first, she developed the Free, a modernized hobby horse swing. The Free expands the features of a traditional hobby horse swing, making the toy also feasible for sitting on, painting on, leaning on and sharing with others. The Free has achieved the goal of combining both entertainment properties with the product function.

王星悦
Wang Xingyue

『用敏锐的视角去发现创新的可能性，用不懈的坚持去实现更美好的未来。
Using keen perspective to find the possibility of innovation, with the unremitting adhere to realize a better future.』

1990年生于浙江杭州，2012年毕业于浙江工业大学艺术学院工业设计系，在校期间曾参与多个学校企业合作项目，通过不断的学习、观察和实践，勇于创新，积累了丰富的设计经验，逐渐成长为一名优秀的工业设计师。

2011年，秉承“关爱社会，关爱灾区同胞”的想法，构思了一款适用于灾区的简易折叠卫生间，通过改变卫生间的遮挡物材料使移动卫生间的体积尽量减至最小，便于灾区运输。同时，抛弃传统的移动卫生间用电机冲水的方法，采用一次性可降解的塑料袋打包，可以尽可能地减少能源的消耗，既卫生又环保。此项设计曾获得2011年浙江省“康大杯”大学生工业设计大赛银奖。

Born in 1990 in Hangzhou Zhejiang, and graduated from Technology Institute of the Arts Department of industrial design, Zhejiang University. During her stay in school, Wang Xingyue has participated in a number of school & enterprise cooperation projects, through continuous learning, observation and practice, she has accumulated rich experience in design and innovative spirit, gradually grew into a fine industrial Designer.

In 2011, stand for an idea to love the world, and take care of the disaster area, she came up with this folding toilet for disaster. It changed the toilet´s cover material to make mobile toilet volume minimize, and abandoned the traditional mobile toilet motor flushing method, instead use of disposable plastic bags packaging waste, so it can reduce energy consumption, help to sanitary and environmental protection. This design has won the 2011 Zhejiang province "Kangda Cup" college students of industrial design competition award with silver medal. Design comments:Using keen perspective to find the possibility of innovation, with the unremitting adhere to realize a better future.

原创ORIGINAL

红星原创奖
Excellent Award

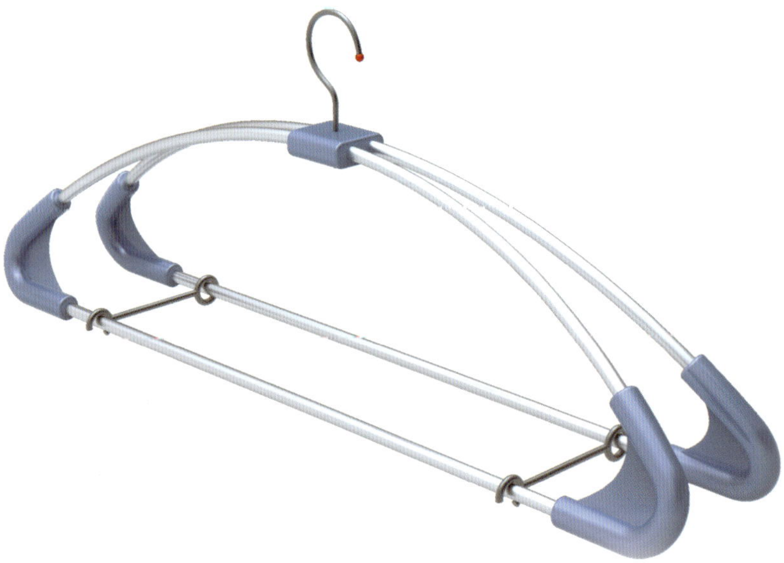

多用速干支撑晾晒架
Useful Rapid-drying Lateral Brace Clothes Rack

设计 / 郝恬、李薪郦

Design / Hao Tian, Li Xinli

该作品能高效利用有限的生活空间，并增加晾晒衣物的蒸发面积，架子中间分开约30° 角，使晾晒的衣物保持一定间距，易通风，从而缩短晾晒时间；其结构坚固，易于收纳，可晾晒大件衣物或多件小衣物。

This works efficiently uses the limited space. It can add the evaporation area of the washed clothing. The rack is split at an angle of about 30° and keeps some space of the washed clothing and easy to dry. It has firm structure and easy to fold, it also can be used to dry big sheet or several small clothes.

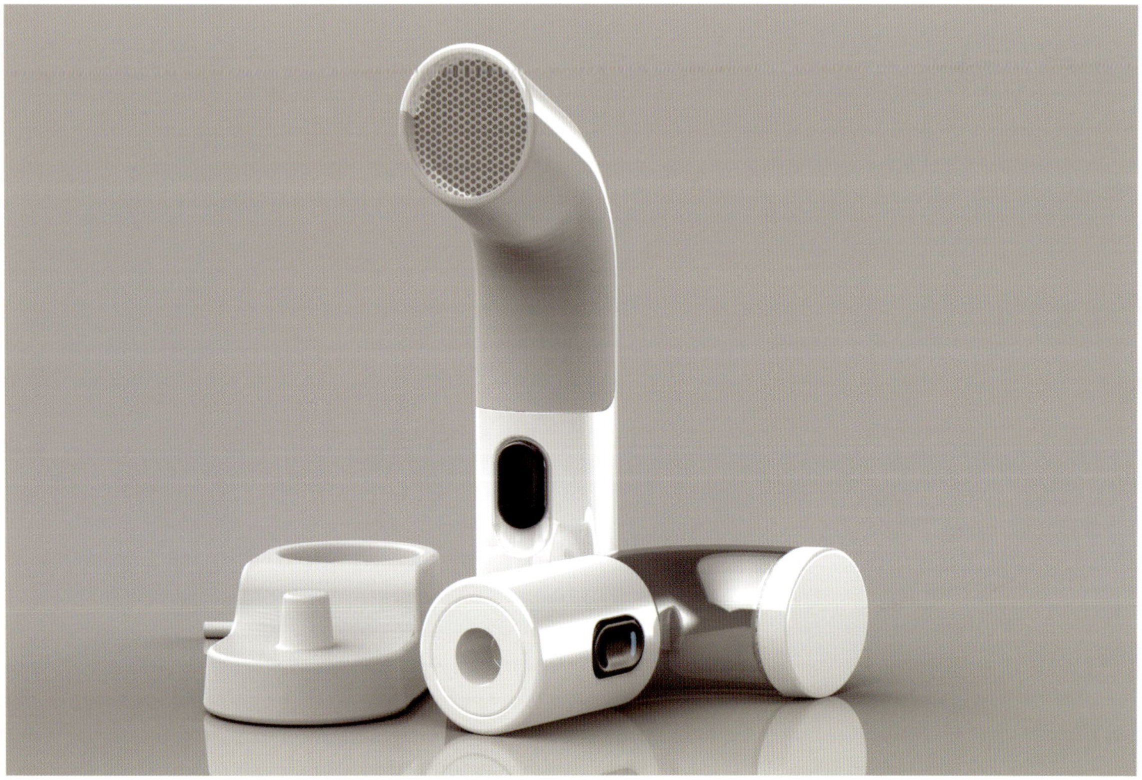

Hand-Washing 手持洗衣机设计
Hand-washing machine

设计 / 周丽雯

Design / Zhou Liwen

当衣服沾染上小面积污渍时，Hand-Washing 手持洗衣机能够让使用者不用脱下衣服便可清理污渍。Hand-Washing 手持洗衣机在形式上采用手持洗衣机部分和干衣吹风组合的套装形式出现，在清洁衣服后能够快捷地烘干衣服。造型上采取圆管式的形态，弯曲的流线型增加了手持的舒适度。

The hand-washing applies users to cleaning small besmirch on the clothes without take off them. It adopts cleaning part and drying part in form, which accelerates the speed of drying clothes. On modeling it chooses the streamline form of circular tube to increase comfortable feeling when handing it.

防滴雨衣
Drop Proof Raincoat

设计 / 曹镒滟

Design / Cao Yiyan

每次我们穿雨衣在雨中行走或骑自行车时，都有被雨水淋湿裤腿的经历。此雨衣设计为防止雨水流到裤腿上，在雨衣下部的边缘处设计了一圈可吹气的气囊，当下雨时穿戴者可先吹足气，这样不管在行走或骑自行车时都可阻止雨水滴到裤腿上，实用且方便。

Every time when we wear raincoat walking or cycling in the rain, we all have the experience of wet trousers. This raincoat is designed to prevent rain from flowing to the lower part of the trousers´ leg. A inflatable ring is designed in the raincoat edge. The ring can be inflated when needs. So that regardless of walking or cycling it could avoid rain to flow into the trousers´ leg. This is both practical and convenient.

灾区简易折叠卫生间
Simple folding toilet for disaster areas

设计 / 王星悦、李璟璐

Design / Wang Xingyue, Li Jinglu

通过改变厕所的遮挡物材料来使移动厕所的体积尽量减到最小，以便于灾区的运输。同时，抛弃传统的移动厕所用电机冲水的方法，用一次性可降解的塑料袋打包，这样可以尽可能地减少能源的消耗，既卫生又环保。

It changed the toilet´s cover material to make mobile toilet volume minimize, and abandoned the traditional mobile toilet motor flushing method, it uses disposable plastic bags packaging waste, so it can reduce energy consumption, help to sanitary and environmental protection.

脚垫灯
Mat Light

设计 / 深圳市鼎典生活用品有限公司
Design / Shenzhen Designdo Daily Use Co.,Ltd

该作品结合了地垫与灯的功能，可放置床边或门口等需要的地方，地垫通过内部触动开关，打开周围的LED灯带，灯光会持续30秒左右。作为辅助光源，灯光并不刺眼，也可照亮周围区域，帮助人们迅速适应黑夜。

This works combines the function of mat and light. It can be placed at the bedside or on the door where needed. It is opened by internal touch switch. The LED lights will last about 30 seconds. As an auxiliary light source, the light is not dazzling, and also illuminates the surrounding area, which can help people to adapt quickly to the night.

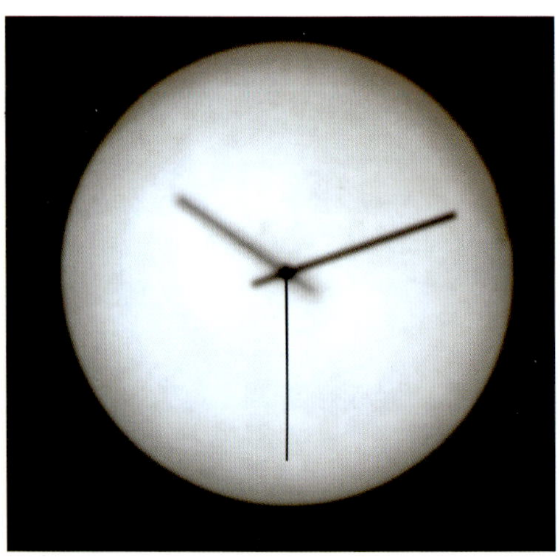

瓷表
China Clock

设计 / 中央美术学院设计学院产品设计系“一起”工作组
Design / "Together" Work Group, Industrial Design, School of Design, Central Academy of Fine Arts

本表的设计灵感来源于骨瓷本身薄如纸、透光性好的特点，温润纯白的骨瓷，加上指针之间的虚实关系，使得作品具有了不同的韵味。钟平时只是一个圆盘，只有秒针在表面转动。当声控打开，内部灯板会照亮表盘，里面指针的影子就会被投在圆盘上，显示出准确时间。

This clock shows a common disk with a rotating second hand on the surface. When the voice-operated-switch is on, the lamp panel inside will light up and cast the shadow of pointer on the disk. Accurate time is presented. The creamy white color, as well as the design of shadow minute-hand, makes a distinguished charm.

FREE——多功能儿童座椅
Free–Multifunction Seat for Children

设计 / 北京林业大学

Design / Beijing Forestry University

在木马“摇”的使用方式基础上衍生出坐、倚、画、享等，完成了从产品的娱乐属性到使用属性的转变。以达到“一个玩具伴随整个童年”的设计目标，并解决儿童玩具浪费的问题。

作品的外形采用抽象仿生的手法意在开发儿童的想象力。

In addition to swinging, the expanded features of the free make this toy also feasible for sitting, painting, leaning and sharing. It is also a great solution to avoid toy overload, which wastes the space and resource.

Furthermore, the shape of it adopts the abstraction simulation which can explore the creativity of the children.

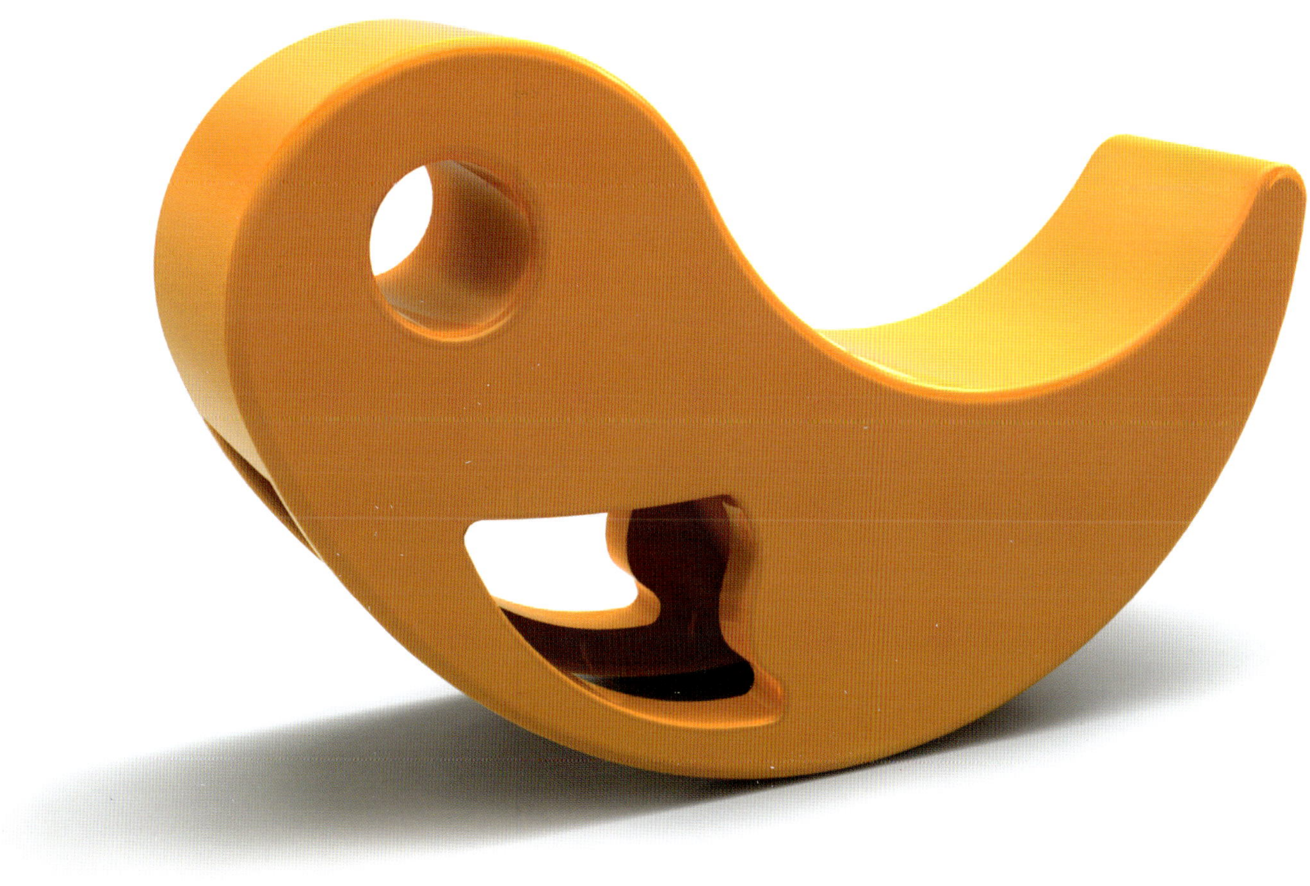

单手挤牙膏器
Single Handed Toothpaste Squeezer

设计 / 浙江科技学院工业设计系
Design / Zhejiang University of Science and Technology Industrial Design Department

该作品是为单手残疾或一只手不方便的用户设计的挤牙膏器套装。设计目的是使他们能够用一只手顺利完成整个刷牙行为。套装包括挤牙膏器和两个牙杯座，靠墙安装，不占用面积。同时此设计亦解决了牙膏快用完时难以挤尽的问题。

It is designed for single-handed handicapped or those who have inconvenience with one hand in daily life. With this, people can finish the toothbrushing with only one hand. The whole set includes a toothpaste squeezer and two bases for cups. It is installed on wall for saving space. And it also helps to squeeze out all the toothpaste without any waste.

眼药水助点器
100% Eye Drop Dispenser

设计 / 尔沃设计整合
Design / Award-Design Integration Studio

使用药水助点器能够精准地滴入适当位置，可以减少因直视眼药水产生眼睛闪避的情况，降低心理恐惧感，减少施点错误与重复率，减少副作用发生率，避免医疗资源浪费，独自使用于行动不便者，能透过医疗辅具，轻松、安全且有效地施点药水。

It can precisely deliver a dose of eye drops into the eye, preventing from blinking and lowering the psychological fear. It can decrease the wrong and repetition rate, reduce the possibility of side effects and medical resources. It is an independent living aid which helps the disabled or the ordinary dose the eye drops easily, safe and effective.

无限刮勺
Scoop Spoon

设计 / 罗琦
Design / Luo Qi

当人们食用瓶装的果酱、沙拉酱、花生酱、巧克力酱时，常常因为不容易刮干净而浪费掉很多酱料，无限刮勺巧妙地改变了勺边缘的形态，这样的设计除了可以当作普通勺使用，还可以轻松地将瓶子边角、侧面、底面的酱料刮下来，避免浪费。形态创新，功能无限。

When people eat bottled jam, salad dressing, peanut butter or chocolate sauce, often waste a lot of jam for it is not easy to scoop. Scoop Spoon subtly changes the shape of the spoon edge, so, other than as an ordinary spoon, it can easily scrape off the jam from corner, side or bottom of the bottle to avoid waste. An innovative form brings plenty of functions.

获奖名单
Winner List

2012中国创新设计红星奖获奖名单

中国创新设计红星奖至尊金奖

消防机器人
生产 / 苏州海伦哲专用车辆有限公司
设计 / 上海轱辘轩工业设计有限公司
008

中国创新设计红星奖银奖

木质拼装榫卯车
生产 / 北京中奥之光科技发展有限公司
设计 / 高天宇
030

Airflow空气背包背负系统
生产 / 设计 / 福建哥仑步户外用品有限公司
032

雅生布鲁克面盆及龙头
生产 / 汉斯格雅欧洲股份有限公司
设计 / 罗南和埃尔文•布鲁克兄弟
034

油烟机CXW-200-F16
生产 / 设计 / 宁波欧琳厨具有限公司
035

垂直对流散热LED路灯
生产 / 勤上光电股份有限公司
设计 / 清华大学美术学院设计战略与原型创新研究所
036

模块化办公及展览展示系统
生产 / 宁波布特坦姆文化传播有限公司
设计 / 宁波柯怡工业设计有限公司
037

康佳9000系列电视
生产 / 康佳集团股份有限公司
设计 / 康佳9000系列设计团队
038

【有余•祝福中国】渔具设计
生产 / 设计 / 北京光彩无限管理咨询有限公司
039

小米手机 MiOne
生产 / 北京小米科技有限责任公司
设计 / 刘德
040

中国创新设计红星奖金奖

LG6210E液压挖掘机
生产 / SDLG (山东临工工程机械有限公司)
设计 / 沃尔沃集团上海设计中心
012

马来西亚城际动车组
生产 / 南车株洲电力机车有限公司
设计 / 南车株洲电力机车有限公司&TRICON Design AG
014

茧-天津万通生态城新新家园零能耗会所
生产 / 天津生态城万拓置业有限公司
设计 / 北京墨臣建筑设计事务所
016

G型透视手术系统
生产 / 北京东方惠尔图像技术有限公司
设计 / 北京智加问道科技有限公司
018

低频磁旋治疗系统
生产 / 山东超瑞施医疗科技有限公司
设计 / 深圳市无限空间工业设计有限公司
020

小天鹅比佛利滚筒洗衣机（06外观）
生产 / 无锡小天鹅股份有限公司
设计 / 小天鹅工业设计团队
022

IdeaCentre A720
生产 / 联想（北京）有限公司
设计 / 联想创新设计中心
024

3D显示器
生产 / LG电子
设计 / LG电子中国设计中心
025

真三维道路智能设计系统
生产 / 设计 / 中交宇科（北京）空间信息技术有限公司
026

最佳团队奖

轱辘轩工业设计团队
042

最佳新人奖

张青
044

Winner List of 2012 China Red Star Design Award

Best of The Gold Prize Of China Red Star Design Award

Fire-fighting Robot
Manufacture / Suzhou Handler Special Vehicle Co.Ltd
Design / Shanghai Guluxuan Industrial Design Co.Ltd
008

Gold Prize of China Red Star Design Award

LG6210E Hydraulic Excavator
Manufacture / Shandong Lingong Construction Machinery Co., Ltd.
Design / Volvo Group Design Center – Shanghai
012

Malaysia SCS EMU
Manufacture / CSR Zhuzhou Electric Locomotive Co.,Ltd
Design / CSR Zhuzhou Electric Locomotive Co.,Ltd&TRICON Design AG
014

Cocoon-Zero-energy Sale Center of Tianjin Vone Shangbei Legacy Homes
Manufacture / Tianjin Eco-City Wantuo Properties Limited
Design / Mochen Architects & Engineers
016

G-type Perspective Surgery System
Manufacture / Beijing Oriental Whale Image Technology Co., Ltd.
Design / ZCO Design CO., Ltd
018

Low-Frequency Rotating Magnetic Therapy System
Manufacture / Shandong CRS Medical technology Co., Ltd.
Design / Shenzhen ND Industrial Design Co,. Ltd.
020

Little Swan Beverly Front-loading Washing Machine
Manufacture / Wuxi Little Swan Company Limited
Design / Little Swan ID team
022

IdeaCentre A720
Manufacture / Lenovo
Design / Lenovo Innovation Design Centre
024

DM92 Series LED Premium 3D TV monitor
Manufacture / LG Electronics
Design / LG Electronics Design China
025

Real 3D Intelligent Road Design System
Manufacture / Design / China Trans Geomatics Co.,Ltd.
026

Silver Prize of China Red Star Design Award

Wood Assembly Tenon Car
Manufacture / Beijing China-Olympics light Technology co.,ltd
Design / Gao Tianyu
030

Airflow Inflatable Outdoor Backpack System
Manufacture / Design / Fujian Kolumb Outdoor Equipment Co., Ltd
032

Axor Bouroullec Basin and Mixer
Manufacture / Hansgrohe SE
Design / Ronan and Erwan Bouroullec
034

RANGE HOOD CXW-200-F16
Manufacture / Design / Ningbo Oulin Kitchen Utensils Co., Ltd
035

Vertical Convection LED Street Light
Manufacture / Kingsun Optoelectronic Co.,Ltd
Design / Institute of Design Strategy and Prototype Innovation, Tsinghua University
036

Modular Office and Exhibition System
Manufacture / Ningbo Beilun Dongren Industrial & Trading Co.,Ltd.
Design / Co-Yes Industrial Design Co.,Ltd.
037

KONKA 9000 Series TV
Manufacture / KONKA Group Co.,Ltd
Design / KONKA 9000 Series design team
038

YOUYU•Blessings China Fishing rod
Manufacture / Design / Shine Design Consultation Center
039

MiOne
Manufacture / Xiaomi Corporation
Design / Liu De
040

Best Team Prize

Guluxuan Design Team
042

Best New Designer Prize

Zhang Qing
044

红星奖 Excellent Prize

电池移动仓
Mobile Storage Battery
生产 / 国家电网
设计 / 杭州汉度工业设计有限公司
Manufacture / State Grid Corporation Of China
Design / HUMTA
048

SY5250GJB3A/12NR搅拌车
SY5250GJB3A/12NR SANY Concrete Truck Mixer
生产 / 三一重工湖南汽车制造有限责任公司
设计 / 湖南大学设计艺术学院
Manufacture / SANY Group Hunan Automobile Manufacturing CO., Ltd
Design / School of Design Hunan University
049

能量隧道
Energy Tunnel
生产 / 香港宝龙科技有限公司
设计 / 北京智加问道科技有限公司
Manufacture / PORON International Ltd
Design / ZCO Design CO., Ltd
050

石墨炉原子吸收分光光度计
Graphite Furnace Atomic Absorption Spectrometry Photometer
生产 / 北京海光仪器公司
设计 / 北京智加问道科技有限公司
Manufacture / Beijing Kechuang Haiguang Instrument Co.,Ltd
Design / Zco Design Co., Ltd
051

数控环保锅炉
Numerical Control Eco Boiler
生产 / 河北新华鑫锅炉制造有限公司
设计 / 北京致翔创新
Manufacture / Sunhouse Boiler Manufactory Co.,Ltd
Design / Aestech Design
052

精密数控电火花成型机 FORM 20
FORM 20 CNC Die Sinking EDM
生产 设计 / 北京阿奇夏米尔工业电子有限公司
Manufacture Design / Beijing Agie Charmilles Industrial Electronics Co., Ltd.
053

汉印——PCB字符喷印机
Hi-print-PCB Legend Inkjet Printer
生产 / 汉印科技
设计 / 贤信堂设计
Manufacture / Hi-print Technology
Design / Sincere Tone Design
053

无人侦察机
Unmanned Reconnaissance Aircraft
生产 / 北京观点航空设备公司
设计 / 姜辛
Manufacture / SKYCAM AIR MATERIAL CO.
Design / Jiang Xin
054

希盟健康护理监控系统
CIM Health Care Monitoring System
生产 / 希盟（中国）科技有限公司
设计 / 上海木马工业产品设计有限公司
Manufacture / CIM (CHINA) TECHNOLOGY INC.
Design / Shanghai Moma Industrial Product Design Co., Ltd
056

利德曼化学发光分析仪
LEADMAN Chemiluminescence Analyzer
生产 / 北京利德曼生化股份有限公司
设计 / 博砚清艺(北京)工业设计有限公司
Manufacture / Leadman Group Co., Ltd.
Design / Beyondesignlab Industrial Design Company
056

KG系列全封闭全自动石油干洗机
KG Series Fully Enclosed Automatic Oil and Dry-cleaning Machines
生产 / 美国百丝特国际集团有限公司
设计 / 北京赛佳图工业设计有限公司
Manufacture / U.S. Best International Group Co., Ltd.
Design / Beyon Design Lab Industrial Design Company
057

顿力多功能医疗床
Dunli Multifunctional Medical Bed
生产 / 杭州顿力医疗器械有限公司
设计 / 上海木马工业产品设计有限公司
Manufacture / Hangzhou Dunli Medical Instruments Co., Ltd
Design / Shanghai Moma Industrial Product Design Co., Ltd
058

牙科综合治疗椅
DENTAL UNIT
生产 / 佛山市思福特医疗设备有限公司
设计 / 佛山市尚致设计有限公司
Manufacture / Foshan Safety Medical Equipment Co.,Ltd.
Design / Foshan Bob Design Co.,Ltd
058

新松智能服务机器人
Siasun Intelligent Service Robot
生产 / 沈阳新松机器人自动化股份有限公司
设计 / 崔亮生
Manufacture / SIASUN Robot & Automation Co.,Ltd
Design / Cui Liangsheng
059

光盘库yeq-001
CD-ROM Library Yeq-001
生产 / 武汉楚活汉工创意科技发展有限公司
设计 / 武汉也琪工业设计有限公司
Manufacture / Wuhan Chu&Han Seiko Creative Technology Development Co.,Ltd
Design / Wuhan YEQ Industrial Design Co,. Ltd
059

数位演讲台
Digital lectern
生产 / 河北海捷现代教学设备有限公司
设计 / 深圳市舵手工业设计有限公司
Manufacture / Hebei Haijie Modern Educational Equipment Co.,Ltd.
Design / Shenzhen Helmsman Industrial Design Co.,Ltd.
059

消防式氧气呼吸器
Fire-Type Oxygen Respirator
生产 / 深圳昊泰气体设备科技有限公司
设计 / 深圳市柏斯工业设计有限公司
Manufacture / Jiangsu Oxtek Air Equipment & Technology Co.,Ltd.
Design / Shenzhen Perth Industrial Design Co.,Ltd.
060

电焊机
Welding machine
生产 / 浙江台州竟添机电有限公司
设计 / 天津市易诺威工业产品策划有限公司
Manufacture / Taizhou Genteck Electric Co., Ltd.
Design / Innova industrial product planning Co., Ltd.
060

煤矿探水雷达
Groundwater Detector System for Coal Mine
生产 / 广西百色美联能源科技有限责任公司
设计 / 洛可可设计集团
Manufacture / Guangxi Baise Myland Technology Co., ltd
Design / LKK Design
061

名菱工业缝纫机
MingLing Industrial Sewing Machines
生产 / 名菱工业自动化科技有限公司
设计 / 广东华南工业设计院
Manufacture / MingLing industrial automation technology Co., Ltd.
Design / South China Industrial Design Institute of Guangdong
061

上海珅铼机电操控箱
Shanghai Sunrise Mechanical And Electrical Control Box
生产 / 上海珅铼机电成套设备有限公司
设计 / 上海木马工业产品设计有限公司
Manufacture / Shanghai sunrise complete sets of m&e equipment Co.,Ltd
Design / Shanghai Moma Industrial Product Design Co., Ltd
062

便携式气相色谱——质谱联用分析仪
Portable Gas Chromatography-Mass Spectrometry Analyzer
生产 / 聚光科技（杭州）股份有限公司
设计 / 杭州汉度工业设计有限公司
Manufacture / Focused Photonics(Hangzhou),inc
Design / HUMTA
062

全智能水表
Radio Frequency Water Meter
生产 / 浙江甬岭供水设备有限公司
设计 / 天津市易诺威工业产品策划有限公司
Manufacture / Zhejiang Younio Water Supply Equipment Co., Ltd
Design / Innova Industrial Product Planning Co., Ltd.
062

碳清风
Car Air Purifier
生产 / 广州市龙曦生物科技有限公司
设计 / 广州深山产品设计有限公司
Manufacture / Guangzhou Longxi Biota Technology Co., Ltd
Design / Guangzhou Sunine Product Design Co., Ltd
063

介入医疗器械手柄
Interventional Medical Device Handle
生产 / 先健科技（深圳）有限公司
设计 / 深圳市四六区工业产品策划有限公司
Manufacture / Lifetech Scientific (Shenzhen) Co., Ltd.
Design / Shenzhen April 6th Industrial Products Design Co.,Ltd
063

工业级信号浪涌防护单元
Unit Surge Voltage Protection
生产 / 北京欧地安科技股份有限公司
设计 / 洛可可设计集团
Manufacture / Beijing Allday Science and Technology Co.,Ltd
Design / LKK Design
063

北京地铁昌平线车辆
Metro Cars for Beijing Metro Changping Line
生产 / 设计 / 南车青岛四方机车车辆股份有限公司
Manufacture / Design / CSR QingDao SiFang CO.,LTD.
064

广州地铁自主知识产权直线电机车辆
LIM Metro Cars With Independent Intellectual Property Right for Guangzhou Metro
生产 设计 / 南车青岛四方机车车辆股份有限公司
Manufacture Design / CSR QingDao SiFang Co.,Ltd
065

混凝土湿喷机外观及人机优化设计
Concrete Wet Spraying Machine Exterior and Human-computer Optimization Design
生产 / 成都市新筑路桥机械股份有限公司
设计 / 徐伯初、高朋飞
Manufacture / Chengdu Xinzhu Road and Bridge Machinery
Design / Xu Bochu, Gao Pengfei
066

长安重汽M系列新能源重卡
CCAT M Series New Energy Heavy Vehicle
生产 / 太原长安重型汽车有限公司
设计 / 周力辉
Manufacture / Taiyuan Changan Heavy Vehicle Co., Ltd.
Design / Zhou Lihui
067

S4200商务艇
S4200 Commercial Vessel
生产 设计 / 太阳鸟游艇股份有限公司
Manufacture Design / Sunbird Yacht Co.,Ltd
068

什刹海游船
Shichahai Pedalo
生产 / 北京市西城区园林市政管理中心
设计 / 北京博蓝士科技有限公司
Manufacture / Garden Municipal Administration Center of Xicheng District, Beijing
Design / IDC design
070

传祺suv GS5
TRUMPCHI SUV GS5
生产 / 广汽乘用车公司
设计 / 广汽集团汽车工程研究院
Manufacture / GAC Motor
Design / GAC Engineering
072

Z-one
生产 / 重庆宗申机车工业制造有限公司
设计 / 重庆蓝海时代产品设计有限公司
Manufacture / Chongqing Zongshen Automobile Industry Manufacturing Co., Ltd
Design / Chongqing Ocean Time Industrial Design Co.,Ltd
073

XMQ6125造型设计
XMQ6125
生产 设计 / 厦门金龙联合汽车工业有限公司
Manufacture Design / Xiamen Kinglong United Automative Industry Co., Ltd
073

生态迷你树屋
Eco-Mini Treehouse
生产 / 合肥德佳节能科技有限公司
设计 / 程曦
Manufacture / Hefei Deka Energy-saving Technology Co.,LTD
Design / Cheng Xi
074

鸽趣
Street lamp-pigeon
生产 / 四川华体灯业有限公司
设计 / 董石羽、王超
Manufacture / Sichuan Huati Lighting Industry Co.,Ltd
Design / Dong Shiyu, Wang Chao
075

高速公路绿色通道车辆检查系统
Freeway Green Corridor Vehicle Inspection System
生产 / 北京华立兴科技有限公司
设计 / 曲建全
Manufacture / Beijing Huali Xing Technology Co., Ltd.
Design / Jianquan Qu
076

Modular Traffic Light System
生产 / Modular Traffic Light System
设计 / Barry Geer
Manufacture / Modular Traffic Light System
Design / Barry Geer
077

电动巴士电池快换设备
Quick Change Battery Device
生产 / 电动巴士科技有限公司
设计 / 北京智加问道科技有限公司
Manufacture / Shanghai Dianba New Energy Technology Co., Ltd.
Design / ZCO Design CO., Ltd
078

ATS自助办税服务终端
Automated Taxation Service Machine
生产 / 广东金赋信息科技有限公司
设计 / 佛山市顺德区潜龙工业设计有限公司
Manufacture / Guangdong Kamfu Information & Technology Co.,Ltd.
Design / Chinno Industrial Design Co.,Ltd
079

CP16老人手机
CP16 Eldly Phone
生产 设计 / 成都嘉兰图设计有限公司
Manufacture Design / ChengDu Newplan Design Co.,Ltd
080

摩托罗拉锋芒 V (MT887 / XT885)
Motorola RAZR V MT887 / XT885
生产 / 摩托罗拉（北京）移动技术有限公司
设计 / 徐国伦
Manufacture / Motorola Mobility
Design / Vincent Shyu
080

手机防辐射听筒GR02
Radiation Receiver for Mobile Phone GR02
生产 / 深圳市高迪信科技有限公司
设计 / 想象力产品策划有限公司
Manufacture / Shenzhen Supertempo Technology Co.,Ltd
Design / Imagination Design Co.Ltd
081

康佳T621芒果手机
Konka T621 Mango Moblie Phone
生产 / 康佳集团通信科技有限公司
设计 / 成亦辉
Manufacture / Shenzhen Konka Telecommunications Technology Co.,Ltd
Design / Cindy Cheng
081

康佳V95
KONKA V95
生产 / 康佳集团通信科技有限公司
设计 / 周雷
Manufacture / Shenzhen Konka Telecommunications Technology Co.,Ltd
Design / Zhou Lei
081

红星奖
Red Star Design Award

运动三防手表手机
Waterproof sports watch mobile
生产 / 深圳市浪尖设计有限公司
设计 / 张东阳、蔡渊洸
Manufacture / Shenzhen ARTOP Design Co.,Ltd
Design / Toyio Zhang, Cai Yuanguangi
082

家用型信息终端
Household Multimedia Phone
生产 / 惠州纳伟仕智能媒体技术集团
设计 / 深圳市柏斯工业设计有限公司
Manufacture / NIVS IntelliMedia Technology Group, Inc.
Design / Shenzhen Perth Industrial Design Co., Ltd
082

方位D800智能VoIP视频电话
Fanvil D800 Smart VoIP Video Telephone
生产 / 方位实通（深圳）科技有限公司
设计 / 广州极至设计有限公司
Manufacture / Fanvil Technology Co.,Ltd
Design / Guangzhou UTOP Design Co.,Ltd.
082

家联网终端
Home Network Terminal
生产 / 石家庄火木科技有限公司
设计 / 北京智加问道科技有限公司
Manufacture / Shijiazhuang Home Technology Co., Ltd
Design / Zco Design Co., Ltd
083

无线路由器
wirolooo routor
生产 / 成都飞鱼星科技开发有限公司
设计 / 成都浪尖工业设计有限公司
Manufacture / Chengdu flying fish star science and technology development Co., Ltd.
Design / Chengdu ARTOP Industrial Design Co.,Ltd.
083

物流PDA
Logistics PDA
生产 / 北京维信通科技公司
设计 / 曲建全、易安定
Manufacture / Beijing Vsimtone Technology Company
Design / Qu Jianquan, YI Anding
084

3防PDA
3 anti-Personal Digital Assistant
生产 / 北京华夏民生科技有限公司
设计 / 曲建全、赵彻
Manufacture / Beijing China Minsheng Sci & Tech Co., Ltd.
Design / Qu Jianquan, Zhao Che
084

恒业世纪-多功能工业手持机
Hy-Multifunctional Industrial Handheld Computer
生产 / 北京恒业世纪科技股份有限公司
设计 / 品物（北京）科技有限公司
Manufacture / Beijing Heng Ye Technology
Design / PER Design&Consultants
085

HHT无线POS
HHT
生产 / 深圳市海维海工业设计有限公司
设计 / 印度 Geoamida公司
Manufacture / Shenzhen hvhi Co.,Ltd
Design / Geoamida
085

FOTA 点钞机
FOTA Money Counter
生产 / 浙江方泰电器有限公司
设计 / 杭州热浪科技有限公司
Manufacture / Zhejiang Fota Electrica Company Limited
Design / Hangzhou Hotid Technology Co.,Ltd
086

智能购物车终端
Intelligent Shopping Cart Terminal
生产 / 北京中汉儒臣国际技术有限公司
设计 / 程旭锋
Manufacture / Beijing China Human International Technology Co.,Ltd.
Design / Cheng Xufeng
086

警用一体化信息采集工作台
Police Integration Information Collection Workbench
生产 / 北京东方金指科技有限公司
设计 / 北京东西创新工业设计有限公司
Manufacture / Easten Golden Finger System
Design / East&West Industrial Design Co.,Ltd
086

WIA工业无线仪表
WIA industrial wireless instrument
生产 / 中国科学院沈阳自动化研究所
设计 / 洛可可设计集团
Manufacture / Shenyang Institute Of Automation Chinese Academy Of Sciences
Design / LKK Design
087

诺基亚西门子通讯三扇区信号基站
Lumina Pico Base-station
生产 / 诺基亚西门子通信
设计 / 深圳市融一工业设计有限公司
Manufacture / Nokia siemens network
Design / Shenzhen RONE Industrial Design Co.,Ltd
087

流动式三维扫描仪
Floating 3D Scanner
生产 / 北京博维恒信科技发展有限公司
设计 / 中国农业大学工学院
Manufacture / 3D CaMega Co., Ltd
Design / College of Engineering, China Agricultural University
088

二代USBKey OnKey193D
the Second Generation USBKey OnKey193D
生产 设计 / 天地融科技股份有限公司
Manufacture Design / Tendyron Corporation
088

警用执法仪
Law Enforcement recorder police camera
生产 / 深圳市高斯贝尔家居智能电子有限公司
设计 / 深圳汉合产品设计有限公司
Manufacture / Shenzhen Gospell Smarthome Electronic Co., Ltd.
Design / RamarkDesign Co., Ltd.
089

太阳能车载警示器
solar car warning device
生产 / 河南天恩太阳能科技有限公司
设计 / 孙合会、陈仕斌
Manufacture / Henan TE Solar Energy Technology Co.,Ltd
Design / Sun Hehui, Chen Shibin
089

手持金属探测仪
Hand-held Metal Detector
生产 / 成都昂讯电子有限公司
设计 / 成都意町工业产品设计有限公司
Manufacture / Chengdu Angxun electric Co.,Ltd
Design / Chengdu IDing industrial design Co.,Ltd
089

自动果蔬面膜机
Automatic Fruit Vegetables Facial Mask Machine
生产 设计 / 北京东西创新工业设计有限公司
Manufacture Design / East&West Industrial Design Co.,Ltd
090

LED深紫外便携式隐形眼镜消毒盒
Led Deep Uv Disinfection Box of Portable Contact Lenses
生产 / 青岛杰生电气有限公司
设计 / 北京东西创新工业设计有限公司
Manufacture / Qingdao Jason Electric CO.,Ltd
Design / East&West Industrial Design Co.,Ltd
090

LED深紫外便携式消毒牙刷盒
Led Deep Uv Disinfection Portable Toothbrush Box
生产 / 青岛杰生电气有限公司
设计 / 北京东西创新工业设计有限公司
Manufacture / Qingdao Jason Electric CO.,Ltd
Design / East&West Industrial Design Co.,Ltd
090

安卓智能高清电视棒 PCTV01
Android Smart HDTV Stick PCTV01
生产 / 韩国三星电子有限公司
设计 / 想象力产品策划有限公司
Manufacture / Samsung Electronics Co., Ltd
Design / Imagination Design Co.,Ltd.
091

博思泰克牵手腕带
Pulsetech Hand-in-hand Wristband
生产 / 无锡博思泰克科技有限公司
设计 / 洛可可设计集团
Manufacture / Wuxi Pulsetech Co,.Ltd
Design / LKK Design
091

快乐童声儿童点读笔
Point to Read Pen
生产 / 湖南快乐童声教育科技发展有限公司
设计 / 深圳市群创工业设计有限公司
Manufacture / Hunan Kuailetongsheng Education Technology Co.,Ltd.
Design / Shenzhen Qunchuang Industrial design Co.,Ltd
091

Transphone
生产 / 华移联科（沈阳）技术有限公司
设计 / 北京致翔创新
Manufacture / China Mobile Internet Technologies Inc.
Design / Aestech Design
092

航天信息加密移动硬盘
Password Encryption Hard Disk
生产 设计 / 航天信息股份有限公司
Manufacture Design / Aisino Corporation
092

TP移动电源2
TP-Power2
生产 / 天宝国际兴业有限公司
设计 / 谭迪明、洪鸿莹
Manufacture / Ten Pao International Ltd.
Design / Daniel Tan, Tim Hung
092

航天标准19寸机柜
Space Standard 19 Inch Of Cabinets
生产 / 航天恒星科技有限公司
设计 / 北京东西创新工业设计有限公司
Manufacture / Space Star Technology Co.,Ltd
Design / East&West Industrial Design Co.,Ltd
093

飞利浦 PicoPix 笔记本电脑投影仪
Philips PicoPix Notebook Projector
生产 / Sagemcom
设计 / 飞利浦设计
Manufacture / Sagemcom
Design / Philips Design
093

寰烁PC投影一体机
United PC Projection Machine Electronic Instrument
生产 / 山西寰烁科技有限公司
设计 / 洛可可设计集团
Manufacture / ShanXiHuanShuo
Design / LKK Design
093

机械翻转屏
Mechanical Flip Screen
生产 设计 / 北京闪图科技有限公司
Manufacture Design / Beijing Bright Vision Digital Technology Co,.Ltd
094

美臀电踏机
Meitun Electric Stepping Machine
生产 / 广州飞达运动按摩器材有限公司
设计 / 深圳市畅为工业设计有限公司
Manufacture / Guangzhou Feida Exercise & Massager Equipment Co., Ltd
Design / Shenzhen Municipal Industrial Design Company Limited
095

现磨全自动咖啡机
Full Automatic Coffee Machine
生产 / 苏州工业园区咖乐美电器有限公司
设计 / 无锡迪可工业设计有限公司
Manufacture / Suzhou Industry Park Kalerm Electric Appliances Co.,Ltd
Design / Wuxi DEEK Industry Design Co.Ltd
096

和锦胶囊咖啡机
Hejin Coffee Machine
生产 / 上海和锦咖啡科技有限公司
设计 / 上海木马工业产品设计有限公司
Manufacture / Shanghai Hejin Coffee Technology Co., Ltd
Design / Shanghai Moma Industrial Product Design Co., Ltd
096

7天滴漏式咖啡机
7 Days Drip Coffee Maker
生产 / 广东美的精品电器制造有限公司
设计 / 广州易用设计有限公司
Manufacture / GD Midea Premium Appliances Mfg.Co.,Ltd.
Design / EASE Design Guangzhou Co.,Ltd
096

“慢生活”饼式咖啡机
"Slow Life" Soft pad Coffee Machine
生产 / 广东美的精品电器制造有限公司
设计 / 广州易用设计有限公司
Manufacture / GD Midea Premium Appliances Mfg.Co.,Ltd.
Design / EASE Design Guangzhou Co.,Ltd
097

“Emotion”胶囊式咖啡机
"Emotion" Capsule Coffee Machine
生产 / 广东美的精品电器制造有限公司
设计 / 广州易用设计有限公司
Manufacture / GD Midea Premium Appliances Mfg.Co.,Ltd.
Design / EASE Design Guangzhou Co.,Ltd
097

智能即热式开水机
Intelligent & Fast Water Machine
生产 / 宁波清清环保电器有限公司
设计 / 宁波柯怡工业设计有限公司
Manufacture / QingQing Environmental Protection Electrical Co.,Ltd.
Design / CO-YES industrial design Co.,Ltd.
097

智能化自动升降厨具机
Intelligent Kitchen Machine
生产 设计 / 宁波柯怡工业设计有限公司
Manufacture Design / CO-YES industrial design Co.,Ltd.
098

天际智能型隔水炖盅
Intellectual-controlled stewpot
生产 / 广东天际电器股份有限公司
设计 / 佛山市顺德区潜龙工业设计有限公司
Manufacture / Guangdong Tonze Electric Co., Ltd
Design / Chinno Industrial Design Co.,Ltd
099

艾美特2.8L电压力锅
Airmate 2.8L electric pressure cooker
生产 / 艾美特电器有限公司
设计 / 佛山市顺德区潜龙工业设计有限公司
Manufacture / Airmate Electrical (Shenzhen) Co., Ltd.
Design / Chinno Industrial Design Co., Ltd.
099

天际陶瓷饭煲
Tonze ceramic rice cooker
生产 / 广东天际电器有限公司
设计 / 佛山市顺德区潜龙工业设计有限公司
Manufacture / Guangdong Tonze Electric Co., Ltd
Design / Chinno Industrial Design Co.,Ltd
099

便携式电蒸锅
Portable Steamer
生产 / 浙江苏泊尔股份有限公司
设计 / 杭州金瑞工业产品设计有限公司
Manufacture / Zhejiang Supor Co.,Ltd
Design / Hangzhou Canew Industrial Design co.,Ltd
100

苏泊尔电蒸锅
Supor Tainless Steamer
生产 / 浙江苏泊尔家电制造有限公司
设计 / 和硕设计
Manufacture / Zhejiang Supor Electrical Appliances Manufacturing Co.Ltd
Design / Pega Design &Engineering
100

便捷系列电蒸锅
Convenient Series Electric Steamer
生产 / 浙江苏泊尔家电制造有限公司
设计 / 马汉、成凯
Manufacture / Zhejiang Supor Electrical Appliances Manufacturing Co.,Ltd.
Design / Vincent Ma, Ck
100

多媒体电源播放器
Multimedia Power Strip
生产 / 深圳航嘉驰源电气股份有限公司
设计 / 深圳航嘉工业设计部
Manufacture / Shenzhen Huntkey Electric Co.,Ltd
Design / Shenzhen Huntkey industrial design department
101

儿童防漏电保护转换器
Children-protective Leakage-preventing Adaptor
生产 / 北京突破电气有限公司
设计 / 杜大勇
Manufacture / Beijing Top Electric Co .,Ltd
Design / Du Dayong
101

原汁机
Slowjuicer
生产 / 浙江苏泊尔家电制造有限公司
设计 / 马汉、杜聪
Manufacture / Zhejiang Supor Electrical Appliances Manufacturing Co.,Ltd.
Design / Vincent Ma, Kevin Du
102

家用豆奶机
Household soy milk machine
生产 / 广东东菱电器有限公司
设计 / 宁波市鄞州潜龙工业设计有限公司
Manufacture / Guangdong Dongling Electrical Appliances Co.Ltd
Design / Ningbo Yinzhou Chinaloog Industrial Design Co.Ltd
102

微压豆浆机
Micro-pressure Soymilk
生产 / 中山市美斯特实业有限公司
设计 / 上海跃意工业产品设计有限公司
Manufacture / Zhongshan Mester Industrial Co.,Ltd.
Design / Shanghai YOY Industrial Design Co.,Ltd
103

九阳豆浆机-D56SG
Joyoung SoyMilk Marker-D56SG
生产 / 九阳股份有限公司
设计 / 和硕设计
Manufacture / Joyoung Company Limited
Design / PEGA Design &Engineering
103

美的凡帝罗滚筒洗衣机
Midea Vandelo Front-loading Washing Machine
生产 / 无锡小天鹅股份有限公司
设计 / 小天鹅工业设计团队
Manufacture / Wuxi Little Swan Company Limited
Design / Little Swan ID team
104

小天鹅迷你机
Little Swan Mini Washing Machine
生产 / 无锡小天鹅股份有限公司
设计 / 小天鹅工业设计团队
Manufacture / Wuxi Little Swan Company Limited
Design / Little Swan ID team
104

美的凡帝罗波轮全自动洗衣机
Midea Vandelo Top-loading Washing Machine
生产 / 无锡小天鹅股份有限公司
设计 / 小天鹅工业设计团队
Manufacture / Wuxi Little Swan Company Limited
Design / Little Swan ID team
104

美的KF双贯流柜式空调
Midea KF Air-Conditioning
生产 设计 / 广东美的制冷设备有限公司
Manufacture Design / Gd Midea Air-Conditioning Equipment Co., Ltd.
105

家庭植物工厂
The Plant Factory for Family
生产 / 北京京鹏环球科技股份有限公司
设计 / 北京博蓝士科技有限公司
Manufacture / Beijing Kingpeng International Hi-Tech Corporation
Design / IDC design
106

新飞BCD-366WV除菌冰箱
Xinfei BCD-366WV Anti-bacteria refrigerator
生产 设计 / 河南新飞电器有限公司
Manufacture Design / Henan Xinfei Electric Co. Ltd
107

第二代“五星”玻璃面板多门冰箱
Five Star 2.0 Glass Panel Multi-door Refrigerator
生产 / LG电子
设计 / LG电子中国设计中心
Manufacture / LG Electroni
Design / LG Electronics Design China
107

物联网智控抽油烟机
Networking Intelligent Control Range Hoods
生产 / 万家乐
设计 / 梁智坚、刘诗锋
Manufacture / MACRO
Design / Benie Liang, Liu Shifeng
108

莲花灶B809C
Lotus Cook Top B809C
生产 / 中山华帝燃具股份有限公司
设计 / 北京圣宝地工业设计有限公司
Manufacture / Zhongshan Vatti Gas Appliance Stock Co.,Ltd.
Design / CBD Group Corp.
108

德意JZDY(T)-299A灶具
DE&E JZDY(T)-299AStove
生产 / 浙江德意厨具有限公司
设计 / 杭州飞鱼工业设计有限公司
Manufacture / Zhejiang DE&E Kitchen Utensils Co.,Ltd
Design / Hangzhou Feish industrial design Co., Ltd.
108

灵劲系列
Dynamica Series
生产 / 中山华帝燃具股份有限公司
设计 / 北京圣宝地工业设计有限公司
Manufacture / Zhongshan Vatti Gas Appliance Stock Co.,Ltd.
Design / CBD Group Corp.
109

25mm 超薄电磁炉
25mm Ultra Slim IH
生产 / 浙江苏泊尔家电制造有限公司
设计 / 马汉、杜聪
Manufacture / Zhejiang Supor Electrical Appliances Manufacturing Co.,Ltd.
Design / Vincent Ma, Kevin Du
109

消毒柜ZTD90B16
Sterilizer ZTD90B16
生产 设计 / 宁波欧琳厨具有限公司
Manufacture Design / Ningbo Oulin Kitchen Utensils Co., Ltd
110

i-FIVE 集成灶
i-FIVE Integrated Environmental Kitchen
生产 / 浙江奥田电器有限公司
设计 / 杭州金瑞工业产品设计有限公司
Manufacture / Zhejiang Aotin Electric Appliances Co.,Ltd
Design / Hangzhou Canew Industrial Design co.,Ltd
110

ROBAM-812
生产 / 杭州老板电器股份有限公司
设计 / 王强
Manufacture / Hangzhou ROBAM Appliances CO.,LTD
Design / Wang Qiang
110

水滴石LED电视
Constant Dropping Wears The Stone Led TV
生产 / 深圳创维——RGB电子有限公司
设计 / 创维创新设计中心
Manufacture / Skyworth-Rgb Electronics Co.,Ltd
Design / Skyworth-Rgb Electronics Co.,Ltd
111

K91
生产 / 联想（北京）有限公司
设计 / 联想创新设计中心
Manufacture / Lenovo
Design / Lenovo Innovation Design Centre
111

“都看”阅读器
Doucon Reader
生产 / 北京当当科文电子商务有限公司
设计 / 洛可可设计集团
Manufacture / Beijing Dangdang Kewen E-commerce Co., Ltd.
Design / LKK Design
112

Asus Padfone Series A66/P02
生产 / 华硕电脑（上海）有限公司
设计 / 华硕电脑设计中心
Manufacture / Asustek Computer, Inc.
Design / Asus Design Center
112

平板电脑
MID
生产 / 深圳市群创电子有限公司
设计 / 深圳市群创工业设计有限公司
Manufacture / Shenzhen Qunchuang Electronics Co.,Ltd
Design / Shenzhen Qunchuang Industrial design Co.,Ltd
112

SKYWORTH-E810 LED TV
生产 / 深圳创维——RGB电子有限公司
设计 / 创维创新设计中心
Manufacture / Skyworth-Rgb Electronics Co.,Ltd
Design / Skyworth-Rgb Electronics Co.,Ltd
113

V6500超窄边3D液晶电视
V6500 Ultra Narrow 3D LED TV
生产 / TCL多媒体科技控股股份有限公司
设计 / TCL多媒体工业设计中心
Manufacture / TCL Multimedia Technology Holdings LTD.
Design / TCL Multimedia Industrial Design Center
113

苹果（iPhone 4/4S）专用高容量后备电源
iPhone 4/4S Mobile energy
生产 设计 / 福建考克电子科技有限公司
Manufacture Design / Fujian Kaoke Electronics Science & Technology Co.,Ltd
114

盲文点读机
Dotty
生产 设计 / 和硕设计
Manufacture Design / PEGA Design &Engineering
114

移动电源2900
Mobile power 2900
生产 / 比亚迪精密制造有限公司
设计 / 岳文龙
Manufacture / BYD Precision Manufacture CO.,Ltd
Design / Yue WenLong
114

华硕变形平板
ASUS Transformer Series
生产 / 华硕电脑（上海）有限公司
设计 / 华硕电脑设计中心
Manufacture / Asustek Computer, Inc.
Design / Asus Design Center
115

IdeaPad Yoga
生产 / 联想（北京）有限公司
设计 / 联想创新设计中心
Manufacture / Lenovo
Design / Lenovo Innovation Design Centre
115

太阳能便携式充电器
Portable Solar Charger
生产 设计 / 成都浪尖工业设计有限公司
Manufacture Design / Chengdu ARTOP Industrial Design Co.,Ltd.
115

光荣使命游戏显卡
Glorious Mission Game Graphics
生产 / 七彩虹科技发展有限公司
设计 / 张美昭
Manufacture / Colorful Technology and Development CO. Ltd
Design / Amei
116

同体点阵鼠标键盘
Lattice Mouse And Keyboard With The Body
生产 / 斯巴科（北京）科技有限公司
设计 / 曲建全、杨哲
Manufacture / SPARK (Beijing) Technology Co., Ltd.
Design / Qu Jianquan, Yang Zhe
116

天秦键盘
TianQin Keyboard
生产 / 天秦
设计 / 何峰枫
Manufacture / TIANQIN
Design / VINCENT HE
116

功能充电防盗支架FU系列
Multifunctional and Theftproof Electrical Source Bracket – FU Series
生产 / 天津市雅铁科贸有限公司
设计 / 洛可可设计集团
Manufacture / Tianjin Yatie Techs &Trade Co., Ltd
Design / LKK Design
117

电视小贝
Television Set-top Boxes
生产 / 永新视博
设计 / 何峰枫
Manufacture / Vovel Supertv
Design / Vincent He
117

哈曼卡顿 BDS 577
Harman Kardon BDS 577
生产 / Harman International Industries,Incorporated
设计 / 哈曼设计中心
Manufacture / Harman International Industries, Incorporated
Design / Harman Design Centre
117

网络视频音箱
Sound Bar
生产 / 惠州纳伟仕智能媒体技术集团
设计 / 深圳市柏斯工业设计有限公司
Manufacture / NIVS IntelliMedia Technology Group, Inc.
Design / Shenzhen Perth Industrial Design Co.,Ltd.
118

哈曼卡顿水晶——无线
Harman Kardon SoundSticks Wireless
生产 / Harman International Industries,Incorporated
设计 / 哈曼设计中心
Manufacture / Harman International Industries, Incorporated
Design / Harman Design Centre
119

豌豆龙
I-bean
生产 设计 / 幻响神州（北京）科技有限公司
Manufacture Design / I-mu Technology Co., Ltd.
119

梅薇思蓝牙音箱
Mavis Bluetooth Speaker
生产 / 西西艾
设计 / 陈波、黄小龙
Manufacture / CCA
Design / Chen bo, bruce-huang
120

K-BOX不插电音响
K-BOX
生产 / 康佳集团通信科技有限公司
设计 / 龚晟宇、卫波
Manufacture / Shenzhen Konka Telecommunications Technology Co.,Ltd
Design / Gong Shengyu, Wei Bo
120

飞利浦桌面对接扬声器 DS6200
Philips Desktop Docking Speaker DS6200
生产 / 荷兰皇家飞利浦电子公司
设计 / 飞利浦设计
Manufacture / Royal Philips Electronics
Design / Philips Design
121

飞利浦 Soundbar 家庭影院 HTS7111
Philips Soundbar Home Theatre HTS7111
生产 / 荷兰皇家飞利浦电子公司
设计 / 飞利浦设计
Manufacture / Royal Philips Electronics
Design / Philips Design
121

蓝牙小音箱
Portable Bluetooth Speaker
生产 / 深圳市钜弘科技有限公司
设计 / 想象力产品策划有限公司
Manufacture / Shenzhen Joyhong Technology Co.,Ltd
Design / Imagination Design Co.Ltd
121

JBL贴耳式耳机 J55i
JBL On-ear Headphone
生产 / Harman International Industries,Incorporated
设计 / 哈曼设计中心
Manufacture / Harman International Industries, Incorporated
Design / Harman Design Centre
122

Antilope
生产 / 浙江魔杰电子股份有限公司
设计 / MOGIC ID TEAM
Manufacture / Zhejiang Mogic Electronic Co., ltd
Design / MOGIC ID TEAM
122

哈曼卡顿NI&AE入耳式耳机
Harman / Kardon NI & AE In Ear Headphones
生产 / Harman International Industries,Incorporated
设计 / 哈曼设计中心
Manufacture / Harman International Industries, Incorporated
Design / Harman Design Centre
122

骨传导助听耳机
Bone conduction hearing aid system
生产 / 北京美尔斯通科技发展股份有限公司
设计 / 洛可可设计集团
Manufacture / Melst Technology co., ltd, Beijing
Design / LKK Design
123

便携式老人音箱
Portable elderly speaker
生产 / 惠州纳伟仕智能媒体技术集团
设计 / 深圳市柏斯工业设计有限公司
Manufacture / NIVS IntelliMedia Technology Group, Inc.
Design / Shenzhen Perth Industrial Design Co.,Ltd.
123

折线桌面音箱
Line desktop speakers
生产 / 惠州纳伟仕智能媒体技术集团
设计 / 深圳市柏斯工业设计有限公司
Manufacture / Nivs Intellimedia Technology Group, Inc.
Design / Shenzhen Perth Industrial Design Co.,Ltd.
123

“Grande”系列无尘袋吸尘器
"Grande" Series Bagless Vacuum Cleaner
生产 / LG电子
设计 / LG电子中国设计中心
Manufacture / LG Electronics
Design / LG Electronics Design China
124

蒸汽式挂烫机
Garment Steamer
生产 / 江苏松桥电器有限公司
设计 / 苏宁电器股份有限公司
Manufacture / Jiangsu Mazuba Co.,Ltd
Design / Suning Appliance Co.,Ltd
124

红星奖
Red Star Design Award

手持式电动吸奶器
Electronic Breast Pump
生产 / 佛山市顺德区美诺电器科技有限公司
设计 / 佛山市尚致设计有限公司
Manufacture / MyCarol Electric Technologies Co.Ltd
Design / Foshan BOB DESIGN Co.,Ltd
125

臻尚剃须刀
Vogue-wit Shaver
生产 / 上海奔腾电工有限公司
设计 / 龙域设计
Manufacture / Shanghai POVOS Electric Works Co.,Ltd.
Design / LOE DESIGN
125

家用理发剪
family electric hair device
生产 / 上海奔腾电工有限公司
设计 / 龙域设计
Manufacture / Shanghai POVOS Electric Works Co.,Ltd.
Design / LOE DESIGN
125

模块化欧式颗粒火炉系列（模块化拆装DIY自由组合）
European Pellet Stoves (Modular combinations & DIY)
生产 设计 / 宁波柯怡工业设计有限公司
Manufacture Design / CO-YES Industrial Design Co., Ltd.
126

自动进纸碎纸机AF650
AF650 Auto Feed Paper Shredder
生产 设计 / 东莞福泰电子有限公司
Manufacture Design / Dongguan Forta Electronics Company Limited
126

口腔CT成像系统
Oral Cavity CT Block Diagram System
生产 / 四川九九瑞迪数字成像技术有限责任公司
设计 / 成都嘉兰图设计有限公司
Manufacture / Sichuan DNDR Digital Radiography Co., Ltd.
Design / Chengdu Newplan Design Co., Ltd.
127

多功能数码保健盒
Multi-functional Digital Health Box
生产 / 广州市原子工业产品科技发展有限公司
设计 / 广州市沅子工业产品设计有限公司
Manufacture / Atomic Industrial Product Technology Development Co., Ltd.
Design / Atom Industrial Design Co., Ltd.
128

易奇糖尿病治疗仪
YiQi Diabetes Treatment Instrument
生产 / 河南易奇生物科技有限公司
设计 / 罗琦
Manufacture / Henan YiQi Biotechnology Co., Ltd.
Design / Luo Qi
128

便携式徒手心肺复苏指导器
Portable Unarmed CPR Guidance Device
生产 / 成都东方人健康产业有限责任公司
设计 / 成都意町工业产品设计有限公司
Manufacture / Chengdu DFR Health Property Industrial Co., Ltd.
Design / Chengdu IDing industrial design Co., Ltd.
129

个人剂量计
Personal Dosimeter
生产 / 成都麦特斯科技有限公司
设计 / 成都意町工业产品设计有限公司
Manufacture / Chengdu Memory Test Technology Co., Ltd.
Design / Chengdu IDing industrial design Co., Ltd.
129

智能小护士
Intelligent Nurse
生产 / 北京盈科通达信息技术有限公司
设计 / 北京智加问道科技有限公司
Manufacture / Beijing Full-tech Way Information Technology Co., Ltd.
Design / ZCO Design Co., Ltd.
129

公牛墙壁开关
Gongniu Decorative Switches
生产 / 公牛集团
设计 / 浩汉工业产品设计（上海）有限公司
Manufacture / Gongniu Group
Design / Nova Design (Shanghai) Ltd.
130

音乐花园
Music Garden
生产 设计 / 创意生活（北京）科技发展有限公司
Manufacture Design / Creatife Corporation
130

直流折叠式台地扇(FSZ-3006Cg7)
DC Folding Wall and Desk Fan
生产 设计 / 格力电器（中山）小家电制造有限公司
Manufacture Design / GREE (Zhongshan) Small Home Appliances Co., Ltd.
130

加湿暖风机NTJ20-12S
Heater with Humidifying Function NTJ20-12S
生产 设计 / 广东美的环境电器制造有限公司
Manufacture Design / Gd Midea Environment Appliances Mfg. Co., Ltd.
131

滑动门式直流冷风扇(KSZ-0801RCgL)
Sliding Door DC Cooling Air Fan
生产 设计 / 格力电器（中山）小家电制造有限公司
Manufacture Design / GREE (Zhongshan) Small Home Appliances Co., Ltd.
131

无叶风扇
Air Multiplier
生产 / 深圳市艾克派特科技开发有限公司
设计 / 想象力产品策划有限公司
Manufacture / Shenzhen Accipiter Gentilis Technology Co., Ltd.
Design / Imagination Design Co., Ltd.
131

飞雨Select 150手持花洒
Raindance Select Shower
生产 / 汉斯格雅欧洲股份有限公司
设计 / 凤凰设计室
Manufacture / Hansgrohe SE
Design / Phoenix Design
132

恒温淋浴器
Thermostatic Shower
生产 / 佛山市安蒙建材科技有限公司
设计 / 唐小平
Manufacture / ABM BUILDING MATERIALS TECHNOLOGY CO., LTD.
Design / Xiaoping Tang
132

时光
Time
生产 / 福建中宇建材集团有限公司
设计 / 李春山
Manufacture / Joyou Group Building Materials Co., Ltd.
Design / Chunshan Li
133

智享未来
Intelligent Future
生产 / 佛山百德嘉卫浴科技有限公司
设计 / 郑文凯
Manufacture / Foshan BDC Sanitary Ware Technology Co., Ltd.
Design / Kevin Zheng
133

IDEAS创想面盆龙头
Ideas Basin Faucet
生产 / 辉煌水暖集团有限公司
设计 / 李建民
Manufacture / Huihuang Plumbing Group Co., Ltd.
Design / Jianmin Lee
134

“清源”单柄双控面盆龙头
"Pure Source" Single Handle Double Control Basin Mixer
生产 / 辉煌水暖集团有限公司
设计 / 孙瑞
Manufacture / Huihuang Plumbing Group Co., Ltd.
Design / Sun Rui
135

“谦·影”面盆水龙头
"Modest Shape Series" Basin Faucet
生产 / 辉煌水暖集团有限公司
设计 / 刘建南
Manufacture / Huihuang Plumbing Group Co., Ltd.
Design / Liu Jiannan
135

“金樽玉宴” 触碰面盆龙头
Golden Grail and Jade Feast Smart Touch Basin Faucet
生产 / 辉煌水暖集团有限公司
设计 / 江镇林
Manufacture / Huihuang Plumbing Group Co., Ltd.
Design / Jiang Zhenlin
135

"轻色"面盆龙头
"Nature Color" Basin Faucet
生产 / 辉煌水暖集团有限公司
设计 / 陈文芳
Manufacture / Huihuang Plumbing Group Co., Ltd.
Design / Chen Wenfang
136

Double-F 两人用单冷面盆龙头
Double-F Single Cold Basin Faucet with Two People
生产 / 佛山市日丰企业有限公司
设计 / 彭江明、黄建元
Manufacture / Foshan Rifeng Enterprise Co., Ltd.
Design / Peng Jiangming, Huang Jianyuan
136

RF-9117TP面盆混合龙头
RF-9117TP Basin Mixer Faucet
生产 / 佛山市日丰企业有限公司
设计 / 蔡增熠、钱星宇
Manufacture / Foshan Rifeng Enterprise Co., Ltd.
Design / Cai Zengyi, Qian Xingyu
136

灵石
Pebble
生产 / 申鹭达股份有限公司
设计 / 杨黎明
Manufacture / Sunlot Shares Co., Ltd.
Design / Yang Liming
137

亚马逊系列面盆水龙头
Amazon Series Faucet
生产 / 珠海威锦卫浴设备有限公司
设计 / 新约设计工作室
Manufacture / Zhuhai weijin Bathroom Equipment Co., Ltd.
Design / New Testament Design Studio
137

天歌面盆龙头
Tiange-Basin Faucet
生产 设计 / 九牧厨卫股份有限公司
Manufacture Design / Jomoo Kitchen & Bathroom Appliances Co., Ltd.
137

蝶恋
Butterfly-Loving
生产 / 惠达卫浴股份有限公司
设计 / 孙辉
Manufacture / Huida Sanitay Ware Co., Ltd.
Design / Sun Hui
138

圆融
Integrate Harmony Without Obstruction
生产 / 惠达卫浴股份有限公司
设计 / 许月娥
Manufacture / Huida Sanitay Ware Co., Ltd.
Design / Xu Yue´e
138

"尊尚" 连体座便器
"Honour Fashion" One-piece Toilet
生产 / 辉煌水暖集团有限公司
设计 / 江镇林
Manufacture / Huihuang Plumbing Group Co., Ltd.
Design / Jiang Zhenlin
138

"霞姿月韵"浴缸
"Afterlight Beauty & Moon Elegance" Bathtub
生产 / 辉煌水暖集团有限公司
设计 / 刘建南
Manufacture / Huihuang Plumbing Group Co., Ltd.
Design / Liu Jiannan
139

水槽OLVA8105
Sink OLVA8105
生产 设计 / 宁波欧琳厨具有限公司
Manufacture Design / Ningbo Oulin Kitchen Utensils Co., Ltd.
140

水槽OLSP5203
Sink OLSP5203
生产 设计 / 宁波欧琳厨具有限公司
Manufacture Design / Ningbo Oulin Kitchen Utensils Co., Ltd.
140

集成水槽
Integrated Sink
生产 设计 / 嵊州爱尔卡厨卫科技有限公司
Manufacture Design / Shengzhou Aier Ka kitchen and Technology Co., Ltd.
140

四合一多功能安全锤
Four in One Multi-function Safety Hammer
生产 / 杭州易舍工业产品设计有限公司
设计 / 孙惠兵、庄振华
Manufacture / Hangzhou Yes Industrial & Products Design Co., Ltd.
Design / Titan Sun, Jevin Zhuang
141

智能无线充手电
The Smart Wireless Rechargeable Flashlight
生产 / 深圳航嘉驰源电气股份有限公司
设计 / 深圳航嘉工业设计部
Manufacture / Shenzhen Huntkey Electric Co., Ltd.
Design / Shenzhen Huntkey Industrial Design Department
141

维易（显示器支架）
Victoria Easily (Monitor Stand)
生产 / 大连三维广界数字科技有限公司
设计 / 初龙梅
Manufacture / Extensive World 3D Technology Co., Ltd.
Design / Chu Longmei
141

一树光阴
Nature Light
生产 / 鹤山市明可达实业有限公司
设计 / 广州易用设计有限公司
Manufacture / Mingkeda Industries Co., Ltd.
Design / EASE Design Guangzhou Co., Ltd.
142

太阳能多功能LED一体灯
Solar Multifunctional Intergration LED Lights
生产 / 厦门冠宇科技有限公司
设计 / 高广德、朱有淋
Manufacture / Xiamen Topunive Technology Co., Ltd.
Design / Gao Guangde, Zhu Youlin
142

"Q" 系列OLED台灯
"Q" Series OLED Desk Lamp
生产 设计 / 南京第壹有机光电有限公司
Manufacture Design / First O-Lite, Inc.
143

便携系列台灯
Portable Series Lamp
生产 设计 / 南京第壹有机光电有限公司
Manufacture Design / First O-Lite, Inc.
143

迷你影院
Mini Cinema
生产 设计 / 北京丹方科技开发有限公司
Manufacture Design / Doon Design
144

通士达LED PAR30 射灯
TOPSTAR LED PAR30 Reflector Lamp
生产 / 厦门通士达照明有限公司
设计 / 洛可可设计集团
Manufacture / Xiamen Topstar lighting Co., Ltd.
Design / LKK Design
144

玉兰花传说
Magnolia Legend
生产 / 霍尼韦尔 朗能
设计 / 朱创艺、刘诗锋
Manufacture / Honeywell
Design / Powell Zhu, Liu Shifeng
144

LED蝴蝶导轨灯
LED Butterflaire Track Light
生产 / 佛山市凯西欧灯饰有限公司
设计 / 吴育林
Manufacture / Foshan Cosio Lighting Co., Ltd.
Design / Yulin Wu
145

可旋转式LED灯管
LED Dimmable Rotatable Tube
生产 / 立碁电子工业股份有限公司
设计 / 李逸启、张哲玮
Manufacture / Ligitek Electronics Co., Ltd.
Design / Yi-Chi Li, Che-Wei Chang
145

飞利浦Arcitone 洗墙灯
Philips Arcitone Wall Washer
生产 / 荷兰皇家飞利浦电子公司
设计 / 飞利浦设计
Manufacture / Royal Philips Electronics
Design / Philips Design
146

快速充气帐篷
Fast Inflatable Base Camp Sleeping Tent
生产 设计 / 福建哥仑步户外用品有限公司
Manufacture Design / Fujian Kolumb Outdoor Equipment Co., Ltd.
147

李宁轻云跑鞋
Li-Ning Cloud Running Shoes
生产 / 李宁（中国）体育用品有限公司
设计 / 刘铮
Manufacture / Li-Ning (China) Sports Goods Co., Ltd.
Design / Axis Liu
148

红星奖
Red Star Design Award

K-FIT全方位保护登山鞋
K-Fit Multifunction Protection Hiking Shoes
生产 设计 / 福建哥仑步户外用品有限公司
Manufacture Design / Fujian Kolumb Outdoor Equipment Co., Ltd.
149

皮佐越野跑鞋
The Pizzo Trail Running Shoes
生产 / 南京边城体育用品股份有限公司
设计 / 左智越
Manufacture / Nanjing B.C. SPORTS Products Co., Ltd.
Design / LORENZO
149

共工60升背包
GongGong 60L Backpack
生产 设计 / 北京探路者户外用品股份有限公司
Manufacture Design / Beijing Toread Outdoor Products Co., Ltd.
150

探路者TiEF SKIN超轻外套
Toread Tief Skin Ultra-Light Coat
生产 设计 / 北京探路者户外用品股份有限公司
Manufacture Design / Beijing Toread Outdoor Products Co., Ltd.
150

无缝线衬衫
Seamless Shirt
生产 设计 / 鲁泰纺织股份有限公司
Manufacture Design / Luthai Textile Co., Ltd.
150

儿童箱包
Children´s Suitcase
生产 / 浙江步步乐箱包有限公司
设计 / 天津市易诺威工业产品策划有限公司
Manufacture / Zhejiang Ppluggage Co., Ltd.
Design / Innova Industrial Product Planning Co., Ltd.
151

江航家用制氧机
Oxygen Concentrator Recommend
生产 / 江苏江航医疗设备有限公司
设计 / 洛可可设计集团
Manufacture / Jiangsu Jianghang Medical Equipment Co., Ltd.
Design / LKK Design
151

阿拉丁挑战者旅行壶
Aladdin Challenger
生产 / 奔迈(上海)国际贸易有限公司
设计 / 上海木马工业产品设计有限公司
Manufacture / Pacific Market International, LLC(´PMI´) LEGAL NOTICE
Design / Shanghai Moma Industrial Product Design Co., Ltd.
152

旋风卷发器
Hair Curler
生产 / 肯威专业美发用品有限公司
设计 / 深圳市鼎典工业产品设计有限公司
Manufacture / Guangzhou Yuexiu District Canway Trading Firm
Design / Shenzhen Designdo Industrial Design Co., Ltd.
152

超声波清洗机CE-7200A
Ultrasonic Cleaner CE-7200A
生产 / 东莞市洁康超声波设备有限公司
设计 / 想象力产品策划有限公司
Manufacture / Jeken Ultrasonic Cleaner Limited
Design / Imagination Design Co., Ltd.
153

特百惠旋风切剁器
Tupperware Speedy Chopper
生产 设计 / 特百惠（中国）有限公司
Manufacture Design / Tupperware Brands Corporation
153

百贴记事叮
The Wall
生产 设计 / P.S.L LTD.
Manufacture Design / P.S.L LTD.
154

螺钉瓶塞
Screw Bottle Cork
生产 设计 / 麦基格瑞（北京）产品设计开发有限公司
Manufacture Design / Magic Graphic Product Developing Co., Ltd. Beijing. China
154

康多多PRO多雅畚斗附盖
DustPan with Lid
生产 / 福州山崎实业有限公司
设计 / 奥田朋义、土井健史
Manufacture / Fuzhou Yamazaki Industry Co., Ltd.
Design / Okuda Tomoyoshi, Doi Takeshi
155

康多多PRO双球除尘掸
Two head- Electrostatic Duster
生产 / 福州山崎实业有限公司
设计 / 奥田朋义、土井健史
Manufacture / Fuzhou Yamazaki Industry Co., Ltd.
Design / Okuda Tomoyoshi, Doi Takeshi
155

绿伞品牌洗衣液系列设计
Brand And Product Design of Lv San
生产 / 北京绿伞化学股份有限公司
设计 / 北京光彩无限管理咨询有限公司
Manufacture / Green Umbrella Chemical Co., Ltd.
Design / Shine Design Consultation Center
155

智能防暴锁
Smart Anti-riot Lock
生产 / 湖南泓达科技有限公司
设计 / 深圳市鼎典工业产品设计有限公司
Manufacture / Hunan Hongda Technology Co., Ltd.
Design / Shenzhen Designdo Industrial Design Co., Ltd.
156

广铝碰锁
GAL´s Latch Series
生产 / 广铝集团有限公司
设计 / 吴志勇
Manufacture / Galuminium Group Co., Ltd.
Design / GAVIN
156

传玺
Reviving
生产 设计 / 惠州季昶五金制品有限公司
Manufacture Design / Genius Champion Enterprises Co., Ltd.
157

君子如意椅
The gentleman you chair
生产 / 北京清美玉尧艺术设计中心
设计 / 杨玉尧
Manufacture / Beijing Kiyomi Yu Yao art and Design Center
Design / Yang Yuyao
157

椅刚柔
Chair Gang Rou
生产 / 北京清庭文创文化发展有限公司
设计 / 石大宇
Manufacture / Dragonfly Design Center
Design / Shi Dayu
157

魔方组合家具
KROS
生产 / 富尔曼（北京）艺术设计中心
设计 / 高强
Manufacture / Form (Beijing) Art & Design
Design / Gao Qiang
158

多功能儿童学习桌B
Multifunctional Desk B
生产 / 北京绿茵天地科技开发有限公司
设计 / 北京智加问道科技有限公司
Manufacture / Beijing Green World Sports Industry Incorporated
Design / ZCO Design CO., Ltd.
159

Cleaf
生产 设计 / 震旦（中国）有限公司
Manufacture Design / Aurora (China) Co., Ltd.
160

儿童身高树
Children Height Tree
生产 / 源聚德实业有限公司
设计 / 广东华南工业设计院
Manufacture / Sunnyworld Industrial Co., Ltd.
Design / Guangdong South China Institute Of Industrial Design
161

动物系列木拼玩具
Wood Spell Toy Animal Series
生产 / 搜主意网
设计 / 曲建全
Manufacture / www.soidea.net
Design / Qu Jianquan
161

幸符、梦享
LUCKY SYMBOL, FANCY DREAM
生产 设计 / 依波精品（深圳）有限公司
Manufacture Design / Ebohr Luxuries International Co.,Ltd.
162

飞亚达摄影师女表四叶草LA8362
Fiyta Photographer Female Watch with Clover LA8362
生产 设计 / 飞亚达（集团）股份有限公司
Manufacture Design / Fiyta Holdings Ltd.
162

洞天福地
Heavenly Place of Good Fortune
生产 设计 / 北京前门文化有限公司
Manufacture Design / Beijing Qianmen Culture Co., Ltd.
162

便携式多功能支架
Portable Multi Function Support
生产 / 余姚艾度影视器材有限公司
设计 / 成都浪尖工业设计有限公司
Manufacture / Yuyao IDO Photographic Equipment Co., Ltd.
Design / Chengdu ARTOP Industrial Design Co., Ltd.
163

宝马MINI礼品深度开发
BMW MINI Gift Depth Customization
生产 / 宝马中国汽车贸易有限公司
设计 / 北京华新意创工业设计有限公司
Manufacture / BMW (China) Trading Co., Ltd.
Design / IDEAS DESIGN CO., LTD. CHINA
163

首饰盒
Jewellery Box
生产 设计 / 北京故宫宫苑文化发展有限公司
Manufacture Design / Beijing Imperial Court Culture Development Company Ltd.
164

《邮票上的书画艺术——感悟之美》
Beauty of Enlightenment – Calligraphy and Painting on Stamp
生产 / 北京雅昌彩色印刷有限公司
设计 / 北京雅昌设计中心
Manufacture / Beijing Artron Colour Printing Co., Ltd.
Design / Beijing Artron Design Center
165

清华大学百年校庆内供酒（高级浓香型）包装设计
Liquor Packaging for Tsinghua University Centenary Celebration(Senior Aroma)
生产 / 中国泸州老窖股份有限公司
设计 / 李淳
Manufacture / Luzhou Laojiao Co., Ltd. China
Design / Li Chun
165

七彩汉字游戏卡系列
Chinese Rainbow Game Cards Series
生产 / 香港亚和文化事业有限公司
设计 / 陈伸
Manufacture / Artwow Group Company Ltd.
Design / Sun Chan
166

斗串「汉英」游戏卡系列
Tri/Quad-color Chinese-English Bilingual Game Cards Series
生产 / 香港亚和文化事业有限公司
设计 / 陈伸
Manufacture / Artwow Group Company Ltd.
Design / Sun Chan
166

三维纸雕工艺画
Paper Craft Three-Dimensional Art
生产 / 艳丽与美同舞文化发展（北京）有限公司
设计 / 秦艳丽
Manufacture / Gorgeous and Beauty with Dance Culture Development (Beijing) Co., Ltd.
Design / Qin Yanli
167

投资币包装设计
A Packaging-design for Investment Coins
生产 / 宝泉钱币投资有限公司
设计 / 程旭锋
Manufacture / Baoquan coin Investment Co., Ltd.
Design / Cheng Xufeng
167

2012中国创新设计红星原创奖获奖名单

中国创新设计红星原创奖银奖

GRAD LED滑动控制灯
设计 / 单峰
170

太阳花LED灯
设计 / LG电子中国设计中心
171

空虚时间指示器
设计 / FABLAB Ltd.
172

ONEPLUG 可用单手拔的插头
设计 / 单峰
173

优秀设计师奖

徐佑荣
174

未来之星奖

李 菁
176

王星悦
176

红星原创奖

多用速干支撑晾晒架
设计 / 郝恬、李薪郦
182

Hand-Washing 手持洗衣机设计
设计 / 周丽雯
182

防滴雨衣
设计 / 曹镒滟
183

灾区简易折叠卫生间
设计 / 王星悦、李璟璐
183

脚垫灯
设计 / 深圳市鼎典生活用品有限公司
184

瓷表
设计 / 中央美术学院设计学院产品设计系“一起”工作组
184

FREE——多功能儿童座椅
设计 / 北京林业大学
185

单手挤牙膏器
设计 / 浙江科技学院工业设计系
186

眼药水助点器
设计 / 尔沃设计整合
186

无限刮勺
设计 / 罗琦
187

Winner List Of 2012 China Red Star Original Design Award

Silver Award of China Red Star Original Design Award

GRAD LED LIGHT
Design / Shan Feng
170

Sun Flower
Design / LG Electronics China Design Branch
171

VOID TIME INDICATOR
Design / FABLAB Ltd.
172

ONEPLUG
Design / Shan Feng
173

Excellent Award

Useful Rapid-drying Lateral Brace Clothes Rack
Design / Hao Tian, Li Xinli
182

Hand-washing machine
Design / Zhou Liwen
182

Drop Proof Raincoat
Design / Cao Yiyan
183

Simple folding toilet for disaster areas
Design / Wang Xingyue, Li Jinglu
183

Mat Light
Design / Shenzhen Designdo Daily Use Co.,Ltd
184

China Clock
Design / "Together" Work Group, Industrial Design, School of Design, Central Academy of Fine Arts
184

Free-Multifunction Seat for Children
Design / Beijing Forestry University
185

Single Handed Toothpaste Squeezer
Design / Zhejiang University of Science and Technology Industrial Design Department
186

100% Eye Drop Dispenser
Design / Award-Design Integration Studio
186

Scoop Spoon
Design / Luo Qi
187

Best Designer Award

Kevin Chu
174

Future Star Award

Li Jing
176

Wang Xingyue
176

主办及专家委员会

Organizer & Jury Committee

中国创新设计红星奖委员会主席
Chairman of China Red Star Design Award Committee

朱　焘 Zhu Tao

闫傲霜 Yan Aoshuang

中国创新设计红星奖专家委员会
Jury Committee of China Red Star Design Award

柳冠中 Liu Guanzhong

何人可 He Renke

Peter Zec

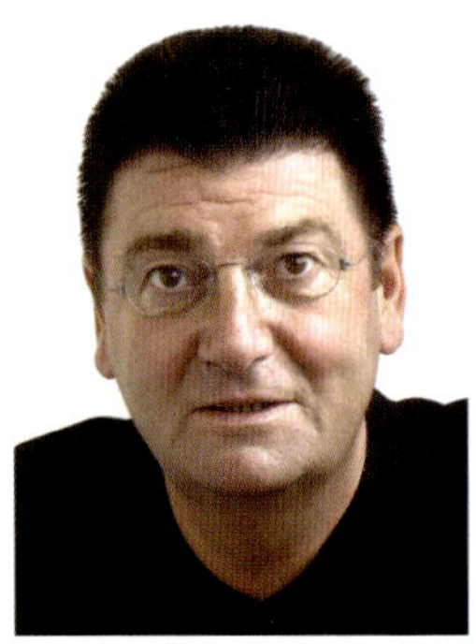

Ralph Wiegmann

Brandon Gien

喜多俊之 Toshiyuki Kita

鲁晓波 Lu Xiaobo

Ernesto Gismondi

Chang Donghoon

童慧明 Tong Huiming

David Kester

陈冬亮 Chen Dongliang

柳冠中 Liu Guanzhong
中国 China

清华大学美术学院责任教授，博士生导师，享受政府津贴学者
清华大学美术学院工业设计系系统设计工作室总设计师
中国工业设计协会副会长
香港理工大学名誉教授
Professor & doctoral supervisor of Art College of Tsinghua University, with governmental subsidies
Chief Designer of System Design Studio of Industrial Design Department of Art College of Tsinghua University
Deputy Chairperson of China Industrial Design Association
Honorary professor of Hong Kong Polytechnic University

何人可 He Renke
中国 China

湖南大学设计艺术学院院长、教授
中国工业设计协会副会长
教育部高等学校工业设计专业教学指导分委员会主任委员
湖南省工业设计创新平台专业委员会委员
Dean & Professor of School of Design, Hunan University
Deputy Chairperson of China Industrial Design Association
Chairman of China National Instructive Committee of Industrial Design Education
President of Design Artists Association of Hunan Province of China

Peter Zec
德国 Germany

2005-2007国际工业设计协会联合会主席
红点设计奖主席
北威设计中心主席
President of ICSID (2005-2007)
President of Red Dot Design Award
Chairman of Design Zentrum Nordrhein Westfalen

Ralph Wiegmann
德国 Germany

德国IF设计奖常务理事
欧洲设计管理奖评委会主席
Managing Director of International Forum Design
European Design Management Award Jury Chairman

Brandon Gien
澳大利亚 Australia

国际工业设计协会联合会当选主席（2011-2013）
澳大利亚优秀设计协会总经理
澳大利亚国际设计奖主席
President-Elect of ICSID (2011-2013)
Managing Director of Good Design Australia
Chair of the Australian International Design Awards

喜多俊之 Toshiyuki Kita
日本 Japan

日本G-mark奖评委会前主席
Former Chairperson of the Jury of G-mark Award

鲁晓波 Lu Xiaobo
中国 China

清华大学美术学院教授、博士生导师
清华大学信息艺术设计系主任
中国工业设计协会常务理事
红点设计奖评委
Professor & Doctoral Tutor of Academy of Arts & Design, Tsinghua University
Director of Information Art & Design of Academy of Arts & Design, Tsinghua University
Committeeman of China Industrial Design Association
Jury of Red Dot Design Award

Ernesto Gismondi
意大利 Italy

阿基米德集团的创始人、总裁
原意大利工业设计协会副主席
Founder & CEO of Artemide Group
Former Vice President of Association of Industrial Design, Italy

Chang Donghoon
韩国 Korea

三星电子集团高级副总裁
三星电子集团手机通讯业务手机设计团队负责人
企业设计中心设计战略团队负责人
亚洲电子艺术和设计协会执委
Senior Vice President of Samsung
Head of Samsung´s Mobile Design Group of Mobile Communications Business, Samsung Electronics Co., LTD
Head of Design Strategy Team of Corporate Design Center
Board member of Asian Digital Art and Design Association (ADADA)

童慧明 Tong Huiming
中国 China

广州美术学院设计学院教授、院长
中国工业设计协会常务理事
广东省工业设计协会副会长
Dean & Professor of College of Design of Guangzhou Academy of Fine Arts
Executive Director of China Industrial Design Association
Deputy Chairman of Guangdong Industrial Design Association

David Kester
英国 UK

英国设计委员会前主席
英国D&AD主席（1994-2003）
英国皇家艺术学院执委
设计商业协会特别顾问
Former Chief Executive of Design Council
Chief Executive of D&AD (1994-2003)
Council member of the Royal College of Art
Special advisor to the Design Business Association

陈冬亮 Chen Dongliang
中国 China

北京工业设计促进中心主任
北京工业设计促进会理事长
中国创新设计红星奖委员会执行主席
中国工业设计协会副会长
意大利设计中国巡展华人评委
韩国好设计奖评委
清华大学美术学院工业设计发展顾问
Director of Beijing Industrial Design Center
Director of Beijing Industrial Design Promotion Organization
Executive Chairman of China Red Star Design Award Committee
Deputy Chairperson of China Industrial Design Association
Jury of Italian Design on Tour
Jury of Korean Good Design Award
Industrial Design Development Consultant of Academy of Arts & Design, Tsinghua University

主办及专家委员会 Organizer & Jury Committee

林衍堂 LAM,Yanta

陈文龙 Wen-long Chen

Tim Fletcher

官政能 Cheng Neng Kuan

辛向阳 Xin Xiangyang

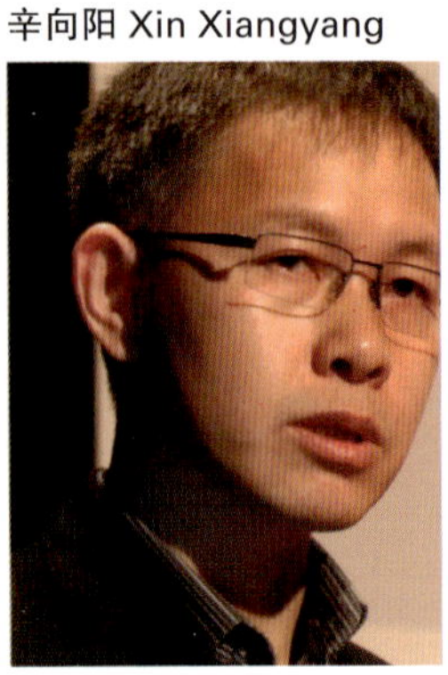

Michael Thomson

娄永琪 Lou Yongqi

许平 Xu Ping

Martin Darbyshire

Francois Lenfant

Lee Soon In

袁岳 Victor Yuan

蔡军 Cai Jun

邱丰顺 Kumo Chiu

Max Burton

Alpay Er

林衍堂 LAM,Yanta
中国香港 China Hong Kong

香港理工大学设计学院副主任
香港设计局董事
Professor of Design & Associate Head school of Design, the Hong Kong Polytechnic University
Director, Hong Kong Design Centre

陈文龙 Wen-long Chen
中国台湾 China Taiwan

2007-2009国际工业设计协会联合会执委会委员
浩汉产品设计股份有限公司总经理
Member of 2007-2009 Executive Board of ICSID
President of Nova Design Co., Ltd

Tim Fletcher
美国 USA

美国工业设计师协会美国政府联络官（2011至今）
美国宾斯法尼亚州匹兹堡Daedalus公司业务发展经理（2009至今）
US Government Liaison Officer of IDSA (Since 2011)
Business Development Manager of Daedalus, Pittsburgh, PA US (Since 2009)

官政能 Cheng Neng Kuan
中国台湾 China Taiwan

台湾实践大学副校长、产品与建筑设计研究所所长
台湾实践大学设计学院首任院长
Deputy Principal of Shih Chien University
Chairman of Institute of Industrial & Architecture Design of Shih Chien University
The First Dean of School of Design of Shih Chien University

辛向阳 Xin Xiangyang
中国 China

江南大学设计学院院长
ICID（国际交互设计会议）学术委员会主任
中国工程学会工业设计分会理事
Professor and Dean, School of Design at Jiangnan University
Director of International Conference on Interaction Design Academic Board
National board member of the Industrial Design Group, Chinese Association of Engineers

Michael Thomson
英国 UK

伦敦Design Connect公司创始人兼负责人
欧洲设计协会（BEDA）办公署副部长
2001-2005国际工业设计协会联合会执委会委员
Founder and Principal of Design Connect London
Vice President of the Bureau of European Design Associations (BEDA)
Member of 2001-2005 Executive Board of ICSID

娄永琪 Lou Yongqi
中国 China

同济大学设计创意学院副院长
同济大学中芬中心执行副主任
芬兰阿尔托大学设计学院客座教授
国际艺术设计与媒体院校联盟执行委员会委员
Vice Dean, College of Design & Innovation, Tongji University,
Executive Vice Director, Sino-Finnish Centre, Tongji University,
Guest professor of Finland Aalto University
Executive Board Member, CUMULUS

许平 Xu Ping
中国 China

南京艺术学院设计学院院长（1999-2002年）
中央美术学院设计学院副院长（2002-2010年）
中央美术学院研究生处处长
Dean of Design School of Nanjing Arts Institute(1999-2002)
Deputy Dean of Design School of China Central Academy of Fine Arts(2002-2010)
Head of Graduate Section of China Central Academy of Fine Arts

Martin Darbyshire
英国 UK

2007-2011国际工业设计协会联合会执委会委员
英国Tangerine设计公司创始人
Member of 2007-2011 Executive Board of ICSID
Chief Executive Officer of Tangerine Design Co.,

Francois Lenfant
法国 France

通用电气医疗全球设计经理
Global Design Manager for Europe & Middle-East (EMEA), GE Healthcare

Lee Soon In
韩国 Korea

2011-2013国际工业设计协会联合会主席
首尔设计中心主席
国际设计高级研究院院长
President of ICSID (2011-2013)
President of the Seoul Design Center
Dean of International Design School for Advanced Studies

袁岳 Victor Yuan
中国 China

零点研究咨询集团董事长
中国信息协会市场研究业分会副会长
北京科技咨询业协会理事长
Chairman of the board, Founder and President of Horizon Research Consultancy Group
Vice President of China Marketing Research Association
President of Beijing Consulting Association (BCA)

蔡军 Cai Jun
中国 China

清华大学美术学院工业设计系教授
清华大学艺术与科学研究中心设计管理研究所所长
清华大学美术学院工业设计系主任（2006-2009）
Industrial Design Professor of Art College of Tsinghua University
Head of Design Management Research Department of Art & Science Research Center, Tsinghua University
Chief of Industrial Design Department of Art College of Tsinghua University (2006-2009)

邱丰顺 Kumo Chiu
中国台湾 China Taiwan

北京艺有道工业设计有限公司创办人及总经理
摩托罗拉亚洲区设计总监（2001-2006）
Founder and President of Idea Dao Design Ltd.
Asia Design Director of Mobile Device , Motorola(2001-2006)

Max Burton
美国 USA

青蛙设计公司执行创意总监
前耐克公司技术实验室创意总监
Executive Creative Director, Frog Design
Former Creative Director for Nike´s Tech Lab

Alpay Er
土耳其 Turkey

伊斯坦布尔技术大学工业产品设计系主任、教授
国际工业设计协会联合会执委（2011-2013）
土耳其工业设计师协会（ETMK）执委会委员
2013年世界设计联盟大会执委会主任
Chair and Professor, Dept. of Industrial Product Design, Istanbul Technical University (ITU)
Member of 2011-2013 Executive Board of ICSID
Executive committee member of the Industrial Designers´ Society of Turkey (ETMK)
Head of Executive Committee for the 2013 International Design Alliance (IDA) Congress

主办及专家委员会 Organizer & Jury Committee

田中一雄 Kazuo Tanaka

Park Youngsoon

石大宇 Shi Dayu

胡越 Hu Yue

殷正声 Yin Zhengsheng

Josyane Franc

Leimei Julia Chiu

Harald Leschke

Tapani Hyvönen

严扬 Yan Yang

Edna dos Santos-Duisenberg

Jeroen Raijmakers

Marie Moreira

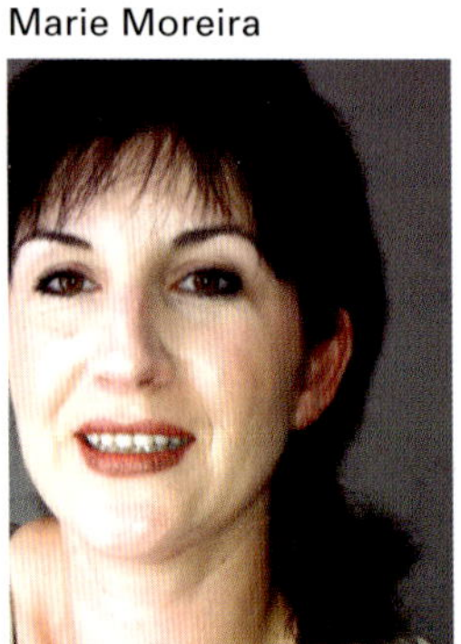

George M. Beylerian

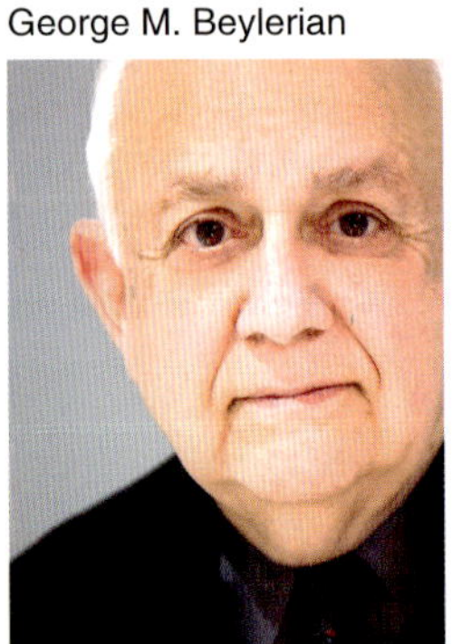

田中一雄 Kazuo Tanaka
日本 Japan
GK设计株式会社总裁
2007-2009国际工业设计协会联合会执委会委员
President of GK Design Group Inc.
Member of 2007-2009 Executive Board of ICSID

Park Youngsoon
韩国 Korea
韩国设计协会联盟主席
韩国设计振兴院理事
2005年韩国好设计奖评委会主席
Chairman of Korea Federation of Design Associations (KFDA)
Director of Korea Institute of Design Promotion (KIDP)
Chairman of Jury committee in Korea Good Design Award(2005)

石大宇 Shi Dayu
美国 USA
清庭设计中心创办人暨创意总监
Dragonfly Design Center Founder and Creative Director

胡越 Hu Yue
中国 China
全国建筑设计大师
北京市建筑设计研究院总建筑师
中国建筑学会理事
National architectural design master
Chief architect of Beijing Institute of Architectural Design
Director of Architectural Society of China

殷正声 Yin Zhengsheng
中国 China
同济大学设计创意学院教授
中国工业设计协会常务理事
上海工业设计协会副理事长
Professor of Design Innovation College of Tongji University
Executive member of China Industrial Design Association
Vice President of Shanghai Industrial Design Association

Josyane Franc
法国 France
圣埃蒂安高等艺术与设计学院国际事务主管
圣埃蒂安国际设计双年展合作创始人
圣埃蒂安UNESCO设计之都协调人
Director of the common Department of International Affairs for the Cité du design and Saint-Etienne higher school of art and design (ESADSE)
Partner founder of the International Design Biennial Saint-Etienne
Chief coordinator for the UNESCO Creative Network for Saint-Etienne

Leimei Julia Chiu
日本 Japan
2011-2013国际平面设计协会联合会主席
日本工业设计振兴会执行主任
武藏野美术大学教授
2011-2013 President of Icograda
Executive Director of Japan Institute of Design Promotion (JDP)
Professor of Musashino Art University (MAU)

Tapani Hyvönen
芬兰 Finland
Destem有限公司、ED设计有限公司CEO
2009-2011国际工业设计协会联合会执委会委员
芬兰设计师协会（Ornamo）主席
CEO of Destem Ltd and ED-Design Ltd.
Member of 2009-2011 Executive Board of ICSID
President of Ornamo, Finnish Designers Association

Harald Leschke
德国 Germany
梅赛德斯奔驰汽车集团设计总监（1978-2007）
Leschke设计公司自由设计师、顾问（2008）
Litex汽车公司总经理 （2008年至今）
Head of Mercedes-Benz Advanced Design (1978-2007)
Freelance designer and consultant in ´leschke.design´ (2008)
General Manager in Litex Motors (since 2008)

严扬 Yan Yang
中国 China
清华大学美术学院工业设计系教授
Professor of Industrial Design Department of Academy of Arts & Design, Tsinghua University

Edna dos Santos-Duisenberg
巴西 Brazil
联合国贸易和发展会议创意经济项目 主任
联合国贸易和发展会议全球数据银行创始人、主任
联合国贸易和发展会议秘书长首席顾问
Chief of Creative Economy Programme of UNCTAD
Founder and Director of the UNCTAD´s global data bank
Chief of Cabinet of the Secretary General of UNCTAD

Jeroen Raijmakers
荷兰 Netherlands
飞利浦医疗全球设计总监
Global Design Director of Healthcare at Philips

Marie Moreira
法国 France
法国工业设计促进会国际项目经理（1999年至今）
埃里克•德•蒙贝尔和茹斯•塞甘当代艺术画廊助理（1998-1999）
International Project Manager of Agency for the Promotion of Industrial Design (Since 1999)
Assistant of Eric de Montbel and Jousse Seguin Contemporary Art Gallery (1998-1999)

George M. Beylerian
美国 USA
Material ConneXion新材料图书馆创始人兼首席执行官（1997年至今）
Culture & Commerce设计咨询公司创始人（1994年）
Founder and CEO of Material ConneXion (Since 1997)
Founder of Culture & Commerce (1994)

中国创新设计红星奖组织机构

主办单位
中国创新设计红星奖委员会

发起单位
中国工业设计协会
北京工业设计促进中心
国务院发展研究中心《新经济导刊》杂志社

项目支持
北京市科学技术委员会

承办单位
北京工业设计促进中心

协办单位
北京光华设计发展基金会
北京工业设计促进会
天津市工业设计协会
上海工业设计协会
重庆工业设计协会
黑龙江省工业设计协会
黑龙江省艺术设计协会
江苏省工业设计学会
山东省企业联合会
河南省工业设计协会
湖南省工业设计协会
广东省工业设计协会
四川省工业设计协会
陕西省工业设计协会
福州市科学技术局
广州工业设计促进会
深圳市设计联合会
宁波市工业设计联合会
青岛市工业设计协会
顺德工业设计协会
无锡工业设计协会
珠海市工业设计协会
海南省艺术设计协会

报道媒体
中央电视台
人民日报
经济日报
中国日报
科技日报
北京电视台·魅力科学
北京日报
北京青年报
Curve杂志
千龙网
新浪尚品
搜狐数码
环球时报
居CASE DA ABITARE
The Journal Of Design
科学时报
北京商报
北京月讯
视觉中国
视觉同盟

Institutes of China Red Star Design Award

Organizer
China Red Star Design Award Committee

Sponsor
China Industrial Design Association
Beijing Industrial Design Center
New Economy Weekly

Support
Beijing Municipal Science & Technology Commission

Host
Beijing Industrial Design Center

Co-organizer
Dragon Design Foundation
Beijing Industrial Design Promotion Organization
Tianjin Industrial Design Association
Shanghai Industrial Design Association
Chongqing Industrial Design Association
Heilongjiang Industrial Design Association
Heilongjiang Province Artistic Design Association
Jiangsu Industrial Design Association
Shandong Enterprise Confederation
Henan Industrial Design Association
Hunan Industrial Design Association
Guangdong Industrial Design Association
Sichuan Industrial Design Association
Shaanxi Industrial Design Association
Fuzhou Municipal Bureau of Science and Technology
Guangzhou Industrial Design Association
Shenzhen Industrial Design Association
Ningbo Industrial Design Union
Qingdao Industrial Design Association
Shunde Industrial Design Association
Wuxi Industrial Design Association
Zhuhai Industrial Design Association
Art Design Association of Hainan Province

Reporting Media
CCTV
People´s Daily
Economic Daily
China Daily
Science And Technology Daily
Beijing Television Station • Funny Science
Beijing Daily
Beijing Youth Daily
Curve
Qianlong.Com
Style.Sina.Com.Cn
Digi.Sohu.Com
Global Times
CASE DA ABITARE
The Journal Of Design
Science Times
Beijing Business Today
Beijing This Month
Chinavisual.Com
Visionunion

中国创新设计红星奖委员会
China Red Star Design Award Committee

主席
朱　焘　闫傲霜

执行主席
黄武秀　陈冬亮

委员
刘　晖　刘　宁　楼晓红
王海宁　邢　雷　崔立祥
刘亚杰　张　伟　张　锡
张震甫　何人可　宋慰祖
林　勇　郑佰森　郑寿平
郑德湘　胡启志　徐和平
蒋国栋　韩选华　程建新
虞汉悦　韩小军　喻湘晖
樊超然　王麒霁　黄　平

Chairman
Zhu Tao/ Yan Aoshuang

Executive Chairman
Huang Wuxiu/ Chen Dongliang

Members
Liu Hui/ Liu Ning/ Lou Xiaohong/
Wang Haining / Xing Lei/ Cui Lixiang/
Liu Yajie/ Zhang Wei/ Zhang Xi/
Zhang Zhenfu/ He Renke/ Song Weizu/
Lin Yong/ Zheng Baisen/ Zheng Shouping/
Zheng Dexiang/ Hu Qizhi/ Xu Heping/
Jiang Guodong/ Han Xuanhua/ Cheng Jianxin/
Yu Hanyue/ Han Xiaojun/ Yu Xianghui/
Fan Chaoran/ Wang Qiji/ Huang Ping

中国创新设计红星奖办公室
China Red Star Design Award Office

楼晓红　左康辉　栾一丞
王　璨　张芸皓　万　菊
王　俊　李　成　张　浩

Lou Xiaohong/ Zuo Kanghui/ Luan Yicheng/
Wang Can/ Zhang Yunhao / Wan Ju/
Wang Jun/ Li Cheng/ Zhang Hao

中国创新设计红星奖与韩国好设计奖的互认，部分选定产品可以使用红星奖与好设计奖的标志。

Selected entries shall be allowed to carry a jointly branded design label with China Red Star Design Award and GD Award as the conclusion of mutual recognition between Red Star and GD.

中国创新设计红星奖与澳大利亚国际设计奖的互认，部分选定产品可以使用红星奖与澳大利亚国际设计奖和澳大利亚好设计奖的标志。

Selected entries shall be allowed to carry a jointly branded design label with China Red Star Design Award and Australian International Design Award™ and Australian Good Design™ as the conclusion of mutual recognition between Red Star and AIDA.

国际工业设计协会联合会认证奖项

ICSID ENDORSEMENT

创新设计服务创新型国家

2012年是中国创新设计红星奖走过的第七个年头，也是红星奖实现自我突破，迈向成熟的一年。在国家、北京和地方政府的亲切关怀下，在设计机构、行业协会和社会各界的大力支持下，红星奖已成长为代表中国优秀设计水平，促进经济增长方式转变，助力建设创新型国家的设计大奖。

一、征集数量和质量均实现历史突破。2012年红星奖共征集到1279家企业的5348件产品。报名企业包括首都机场、中国船舶重工集团、三一重工、广汽集团、联想、海尔、中兴、小米手机等60家国内知名企业；美国戴尔、摩托罗拉、德国宝马、荷兰飞利浦、瑞典沃尔沃，韩国LG电子，芬兰诺基亚等84家外资企业参评，比2011年增长23.5%，非洲企业首次参评。七年来国内参评地域涵盖30个省、市及地区，参评国家累计达到28个。

二、宣传平台更加国际化。2012年红星奖作为亚洲最具影响力设计奖的代表参加2012米兰・中国设计创新展、2012韩国设计展；推荐获奖产品独享优惠价格参评德国红点奖，与澳大利亚国际设计奖实现了标准互认；与《curve》等国际著名媒体建立战略合作伙伴关系；开设红星奖博物馆，永久展览历年获奖产品的精品，对公众免费开放。

三、向产业上端延伸，创办红星原创奖。为建设创新型国家，促进中国制造向中国创造的跨越式发展，弘扬非抄袭模仿的、具有自主知识产权的首创精神，提升中国原创设计水平，红星奖于2012年开始设立红星原创奖。首届红星原创奖共征集到238家单位的559件作品，国内参评地域涵盖21个省、市及地区，并有来自韩国和意大利的企业、设计师参评。

经过严格评审，2012年红星奖共有154家企业的258件产品获奖，其中至尊金奖1名，金奖9项，银奖9项，红星奖239项及1个最佳团队和1名最佳新人。红星原创奖共有14件作品获奖，其中，银奖4项，红星原创奖10项；未来之星2名，优秀设计师1名。

随着国家和地方政府对设计产业支持力度的加大，设计产业发展环境不断优化，2012年北京被批准成为联合国教科文组织创意城市网络设计之都，为红星奖搭建了又一个国际平台。展望未来，十七大报告提出，提高自主创新能力,建设创新型国家。这是国家发展战略的核心，是提高综合国力的关键。面对新时期的机遇和挑战，红星奖将更加努力汇集设计人才和设计资源， 在推动中国制造向中国创造的道路上发挥更加强大的力量。红星奖任重而道远。

红星照耀下的中国，必将是创新的中国。

中国创新设计红星奖委员会

2012年10月8日

Innovation design serving innovative country

2012 is the 7th year of China Red Star Design Award since its establishment which is also a breakthrough, and a key point of being maturity. Under the care of the nation, Beijing municipal government and local governments as well as the great support from the design organizations, industry associations and the society, Red Star has become the very design award representing China excellent design, which promotes the transition of the economy growth, and assists to construct an innovative country.

1. The quantity and quality of the entries has made a historic breakthrough. There are 5,348 entry products from 1,279 enterprises, including the Capital Airport, China Shipbuilding Industry Corporation, SANY, GAC Group, Lenovo, Haier, ZTE, Mione etc 60 domestic well known enterprises and 84 foreign enterprises entered, such as Dell, Motorola, BMW, Philips, Volve, LG and Nokia etc, the amount of the entrants has increased 23.5% comparing with 2011, African companies entered for the first time. In the past 7 years, the applicant enterprises are covering 30 domestic provinces, cities and regions of China as well as 28 countries all over the world.

2. Red Star publicity platform becomes more international. In 2012, as the most influential design award from Asia, Red Star participated 2012 "Milan•New Chinese Design and Innovation Exhibition" and 2012 Design Korea; awarded products can be recommended to apply for Reddot Award with exclusive discounted price. At the same time, Red Star has realized with mutual recognition with Australian International Design Award, and started the strategic cooperation partnership with Curve, one of the most renowned design media. Red Star Museum has also been established; well collected awarded products are chosen to be exhibited permanently in the museum and opened free to the public.

3. Red Star has extended to the upper of the industry, created the Red Star Original Design Award. In order to establish the innovative country, promote leapfrog development from "made in China" to "design in China", carry on the non-copy and non-imitation spirits and have initiative of intellectual property and improve the Chinese original design level, China Red Star Design Award establishes China Red Star Original Design Award in 2012. Totally 559 pieces of works from 238 applicants participated, covering 21 domestic provinces, cities and regions; enterprises and designers from Italy, Korea also submitted works.

Through the strict screening, totally 258 products from 154 enterprises are awarded, including 1 Best of the Gold Prize, 9 Gold Prizes, 9 Silver Prizes, 239 Excellent Prizes as well as 1 Best Team Prize and 1 Best New Designer Prize. 14 Pieces of works won the prizes of Red Star Original Design Award, including 4 Silver Award, 10 Excellent Award, 2 Future Star Award and 1 Best Designer Award.

Along with the increasing support of national and local government of design industry, the industry environment optimizes. In 2012, Beijing is designated as UNESCO Creative Cities Network "City of Design" which is another international platform for Red Star. Looking into the future, the national report puts forward to raise the capability of independent innovation and construct the innovative country which is the core of the national development strategy and the key of raising the comprehensive national strength. Confront the opportunity and challenge of the era, China Red Star will endeavor to bring together design talents and design resources to play a more important role on promoting "made in China" to "design in China". This is Red Star´s mission, and we still have a long way to go.

Red Star over China, will definitely be an innovative China.

China Red Star Design Award Committee

Oct. 8, 2012

中国设计　国际标准

设计在提升企业竞争力、促进城市发展和提高人民生活品质方面正发挥着巨大的作用。世界各国以设计奖项鼓励好设计，推动设计产业的发展也成为了一条成功的经验。

2006年，在中国设立“红星奖”，七年间，参评数量已由400件跃升到5000余件，每年都有200多个企业或个人获奖，在业界产生了极大的影响。红星奖从开始设立，就采用国际化标准，聘请中国和国际著名的设计专家担任评委，红星奖秉承“公平、公开、公益、高水平、国际化”的原则，保证了奖项的国际水准和社会公信力。

2009年红星奖与德国红点奖签署了战略合作协议，同年得到了国际工业设计协会联合会（Icsid）的认证。2010年和2012年，红星奖分别与韩国“好设计奖”、澳大利亚“国际设计奖”实现了标准互认，这使得中国创新设计红星奖在评审标准水平上又迈上了一个新的台阶，对于中国设计超越文化、国界、走向世界，实现基于文化多样性的设计创新具有里程碑的意义。

陈冬亮

中国创新设计红星奖委员会执行主席

2012年10月10日

Chinese Design, International Standard

Design plays an important role on promoting enterprises competitiveness, city development and citizens´ quality of life. Establishing design award has become a successful experience for countries to encourage good design and promote design industry.

In 2006, "Red Star" was established in China. The entrants´ amount has increased from 400 to over 5,000; more than 200 applicants are awarded annually in the past seven years, the improvement has caused great influence in the industry. From the very beginning of its establishment, Red Star adopts international standard, invites domestic and international well known design experts to judge the entry products. Adhering to the principle of "justice, openness, public welfare, high level and international", Red Star guarantees the award´s international level and public credibility.

In 2009, Red Star signed MOU with Red Dot Award, in the same year, Red Star obtained the endorsement of International Council of Societies of Industrial Design (Icsid). In 2010 and 2012, Red Star realizes the mutual recognition with "Good Design" from Korea and "International Design Award" from Australia which brings China Red Star Design Award to a new level of the screening standard. This is a mile stone for Chinese design to cross over culture and national boundaries to stand on the world stage, realize the design innovation based on the cultural diversity.

Chen Dongliang
Executive Chairman of China Red Star Design award Committee
Oct 10, 2012

红星照耀中国　是创新的中国

Red Star over China – Innovative China